Questionnaire Design

THIRD EDITION

Questionnaire Design

How to plan, structure and write survey material for effective market research

Ian Brace

KoganPage

LONDON PHILADELPHIA NEW DELHI

First published in Great Britain and the United States in 2004 by Kogan Page Limited
Second edition 2008
Third edition 2013

120 Pentonville Road	1518 Walnut Street, Suite 1100	4737/23 Ansari Road
London N1 9JN	Philadelphia PA 19102	Daryaganj
United Kingdom	USA	New Delhi 110002
www.koganpage.com		India

© Ian Brace, 2004, 2008, 2013

The right of Ian Brace to be identified as the author of this work has been asserted by him in accordance with the Copyright, Designs and Patents Act 1988.

ISBN   978 0 7494 6779 1
E-ISBN 978 0 7494 6780 7

British Library Cataloguing-in-Publication Data

A CIP record for this book is available from the British Library.

Library of Congress Cataloging-in-Publication Data

Brace, Ian, 1949-
  Questionnaire design : how to plan, structure and write survey material for effective market research / Ian Brace. – 3rd edition.
     pages cm
  Includes bibliographical references and index.
  ISBN 978-0-7494-6779-1 – ISBN 978-0-7494-6780-7 (e-isbn)   1. Market surveys–Methodology.
2. Questionnaires–Methodology.   I. Title.
  HF5415.3.B683 2013
  658.8'3–dc23
                                                                                                    2013006923

Typeset by Graphicraft Limited, Hong Kong
Printed and bound in India by Replika Press Pvt Ltd

CONTENTS

Introduction

It is clear to anyone undertaking data collection through a questionnaire survey that the questionnaire is one of the most crucial elements in its success. You will only collect information that you ask for; and the way you ask the questions will affect the type and accuracy of the responses you receive. This is the case for all methods of data collection, whether there is an interviewer present or the survey is self-completion. However, the full importance of writing a good questionnaire is often underestimated. After all, anybody can write a set of questions, can't they? But if those questions are the wrong questions, poorly phrased, or in the wrong order, the answers obtained may be worse than meaningless: they may be misleading.

In all surveys, there are two generally recognized types of error: sampling and non-sampling error. Sampling error arises from the random variation in the selection of respondents. The extent of it can be calculated and its effects can be taken into account. Sampling error can be reduced, most commonly by increasing the size of the sample, which usually means additional cost. To halve the sampling error requires the sample size to be quadrupled, so achieving a reduction in sampling error can be expensive.

Non-sampling errors arise from mistakes made in areas such as the coding and data entry processes of the survey, and through errors committed by interviewers, but also through mistakes made by the questionnaire writer. Not only can these mistakes be fatal to the success of the survey – if a key question or response code is omitted, or respondents are led to give particular answers – but also they are not always obvious. Even when obvious, the impact is not always quantifiable, nor capable of being measured or corrected for. However, reducing questionnaire error, in contrast to sampling error, need not add significantly to the cost of a survey, provided the questionnaire writer understands how to write a questionnaire; one that will obtain the most pertinent data to address the objectives of the study.

Good questionnaire writing is a no- or low-cost option in any survey, which has major rewards in delivering the best, or most accurate, answers.

What is a questionnaire?

Questionnaires are written in many different ways, to be used in many different situations and with many different data-gathering media. The purpose of this book is to provide some general rules and principles that can be applied to writing any type of questionnaire. The book is written principally with students and practitioners of market research in mind, but it should also be of use to social researchers, political opinion and advocacy pollsters and anyone else who needs to write a questionnaire to collect information by means of a structured interview.

In market research the term 'questionnaire' is used to refer both to questionnaires intended for self-completion by survey participants and to survey instruments intended to be administered by an interviewer, either in a face-to-face interview or by telephone. In other disciplines this is often referred to as an 'interview schedule', with the term 'questionnaire' reserved for the self-completion survey instrument. Throughout this book the market research common usage of questionnaire encompassing both self-completion and interviewer-administered surveys is adhered to.

A structured interview is one in which each subject or respondent is asked a series of questions according to a prepared and fixed interviewing schedule – the questionnaire. Thus this book will not apply to qualitative research interviews, where the interview is carried out to a prepared topic guide, because the interview schedule, although prepared, is not fixed. It will, however, apply to the recruitment interview, usually used in qualitative research to identify eligible subjects to participate in later depth interviews, group discussions or focus groups.

The term 'semi-structured interview' will be avoided as it can mean different things to different people. For some it implies a questionnaire consisting almost entirely of open-ended questions with probing instructions. This provides a framework for a degree of consistency between interviews conducted by a number of different interviewers, while providing them with scope for greater exploration than is normally possible. For other people the term simply means a questionnaire that contains both open-ended and closed questions.

Structured interviews are carried out using a range of different data collection media. Interviewers can be used to ask questions face-to-face with the respondent or subject; interviews can be carried out by telephone; questionnaires can be left with subjects to complete themselves; questionnaires can be mailed to subjects; or questionnaires can be accessed by subjects through the internet on a PC, tablet or mobile phone. Each of these media has its own opportunities and problems, but the general principles of questionnaire construction and writing apply to all of them.

Obtaining the best answers

This book could be called 'Obtaining the best answers' because that is what we are trying to achieve in market research surveys – the 'best' or most accurate answers. We are not, or should not be, trying to obtain particular answers to support our position or our client's position. The role of the researcher is to be as objective as possible in order to provide the ultimate decision makers – whether that is ourselves, our client or our client's client – with the best, most accurate picture that we can paint. That is equally true for researchers in agencies and in client companies. Setting out to tell our clients or sponsors simply what they want to hear is rarely best in the long term, and is questionable ethically.

However, we must recognize that the data we collect through interviews is rarely completely accurate. And why should it be? We are usually asking volunteer respondents to give up their time, frequently for no reward. We ask them to recall events that to them are often trivial, such as the breakfast cereals that they bought, or the choice of flavours of yoghurt offered in the supermarket. We frequently ask them to analyse and report their emotions and feelings about issues that they have never consciously considered, such as their feelings about different brands of paint. Even if they can recognize their feelings and emotions, can they articulate them? Why should they make any effort to do so? The interview may be taking place on a doorstep, or by telephone, when the respondent's first consideration is where the children are, or whether the dinner in the oven is likely to burn; they may be irritated because they have been interrupted while watching a favourite TV programme. Or the interview may be taking place in a shopping mall, where the respondents are anxious to complete their shopping and go home.

As researchers, we have to recognize that we cannot expect to be given perfectly accurate information by our respondents. We must construct and use the questionnaire to help respondents give the researcher the best information that they can. And it is not just the respondent's ability or willingness to provide accurate answers that we must consider. Our own instruments are often blunt and barely capable of assessing what is true or accurate, particularly in relation to attitudes and opinions. This is demonstrated by the way in which different surveys can produce seemingly different assessments of attitude and opinion. This sometimes occurs because of differing objectives but can also be due to differences in the survey instrument itself.

Throughout this book are examples of how question wording, response categories and layout can all affect the results obtained. The book therefore sets out to cover how we can help respondents to provide us with their best answers in which we can reduce unwanted biases and unwanted variations to a minimum or, if we cannot achieve that, to at least make us aware that these biases and variations are likely to exist.

Why do we need a questionnaire?

In all cases the role of the questionnaire is to provide a standardized interview across all subjects. This is so that all respondents are asked the questions that are appropriate to them, and so that, when those questions are asked or presented, it is always in exactly the same way.

Asking the questions in the same way to different people is key to most survey research. Imagine what would happen if the same question were asked differently of different respondents: it would be impossible for the survey researcher to aggregate or interpret the answers. It may be argued that in some instances the same questions should be asked differently of different people, that wording should be tailored to each respondent's vocabulary or knowledge of the topic. Without this tailoring process, respondents will not be able to communicate to the researcher all of the information that is either relevant or that they wish to convey. There is certainly a case for asking a question differently where there are a small number of discrete and identifiable groups covered by the survey, but with large-scale surveys where there is anything more than a few dozen respondents, it is impossible to handle and interpret data without a standardized question format.

What does it do?

The questionnaire is the medium of communication between the researcher and the subject, albeit sometimes administered on the researcher's behalf by an interviewer. In the questionnaire, the researcher articulates the questions to which he or she wants to know the answers and, through the questionnaire, the subjects' answers are conveyed back to the researcher. The questionnaire can thus be described as the medium of conversation between two people, albeit that they are remote from each other and never communicate directly.

Standardized surveys

Many market research companies now use standardized and often branded approaches for some of the more common research requirements – advertising tracking, advertising pre-testing, brand positioning, customer satisfaction – which use standard questionnaires or questionnaire formats. This reduces the need for the researcher to determine and decide on the questions to be asked. However, using standard techniques does not remove the need for the researcher to be aware of the principles of questionnaire design. Standardized surveys are often written with a particular research universe or product sector in mind and need to be adapted for other populations and product sectors. A technique designed for researching fast-moving consumer goods may need considerable alteration for the financial sector.

Many standardized approaches allow some flexibility, often in the way of additional questions that can be added to the end of the standardized interview. The questionnaire writer therefore needs to know what questions can be asked, how to ask them and how to assess their value, given that they follow the standard questions. All researchers therefore need to know how to write a questionnaire.

A remote conversation

The questionnaire has already been described as a medium of remote conversation between researcher and respondent. It is, however, a conversation designed by someone who is not present. For it to work, the respondent must hear or read the question as the writer intended it to be heard or read. It is one of the skills of the questionnaire writer to write questions that have the same meaning to all respondents, regardless of how an interviewer might say them or how they are read on the page or screen.

There is of course a major difference between quantitative survey research and qualitative research, and quantitative researchers must be aware of their remoteness from their subjects and allow for it in all they do. In particular, researchers must not allow their remoteness from respondents to lead them to forget that each respondent is a person. There can be a tendency for researchers to see respondents purely as sources of information, and they write long, complex and boring questionnaires that fail to treat the respondents with the respect that is due.

One of the consequences of the remoteness of researcher from respondents is the difficulty that structured questionnaires have in eliciting creative responses. The lack of interaction between researcher and respondents, and the consequent inability to tailor questions to the specific respondent, means that the questionnaire survey should generally be seen as a reactive medium. It is good at obtaining answers to the questions it asks (although we will see many ways in which it can fail to do even this), but it does not provide answers to questions that are not asked, and it is not a good way of tapping into the creativity of consumers. If that is what is required, qualitative research techniques offer far better solutions.

There are many pitfalls the questionnaire writer has to avoid. Throughout the book, some of the most common errors are illustrated in the 'Seen in print' boxes. These are examples taken from a range of different sources that demonstrate how easy it can be to depart from best practice or even basic principles and collect data that are meaningless or incapable of interpretation. Although called 'Seen in print', the examples come from web-based and telephone interviews as well as from paper questionnaires. Minor changes have been made in many cases in order to spare the blushes of those responsible, but all are taken from live surveys.

01

Objectives in writing a questionnaire

Introduction

This chapter considers *what* the researcher is trying to achieve with the questionnaire. Later chapters will then look at *how* this can be achieved.

The role of the questionnaire is to elicit the information that will enable the researcher to answer the objectives of the survey. To do this the questionnaire must not only collect the data required, but collect it in the most accurate way possible. Collecting accurate data means getting the most accurate responses, so a key objective in writing the questionnaire is to help the respondents provide them. The questionnaire's role does not stop there, though. There are other stakeholders whose interests must also be met.

The questionnaire in the survey process

The questionnaire represents one part of the survey process. It is, however, a very vital part of the process. A poorly written questionnaire will not provide the data required or, worse, will provide data that is incorrect.

The first task with any survey is to define the objectives that the study is to answer. These will relate to the issue at hand and may be very specific, such as to determine which of two alternative product formulations is preferred, or rather broader, such as segmenting the market into different user groups. Where the objectives are specific, the questionnaire writer's task is usually rather more straightforward than where the survey is exploratory in nature. A specific objective usually implies that there is a particular question to be answered and it is the questionnaire writer's job to find the most appropriate way of answering that question.

Where research is exploratory, the questionnaire writer's task is less predetermined, and a major part of the task is establishing what data needs to be collected and how it is best collected. With this type of project it is common to carry out preliminary qualitative research to determine what the issues are within the market, and how subjects in the market view them and talk about them. This will help the questionnaire writer to determine which questions to ask and the type of language to use in order to carry out the 'conversation' with respondents in a way that they will understand and will help them to provide the information sought.

A questionnaire writer who is not familiar with the vocabulary of a market can very quickly come unstuck. This does not just relate to complex business-to-business markets, but can arise almost anywhere. A questionnaire on the subject of bras to be asked of a sample of women was designed by a man, and referred throughout to 'front-opening' and 'back-opening' bras. Very soon after the piloting of the questionnaires had begun, the researcher received a visit from his fearsome head of field, who pointed out in no uncertain terms that, 'while men may "open" bras, women most definitely "fasten" them'.

Before any questions can be asked, though, the sample must be defined, and the sampling method and the data collection medium must be determined. These are all crucial stages in designing a survey that is appropriate to answering the objectives, and although outside the scope of this book, all will have an influence on the way in which the questionnaire is written.

How the data is to be collated and analysed will have an influence on how the questionnaire is written and laid out, as well as determining some of the questions that will need to be asked for analysis purposes. A screening questionnaire for a focus group of eight people will not have to make the same allowances for data input and analysis that a survey of 1,000 people must make, nor ensure that all likely cross-analyses are anticipated and the appropriate questions asked.

Questionnaire writing thus does not exist in a vacuum, but is an integral part of the survey process. How the questionnaire is written affects the remaining survey processes, and what is to happen in those processes affects how the questionnaire is written.

Stakeholders in the questionnaire

Clearly there are a number of different stakeholders in the questionnaire, and the way in which it is written and laid out will have an effect on each of them. There can be up to five different groups of people who have an interest in the questionnaire, and each one has a different requirement of it:

1 The clients, or people commissioning the survey, want the questionnaire to collect the information that will enable them to answer their business objectives.

2 The interviewers, where used, want a questionnaire that is straightforward to administer, has questions that are easily understood by respondents, and has somewhere where they can easily record those responses.

3 Respondents want a questionnaire that poses them questions they can answer without too much effort, and that maintains their interest without taking up too much of their time.

4 The data processors want a questionnaire layout that allows for uncomplicated data entry, where necessary, and for the straightforward production of data tables or other analyses that may be required.

5 The researcher or questionnaire writer has to strive to meet all of these people's needs, and to do so whilst working within the parameters of a budget that has usually been agreed with the client, which in turn means working within an agreed interview length and survey structure.

It is not always possible to meet all of these needs at the same time, and one of the roles of the researcher is to balance the demands of the different stakeholders. The two stakeholders who must be given the highest priority are the client, whose information needs must be met, and the respondent, whose cooperation we rely on to agree to be interviewed and then to answer our questions truthfully, which can sometimes require significant mental effort. Respondents are generally volunteers who are giving their time, frequently for no reward, and, apart from the impact on the quality of the data, we have no right to bore them or antagonize them. To do so is only likely to rebound on their willingness to take part in future surveys. Against their needs, though, we sometimes have to balance those of the interviewer and data processor, in the knowledge that, if we make the questionnaire too complex or difficult for them, we are increasing the risk of errors occurring, or making the required analyses impossible.

The questionnaire writer's job can be summarized, then, as being to write a questionnaire that collects the data required to answer the objectives of the study as objectively as possible and without irritating or annoying the respondents, whilst minimizing the likelihood of error occurring at any stage in the data collection and analysis process.

The objectives of the study

Relating research objectives to business objectives

The brief that the researcher receives may sometimes include the business objectives for the study and the research objectives required to achieve them.

> *Business objective:* to enter the mobile telecoms market with a pricing package that is attractive to at least 60 per cent of the current contract market.
>
> *Research objectives:*
>
> - to determine the distribution of the amount that mobile telecoms users who have a contract pay per month;
> - to determine how that amount is made up from standing charges, call charges and special offers and discounts;
> - to determine level of satisfaction with current supplier;
> - to determine the level of price advantage that would be required for them to consider switching supplier.

However, it is not uncommon for researchers to be given only the business objectives or only the research objectives. If researchers are provided only with the business objectives, they should determine what the research objectives should be in order to meet the business objectives. These should be agreed with the client or business manager, to ensure that there are no misunderstandings about the business objectives and that no areas of information have been omitted.

Sometimes researchers are supplied only with the research objectives. It is perfectly possible for the questionnaire to be written from these alone. However, the more background that questionnaire writers have as to how the data is to be used, the more they are able to ensure that all relevant questions are included, that every question serves a purpose, and that response codes used are appropriate to the business objective. In the above example, the business manager may have had a belief that the target market for the new service should be people aged under 30 years, but nevertheless wished to examine the whole market. This may not have been apparent from the research objectives and could have resulted in the question recording age on the questionnaire having the category 25 to 34 year-olds, and omitting the age break at 30.

Relating the questionnaire to the research objectives

The first task therefore is to determine what the questions are that need to be asked. These will be a function both of the research objectives and of the survey design to be used. It may be clear from the information needs of the study that certain questions must be asked, eg whether or not a car is owned, the number and ages of children in the family, whether or not the respondent ever buys pasta sauce. The research technique to be used may also require certain types of question to be asked, eg a paired comparison product test will almost certainly require questions to compare the respondent's preference between the products, or an advertising awareness study will require questions about advertising recall.

Proprietary or specific techniques will often determine what types of questions must be asked and be quite specific about the format of these questions. Some advertising tracking techniques will not only require that questions be asked about advertising awareness but will also determine the almost exact wording of the question and where in the interview it should be asked.

The objective is not simply to take the study objectives and to write a question against each one. That is generally far too simplistic and can yield facile and misleading information. A series of processes is needed to arrive at the questionnaire from the study objectives. It is one of the skills of the researcher to turn the objectives of the study into a set of information requirements, and from there to create questions to provide that information and then to turn those into a questionnaire.

Study objectives: to determine which of two possible recipes for pasta sauce, A and B, is preferred

At a simplistic level this objective could be answered by asking a sample of the relevant market to taste each of the two recipes and to say which they preferred. However, the first thing to do is to determine what information is required, and that will entail asking questions of the brief. Is it enough to know that x per cent prefer Recipe A and y per cent prefer Recipe B? Do we need to know whether the people who prefer Recipe A differ from those who prefer Recipe B in any way, such as demographic characteristics, weight of usage of pasta sauce, and which brands or recipes they currently use? Can either or both of the recipes be amended following the research to improve their appeal, which would mean that questions about what was liked and disliked about each one should be included? Is it possible to create a new recipe combining some of the characteristics from each of A and B?

Only after the brief has been interrogated in this way can we determine either the final survey design or the information required to address the objective in full.

Recruitment questionnaires

Recruitment questionnaires are used in qualitative research and for recruitment of respondents for some types of quantitative research (eg clinics held in central locations). The purpose of this type of questionnaire is to identify eligible respondents in order to invite them to attend the main research session. Consequently, the data collected should be limited to that required to determine whether or not respondents meet the criteria that would define them as a member of the target group for the research.

The recruitment questionnaire does not, therefore, have to address all of the objectives of the research study but should be limited to the minimum number of questions required to establish eligibility.

Collecting unbiased and accurate data

Clearly, the data collected should be as accurate as possible. However, complete accuracy is almost impossible to obtain in surveys where respondents are asked to report their behaviour or their attitudes. Many problems arise because of problems within the questionnaire itself.

Problems ...

caused by questionnaire writer:

- ambiguity in the question;
- order effects between questions;
- order effects within a question;
- inadequate response codes;
- wrong questions asked because of poor routeing;
- failure of the questionnaire to record the reply accurately or completely.

encountered within the interview

- failure of the respondent to understand the question;
- inattention to the interview because of respondent boredom and fatigue;
- desire by the respondent to answer a different question to the one asked;
- inaccuracy of memory regarding behaviour;
- inaccuracy of memory regarding time periods (telescoping);
- respondents wishing to impress;
- respondents not willing to admit their attitudes or behaviour either consciously or subconsciously;
- respondents trying to influence the outcome of the study and giving answers that they believe will lead to a particular conclusion.

caused by interviewer, where present

- questions asked inaccurately;
- failure to record the reply accurately or completely;
- mistakes made because of boredom and fatigue.

Some of the main biases are analysed by Kalton and Schuman (1982).

Ways in which the questionnaire and questions can be written and structured to minimize the effects of these phenomena will be covered in later chapters on questionnaire construction and question writing. In this chapter we will consider the problems that each of these causes, with the exception of the last three of the respondent issues, which are part of a subject known as 'social desirability bias'. This, and the ways in which it can be countered, is a sufficiently important subject to warrant its own chapter, Chapter 15.

Failure of the respondent to understand the question

Long and complex questions will be the most likely to cause problems, or questions that use words that are not part of the respondent's everyday vocabulary.

Respondents may fail to understand a question because it is not in their competence to answer it. Thus it would be a mistake to ask people what they think is a fair price for certain high-specification audio equipment if they do not own any, have no intention of owning any and do not understand the implications of the high-specification features.

Ambiguity in a question can mean that the respondent cannot understand what is being asked or understands a different question from the one intended.

Inattention to the interview because of respondent boredom and fatigue

Response mistakes made by respondents because of failure to understand the question or to give sufficient thought to their response are exacerbated when they become tired of or bored by the interview. When that happens, respondents will adopt strategies to get them to the end of the interview quickly and with as little thought or effort as possible. Thus with repeated questions, such as rating scales, they will often go into a pattern of response that bears little or no relationship to their true answers.

With behavioural questions less thought is given to the responses as fatigue sets in. Sometimes any answer will be given just to be able to proceed to the next question. Towards the end of a long interview answers are sometimes given that contradict those given earlier.

The point at which boredom and fatigue will set in can be difficult to judge beforehand. It will depend on the level of interest of the respondent in the subject matter and the skill of the questionnaire writer in providing a varied and interesting experience. Few structured interviews can retain the interest of any respondent for as long as 90 minutes (with the possible exception of cars or a hobby subject), and a realistic expectation for most topics is that fatigue will set in after about 30 minutes for most respondents on most subjects.

With interviewer-administered surveys, respondents will often continue to the end, encouraged and cajoled by the interviewer for whom only a completed interview counts. Online, respondents who are bored or fatigued simply log off, even if they lose the financial or other incentives to complete the questionnaire. Figure 1.1, taken from Cape *et al* (2007), shows how drop-out is a function of length of questionnaire, as respondents become bored and fatigued. It can be seen that in a large number of projects more than 20 per cent drop out. With an interviewer-administered interview, many of these would have continued reluctantly to the end, providing potentially unreliable data.

Figure 1.1 also demonstrates that the length of the questionnaire is not the only factor in the decision to drop out. Cape *et al* attribute this largely to the quality of the questionnaire design. This shows that with poor questionnaire design, fatigue is likely to set in earlier and results become unreliable sooner in the interview. The importance of good questionnaire design in gaining good quality data is demonstrated. No matter what the subject, interest is retained longer if the interview experience is itself interesting (maintaining respondent engagement is discussed in Chapter 12).

Desire by the respondent to answer a different question to the one asked

Sometimes respondents will 'interpret' the question in a way that fits their circumstances. When asked how often they go to the cinema, respondents who see films at a club may choose to include those occasions in their response because that is the closest they come to going to a cinema. If the interviewer is made aware of this, a note can be made and a decision taken later by the analyst as to whether to include this or not. However, often the interviewer will not be told and, with most computer-aided systems, including web-based surveys, there is no mechanism provided for respondents to alert the researcher to their interpretation of the question.

FIGURE 1.1   Online drop-out rate by length of interview
(Cape *et al*, 2007)

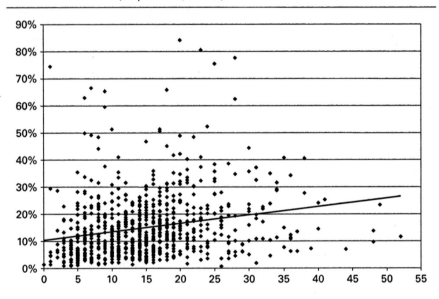

Asking respondents to describe attitudes on subjects for which they hold no conscious attitude

Researchers often ask respondents to reveal their attitudes about a range of subjects that the respondents have never before given conscious thought to. Many respondents may feel that they have an attitude on issues such as street crime and how to deal with it, but few will have consciously thought about the issues surrounding the role of pizza in their lives. Questionnaires frequently present respondents with a bank of attitude statements on subjects that, while of importance to the manufacturer, are very low down on the respondents' list of burning issues. Studies have shown that the data reported is more stable over time where respondents are not given time to think about their attitudes but are asked to respond quickly to each statement (Tourangeau *et al*, 2000). Attitudinal questions will often include an instruction to respondents to give their first reaction and not to spend time considering each statement.

Questions asked inaccurately by the interviewer

It is not uncommon to hear an interviewer paraphrase a question to make it sound more conversational. Anyone who has written a questionnaire and then used it to interview a number of people is likely to have found themselves doing it, as they realize that a question that looks accurate on paper often sounds stilted when spoken.

However it is paraphrased, it is likely that some aspects of the question change, and the response will be different to the one that would have been obtained from the original question. Good interviewer training will instil into the interviewer that the wording on the questionnaire is to be kept to. If, after that training, the interviewer feels the need to alter the wording, then it is a sign of a poorly written question. The role of the interviewer is to hold a conversation with the respondent on behalf of the researcher. The question writer must ensure that this is what happens.

Interviewers can ask questions wrongly because they do not understand them themselves, or because they are too long, and particularly if they involve many sub-clauses. With some business-to-business interviews, the interviewer may not understand the terminology used. A thorough briefing of the interviewers should be carried out and it may be advisable to provide a glossary of terms that respondents may use when giving open-ended verbatim comments. These can be made available on-screen or on paper. They may also be of benefit to coders and editors at the analysis stage of the survey.

Failure of the interviewer to record the reply accurately or completely

Interviewers record responses inaccurately in many ways. They may simply mishear the response. This is particularly likely to happen where, on a paper questionnaire, there is a long and complex routeing instruction following a question. The interviewer's attention may well be divided between listening to the respondent's answer and determining which question should be asked next. The interviewer may be trying to maintain the flow of the interview and not have it interrupted by a lengthy wait while the subsequent question is found, but this is bound to increase the risk of mishearing the answer. This is not an issue with computer-based questionnaires where routeing to the next question is automatic.

With open-ended (verbatim) questions, interviewers may not record everything that is said. There is a temptation to paraphrase and précis the response, again to keep the interview flowing and so as not to make the respondent wait while the full response is recorded.

It is common to provide a list of pre-codes as possible answers to an open question. Interviewers scan the list and code the answer that most closely matches the response given. This is open to error on two counts. First, none of the answers may match exactly what the respondent has said. The interviewer (or respondent, if self-completion) then has the choice of taking the one that is closest to the given response or there is frequently an option to write in verbatim responses that have not been anticipated. There is a strong temptation to make the given response match one of the pre-coded answers, thus inaccurately recording the true response. To minimize the chances of this happening, the pre-coded list may contain similar, but crucially different, answers. The danger then is that when the interviewer (or respondent) scans the list he or she sees only the answer that is close to but different from the given response and codes that as being 'near enough'. In many ways, this is a worse outcome, as it misleads the researcher.

Mistakes made by the interviewer because of boredom and fatigue

A long and tedious interview affects not only the respondent but also the interviewer. Like everybody else, interviewers make mistakes. Whether the interview is on the telephone or face-to-face, responses can be misheard, or a wrong code recorded, and these errors become more frequent if the interviewer is tired of or bored with the interview. An interview that is tedious for the respondent is also tedious for the interviewer. This can be made worse for the interviewer by the embarrassment felt in boring the respondent. The interviewer responds by reading the questions more quickly, leading to an increase in the number of errors of misunderstanding as well as recording errors on the part of the interviewer.

The questionnaire writer has much to consider. The overriding objective is to achieve the most accurate data that will satisfy the research objectives and the business objectives, by avoiding all of these reasons for inaccuracy, at the same time as meeting the needs of all the various stakeholders in the questionnaire.

The data collection media

02

Introduction

The researcher has a continually growing array of different ways in which to collect the data. The data collection modes can be broadly divided into two categories: interviewer-administered; and self-completion. It is not unusual, though, for interviewer-administered interviews to contain self-completion sections, and a third category could be added: interviewer-supervised self-completion. These are interviews where the respondents are left to complete the interview themselves, but with an interviewer in attendance to answer any queries. Each of the types of data collection media provides its own opportunities of questionnaire construction, but equally each has its own drawbacks.

Interviewer-administered interviews

There are a number of benefits to having an interviewer conduct the interview.

Queries about the meaning of a question can be dealt with

Sometimes a question can be unintentionally ambiguous. Although this should have been spotted and corrected before the questionnaire was finalized, it is possible for such questions to slip through. If respondents cannot answer because of the ambiguity, then they are able to ask the interviewer for clarification. Interviewers, though, must be careful not to lead respondents to a particular answer when giving their clarification, and should report back to the researcher that clarification was required.

A misunderstood question can be corrected

Interviewers can sometimes spot that respondents have misunderstood the question by the response they give. This may be because of the answer given or because it is inconsistent with previous answers, or simply inconsistent with what the interviewer already knows (or suspects) about the respondent. Such inconsistencies can be challenged, the question repeated and the response corrected if necessary.

Respondents can be encouraged to provide deeper responses to open questions

An interviewer administering the questionnaire gives the questionnaire writer an opportunity to probe for information on open questions. At the simplest level, a series of non-directive probes (eg 'What else?') can be used to extract as much information as possible from the respondent. If a bland and unhelpful answer is anticipated, the interviewer can be specifically asked to obtain further clarification. For example, the question, 'Why did you buy the item from that shop in particular?' is likely to get the answer, 'Because it was convenient.' An interviewer can be given an instruction not to accept an answer that only mentions convenience, and the questionnaire will supply the probe: 'What do you mean by convenient?'

Interviewer-administered questionnaires can be used in either face-to-face interviews or in telephone interviews. Each of these has its advantages and disadvantages in questionnaire writing. The choice of which is to be used will have been strongly influenced by the overall survey design, but the appropriateness of the medium to the questions to be asked will also play a part (see Table 2.1).

TABLE 2.1   Advantages and disadvantages to questionnaire writer of medium

Face-to-face interviewing		Telephone interviewing	
Advantages	Disadvantages	Advantages	Disadvantages
Ability to show response cards	Self-presentation bias	Relative anonymity can reduce bias	Use of prompts can be difficult
Ability to show stimulus material	Selection bias		Difficult to show stimulus material
More complex questions can be asked	Third-party bias		

Face-to-face

In the UK, face-to-face interviewing had been the dominant mode of data collection for many years. This dominance has been challenged by online web-based surveys, and it is likely that more questionnaires are now completed online than with a face-to-face interviewer. In the United States, face-to-face interviewing has never accounted for the same high proportion of interviews.

Many of the advantages of telephone interviewing are associated with access to respondents, survey control and speed. These do not relate to questionnaire design but can be deciding factors in the survey design.

Advantages of face-to-face interviewing

One clear advantage of face-to-face over telephone interviewing is the ability to show prompt cards to respondents. These cards can be used in questions where prompted awareness or recognition of names is required, where respondents are being asked to select their answer from a scale, or where it is desirable to prompt with a list of possible responses.

The ability to show things also means that products and ideas can be shown to respondents for their reactions. This is obviously important for evaluating any product or advertising, or where reaction to new ideas or concepts for products or advertising is required. Frequently, surveys evaluating products will be carried out in a central location. This facilitates:

- transporting the product – particularly if it is something bulky like a washing machine;
- demonstration of the product – making sure it is cooked or served correctly;
- security of a concept or a new product that might be of significant interest to a competitor.

Where the product is portable, or where the product is left with the respondent to be tried, in-home face-to-face interviewing is often preferred.

Face-to-face CAPI

CAPI (computer-assisted personal interviewing) is the use of a portable computer that provides the questions and pre-codes on the screen. The computers can be either tablet computers with a touch screen or laptop personal computers where answers are recorded by clicking the cursor on the appropriate box. Laptops may have multimedia capabilities. In central locations, desktop personal computers may be used. Personal digital assistants (PDAs) or even smart phones can be used in some circumstances where the number of questions is relatively small (Anderson *et al*, 2011). PDAs have also been used successfully as a self-completion medium.

Whichever type of computer is used, it can either provide the interviewer with a questionnaire and means of recording responses, or allow the respondent to participate in the interview through self-completion of part or all of the questionnaire. Either way, it brings a number of advantages for the questionnaire writer, the main one being the ability to include complex routeing between questions. Thus, the next question to be asked of the respondent can be determined by a combination of answers from a number of previous questions. Such complex routeing would have resulted in a significant level of error if the interviewer had had to determine which question was to be asked.

With CAPI, calculations can be programmed into the questionnaire, which it would not have been possible to ask the interviewer to do without risking a high level of error. Thus an estimate of a household's annual consumption of a grocery product can be calculated; this would be impossible for respondents to estimate accurately. However, they may be able to make more accurate estimates of short-term consumption for each member of the family, from which total household consumption can be calculated. In business-to-business interviewing, volumes of consumption or output can be summed either as a total or within predetermined categories, for the interviewer to read back to the respondent to check the accuracy. This information can be used both as inputs to future questions and for question routeing.

The questionnaire writer has to worry less about the layout of the questionnaire with CAPI than with paper questionnaires. Eliminating many interviewer instructions and providing the means of recording pre-coded or numerical data makes this part of the questionnaire writer's task easier.

With pre-coded prompted questions, CAPI can randomize or rotate the order in which the response list is presented to the respondent on-screen. Some researchers prefer to use prompt lists on cards that can be handed to and easily read by the respondent. However, where the respondent is asked to read response lists from the screen, randomization and rotation of response lists can present a significant advantage.

The combination of being able to make calculations and to randomize response lists has led to the development of some complex techniques such as adaptive conjoint analysis. With this technique, the responses to questions asked at the beginning of the sequence are used to construct scenarios shown at later questions where the respondent is asked to provide preferences between them. Even the number of scenarios asked about is determined by the respondent's pattern of answers. While this is theoretically possible with paper questionnaires (and a lot of show cards), the adaptive conjoint questionnaire is made easy to administer with the use of a computerized questionnaire.

Multimedia CAPI provides the questionnaire writer with more opportunities to present colour images, moving images and sound. Thus TV or cinema advertisements can be played as stimuli either for recognition or for evaluation. When evaluating TV or cinema advertisements on CAPI, care must be taken to ensure that all parties involved in implementing the findings are happy with the quality of the reproduction of the ad on the computer screen.

CAPI also presents self-completion options such as having icons or representations of brands that can be moved on the screen and placed in appropriate response boxes by the respondent. Packs can be displayed, and supermarket shelves simulated. This creates opportunities to simulate a presentation, as it would appear in a store, with different numbers of facings for different products, as an attempt to reproduce better the actual in-store choice situation. Three-dimensional pack simulations can be shown and rotated by respondents, while they are asked questions about the simulations.

Electronic questionnaires thus provide the possibility of showing improved stimuli; of offering new ways of measuring consumer response; and of making the process more interesting and involving for the respondent.

Disadvantages of face-to-face interviewing

The main disadvantage of face-to-face interviewing is generally the cost of obtaining a sufficiently representative sample of the survey population. However, that is an issue of survey design and does not relate directly to the interview process.

The accuracy of the data can be influenced by the interaction between interviewer and respondent. Carefully chosen and well-trained interviewers are essential if the quality of the data is to be maximized. The biases that can be introduced by the presence of the interviewer, and the inaccuracies that can be caused if the interviewers fail to ask questions and record responses as they should, have already been discussed in Chapter 1. How to minimize these is part of the skill of the questionnaire writer.

Telephone-administered questionnaires

Advantages of telephone interviewing

Most of the advantages enjoyed by telephone interviewing are to the benefit of the survey design rather than to the questionnaire design. Thus there are efficiencies in cost and speed, particularly where the sample is geographically dispersed, or where, as often happens in business-to-business surveys, the respondents are prepared to talk on the telephone but not to have someone visit them.

One advantage for data accuracy is that the telephone as a medium gives more anonymity to the respondents in respect of their relationship to the interviewer. This can help to diminish some of the bias that can occur as a result of respondents trying to impress or face-save in front of interviewers (see Chapter 15). It is also the experience of many researchers that respondents are more prepared to discuss sensitive subjects such as health on the telephone than face-to-face with an interviewer. Fuller responses are achieved to open questions, and they are more likely to be honest because the interviewer is not physically present with the respondent. Telephone interviewing thus becomes the medium of choice for interviews where there is a need for an interviewer-administered interview, coupled with a sensitive subject matter.

Computer-assisted telephone interviewing (CATI) brings many of the same advantages to this medium as CAPI does to face-to-face interviewing. These include an ability to include complex routeing and calculations within the interview, and the automatic randomization or rotation of question order and of prompt lists within questions.

Disadvantages of telephone interviewing

From the point of view of the questionnaire writer, telephone interviewing has a number of disadvantages.

First, there is limited ability to show material such as prompt lists or stimuli. However, where the list is short it can be read out by the interviewer and remembered by the respondents. When it is straightforward for the respondents to understand, they can hold the question and answer in their head until the time comes for them to respond. It is important that the interviewer reaches the end of the options before the respondent answers, so that the complete list of possible responses is read out. For longer lists of response options, or repeated lists such as scales, respondents can be asked to write them down.

The inability to show material such as concepts or advertising is another drawback to telephone interviewing. Radio ads or the soundtrack from TV ads can be played over the telephone as a prompt for recognition. Care must be taken to distinguish responses that arise because of the quality of the recording as heard by the respondent, which can be variable, from those relating to content. Other ways must be sought, though, for visual material.

It is possible to mail material to respondents for them to look at during the interview. This creates a lengthy and more expensive process. The respondents have to be recruited and agreement obtained in an initial interview; the material then has to be sent; the main interview can only be carried out once the material has arrived.

It may be desirable for respondents not to see the material before a certain point in the interview. In that case, the initial contact would complete the interview up until that point, when respondents would be asked permission for the researcher to send them material and to call them again to complete the interview. This procedure runs the risk of a high proportion of respondents refusing the researcher permission to send the material.

With some populations, it is possible to speed up this process. In business-to-business studies, it is now common to e-mail material to respondents. This means that the gap between the first and second contacts or parts of the interview can be reduced to minutes. By reducing that period, fewer respondents are lost between the two stages.

A possible method of showing material, particularly in business-to-business surveys, is to ask the respondent to log on to a website where the material is displayed. The respondent can log on while the interviewer continues to talk on the telephone, so there is no loss of continuity in the interview. Interviews started on the telephone can be continued on the internet, by asking the respondent to log on to a website that contains the remainder of the questionnaire together with the prompt material.

Self-completion surveys

Self-completion methods, whether paper based or electronic, can benefit from the absence of an interviewer from the process. This removes a major source of potential bias in the responses, and makes it easier for respondents to be honest about sensitive subjects. However, self-completion studies can also suffer from there being no interviewer to identify when a respondent has misunderstood, or to ask for clarification where there are inconsistencies, or to probe for fuller answers.

From the aspect of the survey design, self-completion questionnaires are often considerably cheaper per interview to administer than interviewer-administered ones. Against that must be balanced the difficulties of achieving a representative sample when a high degree of self-selection is typical with self-completion studies, and particularly when there is a low response rate.

Paper questionnaires

Paper self-completion questionnaires are typically sent by mail to people who qualify or are thought to qualify as eligible for the study. They may be members of a panel who have agreed to take part in surveys, or they may be taken from a database such as customers of a company or members of an organization.

Advantages of paper questionnaires

With a paper self-completion questionnaire, respondents have time to consider their answers. They can leave the questionnaire while they think about an issue, or while they go away to check something or look up some information. With little time pressure on them, they can write lengthy and full answers to open questions if they wish to do so.

Descriptive material can be included for evaluation. Written descriptions and pictures of new concepts, products or ideas can be included, and again the respondents have the time to read and digest these before giving their responses. For photographs and drawings, as well as written material, a level of production quality can be achieved that is appropriate to the study.

Disadvantages of paper questionnaires

With a paper self-completion questionnaire, it is impossible to stop respondents from reading through all of the questions before responding. In other modes the question sequence is often carefully chosen by the questionnaire writer to reveal certain pieces of information at a specific point in the interview. That is impossible with this type of questionnaire. Certain questions therefore cannot be included. It is not possible to ask a spontaneous brand awareness question if the questionnaire includes brand names in any of the other questions. Respondents may have read through the questionnaire and will have been prompted by mentions of a brand.

Having time to consider answers, while often an advantage, is not always what the questionnaire writer wants. With attitudinal and image questions, it is often the first reaction that is sought, rather than a considered response. An instruction in the question for respondents to give their first reaction cannot be enforced, nor encouraged in the way that an interviewer can, either face-to-face or by telephone.

Where prompt material has been sent to the respondents for their reaction, it is difficult to retrieve all of it. This can present a security concern if the material is commercially sensitive.

Web-based self-completion

There are several different ways of carrying out surveys using the internet. The questionnaire can either be delivered by e-mail or accessed via a web page. The main approaches are summarized by Bradley (1999) as follows.

Types of internet questionnaires

Open web – a website open to anyone who visits it.

Closed web – respondents are invited to visit a website to complete a questionnaire.

Hidden web – the questionnaire appears to a visitor only when triggered by some mechanism (eg date, visitor number, interest in a specific page). This includes pop-up surveys.

E-mail URL embedded – a respondent is invited by e-mail to the survey site, and the e-mail contains a URL or web address on which respondents click.

Simple e-mail – an e-mail with questions contained in it.

E-mail attachment – the questionnaire is sent as an attachment to an e-mail.

The last two of these, the simple e-mail and e-mail attachment, are rarely used in commercial research for a variety of practical reasons. Attachments require respondents to download the questionnaire, complete it and then return it. This requires a lot of cooperation and has been shown to lead to low response rates. Questionnaires embedded within e-mails can have their layout distorted, depending on the e-mail software with which it is opened. This can lead to the questionnaire being incomprehensible to the recipient. Both of these approaches also suffer from the inability to include complex routeing. Most practitioners now use questionnaires hosted on a website to which respondents are invited or routed in some way. This book will therefore concentrate on the web-based questionnaire.

The invitation to the website or questionnaire can be delivered in a number of ways:

- By link in an e-mail to people on a panel or to a mailing list of customers or people who might qualify for the survey.
- Pop-ups used to direct respondents to the questionnaire while they are visiting another site.
- Invitations can be posted as banner ads on other sites (eg ISP home pages).
- Respondents can be directed to the site following a recruitment interview by telephone, face-to-face or responding to an online advertisement for respondents (Nunan and Knox, 2011).

There are many different ways of capturing a sample online. There are also many issues regarding how representative such samples are of a population that contains people other than those with internet access. These issues are outside the scope of this book and are well covered elsewhere.

Advantages of web-based self-completion

Web-based questionnaires have the same strength as paper self-completion questionnaires in that, in theory at least, respondents can complete the questionnaire in their own time, going away from it if they are interrupted and returning to it later. In practice, there is little evidence that respondents leave a questionnaire while they think about it and return later.

In terms of data collection, the major differences between online surveys and other forms are the same as between postal self-completion and inter-viewer-administered surveys. Any advantages are those that come from being technology driven (Ilieva *et al*, 2002). Some of the differences between online and other forms of data collection given by Taylor (2000) are shown in the box.

Differences between online and other forms of data

- It is a visual medium, allowing images, messages and longer lists of response options. (One survey of motorists has a list of more than 90 different car makes and models for respondents to code their vehicle against. This level of detail would be difficult in any other medium.)

- It captures the unedited voice of the consumer, so that open-ended responses can be richer, longer and more revealing.

- It may be more effective in addressing sensitive issues (medical issues, in particular, may be more easily discussed).

- Scales may elicit different response patterns – it has been the experience both of Taylor and of other researchers that the extremes of scales are used less often.

- More 'Don't knows' may be generated, which is likely to be a function of the 'Don't know' code appearing as a response option.

In addition to online surveys being more effective with sensitive issues, evidence from Kellner (2004) and Basi (1999) supports the view that because there is no interviewer there is less social desirability bias and the respondents answer more honestly (see Chapter 15). This means that data on 'threatening' questions, where respondents feel a need to appear to be socially acceptable, is likely to represent better how the survey population really feels.

The distribution of usage of the points on rating scales has been shown to be different, with less use of the extreme points than is found with face-to-face or telephone interviewing. However, Cobanoglu *et al* (2001) have shown that mean scores for data collected via a web-based questionnaire are the same as for other self-completion methods, postal and fax surveys. This supports the view that using a web-based questionnaire should be seen as an alternative method of administering a self-completion survey.

Most studies of how people respond to web-based questionnaires have found that they are completed more quickly than their equivalent telephone or face-to-face administered versions. Being quicker can help to make it a more pleasurable experience for respondents.

The presentation of the questionnaire can also help to make its completion pleasurable. With a little flair and imagination, web questionnaires can be designed to have visual appeal, an equivalent level of which is often too costly to achieve with paper questionnaires. In addition to the page design, techniques such as showing icons to represent each brand can be used for respondents to move around the screen and drop into the appropriate response box. By involving the respondents more, the interview is more likely to keep their attention and continue to provide good-quality data through to the end of the questionnaire. This is returned to in Chapters 11 and 12.

Demonstration of material can also be achieved with a web-based survey in many of the same ways as with CAPI surveys. TV advertisements can be shown, although the quality with which they are seen will depend on the equipment the respondent is using to view them. There is software available that allows the respondent to rotate the pack representation in three dimensions and even to change elements of it such as colour or text.

With web-based questionnaires there is no possibility of the participant looking ahead and the questions are presented in the sequence that the researcher wants them to be answered. Generally, web-based questionnaires will allow respondents to go back over questions already answered either to check or to change previous answers. However, it is unlikely that respondents will go completely through the interview and then go back to the beginning and change all of their answers.

As with other electronic questionnaires, the web-based questionnaire can:

- change the order of questions between respondents;
- rotate or randomize response lists;
- customize response lists against previous answers;
- cope with complex routeing;
- carry out calculations within the interview.

Disadvantages of web-based self-completion

As with all self-completion media, a major disadvantage is not having an interviewer on hand to clarify questions or to repair misunderstandings. This reinforces the demands made on the questionnaire writer to make the questionnaire clear, unambiguous and engaging.

It might be thought that an issue with web-based questionnaires would be the difficulty of recording open-ended verbatim responses. Most respondents are not accomplished typists, and it might be expected that questions that require responses to be typed in verbatim would be poorly completed, and be at best completed perfunctorily and in abbreviated fashion. However, experience has shown that, while this is undoubtedly an issue with some respondents, the overall level of detail to which this type of question is completed is high. The ability of respondents to take their time and think about their answer appears to more than cancel out any typing difficulties, and responses are generally as complete as for interviewer-administered questionnaires.

Web-based surveys have other disadvantages compared to face-to-face surveys, such as the inability to touch or smell stimuli, but these tend to be issues of survey design rather than questionnaire design.

03 Planning the questionnaire

Introduction

Whatever the type of data collection used, a questionnaire that is going to provide accurate, good-quality information needs to be thought about and planned before any questions are written. The sequence of the different topics that may be covered by the questionnaire, the sequence of individual questions and the sequence in which prompted responses are given can all dramatically affect the accuracy and reliability of the collected data. It is also essential to plan the routeing so that respondents are asked the questions that they should be asked and are not asked those that are irrelevant to them.

From the research objectives plus, if possible, the business objectives, it should be clear what data needs to be collected, in outline if not in detail. Once the researcher knows the definition of the research universe, the data collection medium and the survey design, the questions themselves can be drafted. The steps in planning are:

1 Define the principal information that is required.
2 Determine the secondary information that is required for analysis purposes.
3 Map the flow of the subject areas or sub-sections within the questionnaire.

The questionnaire writer should ask the questions that are relevant to the objectives and not be tempted to ask questions of areas that might be of interest but not relevant to the objectives. To do so is to waste resources in terms of the time of everyone involved, including the respondents, and to spend money unnecessarily.

Defining the information required

It should be clear from the research objectives and the business objectives what information areas the questionnaire needs to cover. This is the principal information such as product and brand awareness and usage, behavioural patterns, attitudes, satisfaction with service, response to concept or test product, etc. The level of detail that is required should also be apparent from the research and business objectives.

Other information required

It may not always be obvious from the research objectives what additional information is required for analysis purposes. This may include demographic or classification data, but could be far broader. In an attitudinal study, for example, it could include brand and product usage so that attitudes can be cross-analysed by products used and weight of usage.

Information may be required to weight the data at the analysis stage to transform it from a sample of product users to represent weight of usage, for example. It is important that the ways in which the data are to be analysed is thought about at the planning stage. If the appropriate data is not collected, the analysis cannot be carried out.

Sequencing the sections

The questionnaire can be properly planned once the principal and analysis information requirements have been decided. It is most commonly divided into three sections: exclusion or security question, screening questions and then the main questionnaire.

Exclusion question

A common though not universal practice is to exclude respondents from research surveys who work in market research, marketing or the client's industry. This will normally be the first question, so that they can be identified and excluded as quickly as possible and neither the respondent's nor the interviewer's time is wasted.

Exclusion by industry or profession is carried out partly to protect the confidentiality of the content of the survey, which could find its way to the desk of a competitor through any one of these routes. It is also carried out to avoid over-representation of unusual behaviour and attitudes.

Someone who works in marketing or market research is likely to differ from the public at large in terms of patterns of behaviour, particularly in relation to new products, higher levels of brand awareness and response to attitudinal questions. People who work in the industry that is the subject of the survey pose not only a threat to the security of the study, but may well have behavioural characteristics that are very different from the rest of the population. Their different behaviour could be due to staff discounts on the products in question or to a high degree of familiarity with the product.

Some companies take the issue of security further and exclude journalists from some or all of their surveys. There is a risk that if journalists are shown a new concept or product, they might be tempted to write a story about it, and what was a closely guarded new idea could quickly become the subject of a press article.

The researcher should decide whether or not to exclude any profession based on the risk posed to the project. A behavioural study of the consumption of bread is unlikely either to reveal any new concepts to respondents or to stimulate the writing of an article. However, a study evaluating a new design for a car is likely to arouse a great deal of interest.

The security question is usually asked as a prompted question, with respondents shown a list of industries and professions. It is advisable to include jobs and professions in addition to those you wish to exclude; this reduces the possibility of a respondent trying to manipulate the outcome. Sometimes respondents will do this unintentionally. Most people's natural inclination is to try to be helpful and answer questions positively. Some people will 'stretch' the eligibility of someone in their household and say that they work in one of the industries or professions, believing that they are being helpful. If the only industries and professions offered are the exclusions, respondents may be eliminated from the study unnecessarily.

Some respondents will deliberately try to manipulate the outcome by saying that someone in their family works in one of the professions or industries because they realize that this is a screening criterion. They may wish not to be interviewed and, correctly, think that by saying that someone in their household works in one of the professions or industries they will be excluded. Or they may want to be interviewed and, mistakenly, think that qualification depends on someone in their household qualifying at this question.

Including a number of professions or industries in which many people work can reduce the effect of all of these biases, by allowing more people to answer positively without unnecessarily excluding themselves.

Typical exclusion question

SHOW CARD A.

Do you or anybody in your household work in any of the industries or professions on this card?

ACCOUNTANCY

ADVERTISING*

COMPUTERS OR INFORMATION TECHNOLOGY

MARKETING/MARKET RESEARCH*

ALCOHOLIC DRINK PRODUCTION OR RETAILING*

BANKING OR INSURANCE

GROCERY RETAILING

NONE OF THESE

* RESPONDENT TO BE EXCLUDED FROM INTERVIEW.
(Asterisks are not shown on the card.)

Screening questions

Following the exclusion question, the next part of the questionnaire will be to screen the respondents for eligibility for the survey, depending on whether or not they belong to the research population. In many surveys the researcher only wants to interview people with certain characteristics – demographic, behavioural or attitudinal. We do not want to find out at the end of the interview that the respondent does not meet the criteria to be included in the sample definition.

Even where the sample is defined as being all adults, there will often be quota requirements on age or social grouping that have to be determined before proceeding with the interview. If drawing a sample from an access panel, much of this will be known beforehand and the sample selected accordingly.

It is common with face-to-face interviewing for demographic criteria not to be asked at the beginning but estimated by the interviewer, who confirms them only at the end of the interview. For gender this usually runs little risk, but for age and social grouping there is a clear risk that the estimation is incorrect. The interviewer discovers this error usually at the end of the interview when completing the classification details. The respondent may then fall into a different quota group than expected, or in a quota group that is already full, or outside any required quota grouping.

Eligibility criteria often include both behavioural and attitudinal questions, or complex behavioural criteria. The screening questions can take several minutes to administer and seem like an interview in their own right to respondents. Lengthy screening also takes up interviewer time, and if paper questionnaires are being used, may lead to errors in the assessment of eligibility. The complexity of the eligibility criteria should be a consideration in the survey design, and kept as simple and as straightforward to administer as possible.

The main questionnaire

The main questionnaire can now be planned.

Once into the main questionnaire, the writer must consider the order in which the various topics are presented to the respondents. As a rule, it is better to work from the most general topics through to the most specific. Thus, the interview might start with questions about the respondent's behaviour in the market in general, before proceeding through to specific questions about the client's product and then to reaction to a new proposition for the client's product. There are two reasons for this.

First, if the questions on the specific product or brand of interest were asked first, the respondents would be aware of the question writer's interest and this would bias their answers to the more general market questions that come later. Raising the respondents' consciousness of the product or brand in question will tend to lead to it being over-represented as a response to any questions that follow. This may include questions about consumption of products or brands in the market generally and lead to overestimation of consumption of the brand of interest.

Second, starting with general questions allows the respondents to think about their behaviour in the market before getting into the detail. Respondents are rarely as interested in the market as are the researcher and client. They may find it difficult to respond immediately to questions about the detail of a particular brand or product. Starting with questions that are more general helps the respondents to ease into the subject, recalling their overall behaviour and how they feel about brands and products before reaching the detailed questions. There are many exceptions to this general rule when there is a good research reason for not starting with the more general questions, but the questionnaire writer should always be prepared to justify the decision.

It is important to map the questionnaire so that it flows logically from one subject area to the next. Avoid returning to a topic area previously asked about. This makes the questionnaire appear not to have been thought through, can confuse respondents who think that they have dealt with this already and, with paper questionnaires, can frequently require interviewers to refer back for information already given, which may lead to errors.

A flow diagram can assist in ensuring that all topics are covered and that respondents are asked the sections that are relevant to them. In the example flow chart (see Figure 3.1), the objective is to establish what journey types buses are used for; to determine why the bus or other public transport is preferred to using a car; and to obtain a rating of different types of public transport. People who do not use any form of public transport are not to be asked this last section. This diagram does not tell us precisely what questions need to be asked. What it determines is how the question areas that the different categories of respondents (bus users, non-bus users who use other public transport, and people who use no public transport) need to be asked will flow.

FIGURE 3.1   Flow chart to plan questionnaire

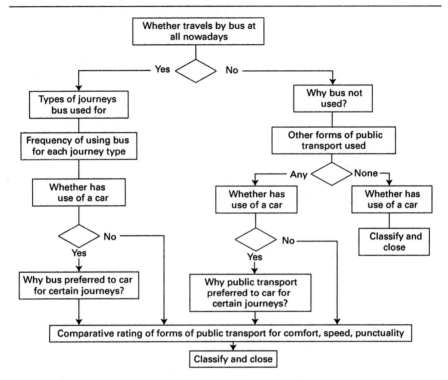

The flow chart also demonstrates that there will be some routeing issues. Whether or not the respondent has use of a car appears three times in different paths. Complex routeing will be required if the questionnaire writer decides that this question should appear only once, to facilitate analysis. Alternatively, the same question can appear three times, once in the path of each respondent category. The latter approach is less likely to result in interviewer error if using paper questionnaires, or in routeing errors within electronic questionnaires.

The flow chart is a very useful aid in checking the routeing in computer-aided questionnaires. Without a chart, it can be difficult to determine whether every routeing has been correctly defined in the script, and there are many examples of important questions not being asked because of routeing errors not picked up in script checking.

Behaviour before attitude

It is generally advisable to start any section of the interview with behavioural questions before going on to ask about attitudes and images. This is in part to allow the respondents to assess their behavioural position and then to explain their behaviour through their attitudes. Behavioural questions are usually easier to answer because they relate to fact and require only recall. If respondents find it difficult to answer behavioural questions, this is usually because the questionnaire writer has been too ambitious in the level of detail expected, and the reliability of the information that is being reported will be in doubt.

If attitudes are asked first there is a danger that respondents will take a position that is not thought through and that is contradicted by their behaviour. They may well then misreport their behaviour in order to justify their attitudes.

Spontaneous before prompted

It may appear obvious, but great care must be taken not to prompt respondents with possible answers before asking questions designed to obtain their spontaneous response. Thus you cannot ask, 'Which brands of instant coffee can you think of?' if you have already asked, 'Which of the brands of instant coffee on this list do you buy?'

Sometimes it can be virtually impossible to obtain a 'clean' measure of spontaneous brand awareness, particularly where purchase or consumption of a brand is one of the screening criteria for eligibility. This is because respondents will have been exposed to a list of brands in the screening questions. This is a particular issue with certain types of surveys such as advertising testing. Here respondents may be recruited based on their brand consumption in order to evaluate a new advertisement. Part of that evaluation may be to show the test advertisement among other ads. For TV ads this would be as part of a clutter reel; for press ads they would be contained within a mock-up of a newspaper or magazine. The test ad will, however, stand out from the rest if the respondents have been sensitized to the brand or the category through the screening questions. To ameliorate this, a series of mock screening questions are sometimes asked that relate to the products and categories shown in the other ads. While this is unlikely to reduce the sensitization of the respondents to the test ad's category, it does raise the level of sensitization so that it is the same for all the ads, thereby cancelling out the differential effect. This type of strategy often needs to be adopted where it is essential that prompting occurs earlier than is desirable.

Prompting also extends to attitudes. A questionnaire may include a series of attitude statements to which respondents are asked to respond. If attitudes on the same subject are to be assessed spontaneously, that must be asked before the attitude statements have been shown or respondents will continue to play back the attitudes with which they have been prompted.

Sensitive sections

If the interview is to include questions of a sensitive nature, if possible they should not be asked at the beginning of the interview. Where the questionnaire is interviewer-administered, this allows a relationship to be built between interviewer and respondent, so that the respondent is more willing to disclose sensitive information. The trust that has hopefully been built between them reassures the respondent that the information will not be abused.

With web-based questionnaires, these questions should also be positioned towards the end of the interview. Although there is no interviewer, there is still a relationship built between the respondent and 'the survey'. Having been prepared to divulge less sensitive information in earlier questions, it may be less difficult for respondents then to disclose data that are more sensitive. Such questions at the beginning of the interview are likely to be seen as more intrusive and provoke a greater level of non-response or termination of interview.

A further reason for asking sensitive questions later in the interview is that if the interview is terminated at this point by the respondent, most of the data has already been collected and may be usable. In extreme cases where it is expected that the level of termination due to intrusiveness of the questions will be high, being able to salvage as much information as possible will be part of the questionnaire writer's strategy, and all key questions required for analysis will have already been asked. However, if questions are so intrusive as to cause a significant level of offence, the questionnaire writer should consider the ethical position carefully before including them. (See Chapter 14 for what may constitute a sensitive topic.)

Classification questions

Partly because they can be seen as intrusive, classification questions are normally asked at the end of the interview. They are also positioned here because they are usually disconnected from the subject matter of the interview. Asking them earlier in the interview would disrupt the flow of the 'conversation'. Information such as gender, age, income, social grouping, final level of education, TV viewing, number of children in household, etc rarely relate directly to the subject of the study. However, they are proven discriminators in many behavioural and attitudinal fields and so are invaluable for cross-analysis purposes.

The researcher should resist the temptation to ask for more classification data than are needed simply because it might be useful for cross-analysis. This is often personal information and respondents do not always understand why it is needed.

04

Types of question

Introduction

Questions can be asked and data recorded in many ways. Different types of questions are appropriate for different purposes and different types of data can be used and analysed differently. It is important for the questionnaire writer to understand the range of question types available because the choice of question type will determine the information that is elicited. It is also important to understand the different types of data that will be generated, because that will determine the types of analysis that can be carried out.

Question types

Any question in an interview can be classified in a number of different ways:

- open or closed, depending on whether or not the answer can come only from a finite number of possible responses;
- spontaneous or prompted, depending on whether respondents are asked to reply in their own words or given a number of options from which to choose a response;
- open-ended or pre-coded, depending on whether the answer is recorded verbatim or against one or more of a number of predetermined answers.

We are using here the definition of an open-ended question that is commonly used in market research, which is that the responses are recorded verbatim, and distinguishing it from an open question, which seeks a response that may or may not be recorded verbatim. Whether a question is open-ended or pre-coded is determined by how responses are recorded rather than the question itself.

Open questions are usually asked spontaneously, and any prompted question is likely to be closed. Prompted questions will usually be pre-coded, but open questions can be recorded either as open-ended (verbatim) or pre-coded responses.

Open and closed questions

An open question is one where the range of possible answers is not suggested in the question and which respondents are expected to answer in their own words:

'Tell me what you ate for breakfast today.'

'How did you travel here?'

'What did you like about this product?'

An open question may elicit a short answer, where the anticipated answer would simply be one or more products, or it may lead respondents to talk as long as possible using their own words in order to give fully their answer, as in, 'Why do you eat that brand of breakfast cereal more than any other?' Open questions always seek a spontaneous, that is unprompted, response. In conversation, one person trying to start another person talking about a topic would use an open question.

The responses may be recorded verbatim as an open-ended question ('Why do you eat …?') or, with interviewer-administered surveys, a list of the most commonly given responses may be provided that can be coded ('Which brand did you eat …?'). Open pre-coded questions often require the interviewer to match the response given to one of the codes available in the questionnaire. The questionnaire writer must make sure that the code list is clear, comprehensive and unambiguous.

Closed questions, on the other hand, tend, in conversation, to bring it to a stop. This is because there is a predictable and usually small set of answers to a closed question that the respondent can give. Any question that simply requires the answer 'yes' or 'no' is a closed question, and not helpful to opening out a conversation. An evening spent with a new acquaintance with both of you asking only closed questions would be very dull indeed.

In a research interview, closed questions also include any question where the respondent is asked to choose from a number of alternative answers. Thus any prompted question is a closed question. Examples of closed questions are:

'Have you drunk any beer in the last 24 hours?'

'Are you aged under 25?'

'Which of these brands of tinned meat do you buy most often?'

'Which of the phrases on this card best indicates how likely you are to buy this product?'

These are all closed questions, the first two because they can only be answered 'yes' or 'no', and the last two because there is a frame of possible responses from which the respondent is asked to choose.

Closed, and therefore pre-coded, questions are popular with researchers and interviewers alike because there is a set of answers known beforehand that can be listed on the questionnaire. With a paper questionnaire the interviewer only has to circle the appropriate code and that code can easily be entered into the data file by those responsible for data entry. With an electronic questionnaire, either the interviewer or the respondent only has to check the appropriate box and the data is automatically recorded and stored, ready for analysis. This type of question is usually easy to administer and cheap to process.

A questionnaire that measures behaviour is likely to consist mostly of closed questions ('Which of these brands ...?', 'When did you last ...?', 'How many did you buy?'), whereas one exploring attitudes is likely to have a higher proportion of open questions. From the point of view of maintaining the involvement of the respondent, the interview should consist of a mixture of both types of question (see Figure 4.1).

FIGURE 4.1   Examples of question types

OPEN QUESTIONS CAN APPEAR AS EITHER OPEN-ENDED OR PRE-CODED QUESTIONS		
OPEN QUESTION	OPEN-ENDED	Why do you prefer Product A to Product B? Please write in your answer in your own words
	PRE-CODED	Why do you prefer Product A to Product B? INTERVIEWER: CODE RESPONSE AGAINST LIST OF ANSWERS
CLOSED QUESTION	PRE-CODED	For which of these reasons do you prefer Product A to Product B? Please mark as many reasons on the list below as apply

Spontaneous questions

A spontaneous question is any question for which the respondent is not given a repertoire of possible answers from which to choose. All open-ended questions are by their nature spontaneous, but not all spontaneous questions need be open-ended.

Spontaneous questions will be used when the questionnaire writer does not know what the range of responses is likely to be, or wants to collect the response in the respondent's own words. These will be open-ended questions with the response recorded verbatim for later coding.

The decision whether or not to make a spontaneous question open-ended depends on whether it is important to record the response verbatim and whether the full range, or at least the majority, of likely responses is known.

A spontaneous question will also be used where the researcher wants to find out what the respondent knows without being prompted.

One of the difficulties with spontaneous questions is that the amount of effort that respondents are prepared to make with their answers varies depending on how interested they are in the subject and on the medium of the interview.

Common uses of spontaneous questions

Spontaneous open questions are frequently used in market research to measure awareness and attitudes, for example:

- brand awareness;
- awareness of brands seen advertised;
- recall of brands or products used or bought;
- advertising content recall;
- attitudes towards a product, or activity or situation;
- likes and dislikes of a product or concept.

The first three in this list would normally be pre-coded on an interviewer-administered questionnaire, where the interviewers can easily code the response without prompting the respondents.

With spontaneous questions we are trying to determine what is at the forefront of people's minds; information they can easily access. We interpret this as *saliency* in the case of brands, or as *importance* in the case of attitudes. Spontaneous questions are not a good measure of all of the brands people have heard of, nor of behaviour, nor of the full range of attitudes or emotions. Prompted questions usually elicit more complete and accurate responses in terms of behaviour.

Spontaneous brand awareness

Spontaneous brand awareness is a measure of which brands are the most salient in the respondents' minds. It would be the result of the following or similar questioning: 'Which brands of breakfast cereal have you heard of?' The objective here is to obtain every brand that the respondent can think of, and so probes asking for 'What else?' or 'Any more?' will be used extensively in interviewer-administered interviews. The list of possible brands will usually be given as pre-codes on the questionnaire for the interviewer to record responses. Frequently the first brand mentioned will be recorded separately, to give a measure of 'top of mind awareness'.

With self-completion questionnaires (including web-based), spontaneous questions must be recorded as open-ended responses to avoid prompting the respondents. With paper self-completion questionnaires, it is not possible to obtain spontaneous awareness if any brands are mentioned anywhere in the questionnaire. Respondents will read through the questionnaire and will be prompted by any brand names that appear.

Sometimes we wish to know precisely how respondents refer to a brand. Then, in any data collection medium, the responses will be recorded verbatim. The researcher can then determine whether it is the brand, sub-brand or variant that is mentioned, or what combination of these. This is particularly used in advertising research where it can be important to know precisely what level of branding is being communicated.

Spontaneous brand awareness is subject to the effort that respondents are prepared to make. This can vary according to where the interview takes place. It has been demonstrated on numerous occasions that the average number of brands that are given spontaneously in face-to-face street interviews is significantly lower than with face-to-face in-home interviews, which is in turn lower than with online surveys. Not only is the average number lower in the street, but the distribution of the brands mentioned is also different. In the street, where less effort is made, the dominant brands in a market will tend to be mentioned. Their spontaneous brand awareness figures may be similar to those obtained elsewhere, but the smaller and newer brands get lower prompted awareness levels.

Spontaneous advertising awareness

When evaluating the effect of an advertising campaign, spontaneous advertising awareness is usually a key measure. Exactly how this is measured, though, differs between researchers.

One way is to ask spontaneous brand awareness first, followed by a spontaneous awareness of brands seen advertised, followed by content recall of the advertising claimed to have been seen. All questions require spontaneous responses; the first two are likely to be pre-coded with a list of brands, and the third question will be open-ended:

'Which brands of breakfast cereal have you heard of?'

'Which brands of breakfast cereal have you seen or heard advertising for recently?'

'What did the advertising say, or what was it about?'

Repeat the last question for all brands for which advertising has been seen.

An alternative approach is not to ask brand awareness first, but to ask the respondent to recall spontaneously any advertising for any brand in the category:

'Please describe to me any advertising that you have seen recently for a breakfast cereal. What did it say? What was it about? What brand was that for?'

Repeat until the respondent can recall no more advertising.

'Please tell me any other brands of breakfast cereal that you have seen advertising for.'

Proponents of this approach argue that, by leading with the brand recall in the first approach, the best-known brands score well as respondents assume that they have seen advertising for them, whether or not they have actually been advertising. By leading with advertising content recall, without mentioning any brands, the second approach claims to attain a truer measure of memorability of the advertising.

Spontaneous attitudinal questions

Spontaneous questions regarding attitudes can be either open-ended or pre-coded. Typical spontaneous attitudinal questions are:

'What, if anything, do you like about ...?'

'What, if anything, do you dislike about ...?'

'How do you feel about ...?'

'Please describe to me your feelings about ...'

The responses to these questions would most likely be recorded verbatim as open-ended answers. This enables the capture of the full range of answers in the code frame, which may include some that were not anticipated. This also allows the researcher to see the precise language used by respondents to describe their feelings and attitudes.

Preliminary qualitative research may have been carried out so that the full range of attitudes held on the issue in question has been determined. The study may be a repeat of a previous one in which the attitudes were defined. In these cases summaries of the main attitudes may be pre-coded on interviewer-administered questionnaires, to save the time and expense of coding the responses at the analysis stage. With any kind of self-completion questionnaire pre-coding is not a possibility if the attitudes are to be expressed spontaneously.

Prompted questions

Spontaneous responses rarely give the researcher the complete picture regarding what the respondent knows or feels, but only what is front-of-mind. However, most people find it difficult to articulate everything that they know or feel about a subject, or they forget that they know something, or they have given one answer and aren't prepared to make further effort to think of additional answers. Prompting with a set of options tells the researcher what people know or recognize, rather than what is front-of-mind, if we are measuring awareness or recognition. Alternatively, prompting helps people to recall actions and behaviour, and to express their answers in the framework desired by the researcher.

For prompted awareness questions that follow a spontaneous question on the same issue it may sometimes be helpful to include the phrase 'including any that you have already mentioned'. Whether or not this phrase is

used, the analysis should always re-record any answers mentioned spontaneously on to the prompted recognition answer for each respondent.

Open-ended questions

An open-ended question is an open question where the response is recorded
verbatim. An open-ended question is nearly always also an open question.
(It would be wasteful to record yes/no answers verbatim.) Open-ended questions are also known as 'unstructured' or 'free-response' questions. Open-
ended questions are used for a number of reasons:

- The researcher cannot predict what the responses might be, or it is
  dangerous to do so. Questions about what is liked or disliked about
  a product or service should always be open-ended, as it would be
  presumptuous to assume what people might like or dislike by having
  a list of pre-codes.

- We want to know the precise phraseology that people use to respond
  to the question. We may be able to predict the general sense of the
  response but wish to know the terminology that people use.

- We may want to quote some verbatim responses in the report or
  presentation to illustrate something such as the strength of feeling
  that respondents feel. In response to the question, 'Why will you not
  use that company again?', a respondent may write in: 'They were …
  awful. They mucked me about for months, didn't respond to my
  letters and when they did they could never get anything right. I shall
  never use them again.' Had pre-codes been given on the questionnaire
  this might simply have been recorded as 'Poor service'. The verbatim
  response provides much richer information to the end user of the
  research.

Through analysis of the verbatim responses, clients can determine if the
customer is talking about a business process, a policy issue, a people issue
(especially in service delivery surveys), etc. This enables them to determine
the extent of any challenges they will face when reporting the findings of the
survey to their management.

Common uses for open-ended questions include:

- likes and dislikes of a product, concept, advertisement, etc;
- spontaneous descriptions of product images;
- spontaneous descriptions of the content of advertisements;
- reasons for choice of product/store/service provider;
- why certain actions were taken or not taken;
- what improvements or changes respondents would like to see.

These are all directive questions, aimed at eliciting a specific type of response to a defined issue. In addition, non-directive questions can be asked,

such as what, if anything, comes to mind when the respondent is shown a visual prompt, and whether there is anything else that the respondent wants to say on the subject. Questions that ask 'What?', 'Why?' or 'How?', or for likes and dislikes, will commonly be open-ended.

Open-ended questions are easy to ask but suffer from several drawbacks:

- In interviewer-administered surveys they are subject to error in the way and the detail with which the interviewer records the answer.

- Respondents frequently find it difficult both to recognize and to articulate how they feel. This is particularly true of negative feelings, so asking open-ended questions about what people dislike about something tends to generate a high level of 'Nothing' or 'Don't know' responses.

- Without the clues given by an answer list, respondents sometimes misunderstand the question or answer the question that they want to answer rather than the one on the questionnaire.

- Analysing the responses can be a difficult, time-consuming and relatively expensive process.

In addition, some commentators (Peterson, 2000) see verbosity of respondents as a problem with open-ended questions. It is argued that if one respondent says only one thing that he or she likes about a product, but another says six things, the latter respondent will be given six times the weight of the former in the analysis. To even this up, only the first response of the more verbose respondent is counted. In practice, interviewers are trained to extract as much detail as possible from respondents to open-ended questions. The objective is to identify the full range of responses given by all respondents and to determine the proportion of the sample that agrees with each of them.

To analyse the responses, a procedure known as 'coding' is used. Manual coding requires a sample of the answers to be examined and the answers grouped under commonly occurring themes, usually known as a 'code frame'. If the coder is someone other than the researcher, that list of themes needs to be discussed with the researcher to see whether it meets the latter's needs. The coder may have grouped answers relating to low price and to value for money together as a single theme, but the researcher may see them as distinct issues and want them separated. The researcher may be looking for specific responses to occur that have not arisen in the sample of answers listed. It may be important for the researcher to know that few people mention this, but to be sure that this is the case the theme must be included on the code frame. When the list of themes has been agreed, each theme is allocated a code and all questionnaires are then inspected and coded according to the themes within each respondent's answer.

Manual coding is a slow and labour-intensive activity, particularly when there is a large sample size and the questionnaire contains many open-ended questions. Most research agencies will include a limit to the number of open-ended questions in their quote for a project, because it is such a significant variable in the costing.

There are a number of computerized coding systems available that are increasingly used by research companies (Esuli and Sebastiani, 2010). Word recognition software has also helped to automate this process. These reduce but do not eliminate the human input required. Responses to open-ended questions can be input to word cloud software producing a visually appealing demonstration of the most frequent terms used.

Probing

With most open questions it is important to extract from respondents as much information as they can provide. The first reason they give for having bought that brand may be the same for all brands and will not discriminate. Although it is the first that comes to mind, it may not be the one in which the researcher is most interested. First responses given to open questions are often very bland, and non-directional probing is required to try to fill out the answer.

Probing is very different from prompting, and the two must not be confused. In prompting, respondents are given a number of possible answers from which to choose, or are given clues to the answers through visual or picture prompts. Probing makes no suggestions regarding answers to the respondent. A typical probe with instructions is:

'What else did you like about the product?' PAUSE. THEN PROBE: 'What else?' CONTINUE UNTIL NO FURTHER ANSWERS.

The object here is to keep respondents talking in reply to the initial question in their own words until there is no more that they can or wish to say. They are not led in any direction.

Do not use phrases such as, 'Is there anything else?' as a probe. That form of probe allows or even encourages the respondents to say, 'No, nothing else.' If the probe is, 'What else?' this makes a presumption that there is more that the respondent wants to say and puts the onus on the respondent to indicate that he or she has no more to say. This helps the researcher to obtain the fullest answer rather than helping the respondent to say as little as possible. With self-completion questionnaires, either paper or online, the size of the space allowed acts as a visual probe, encouraging respondents to keep answering for longer (Christian and Dillman, 2004).

It is occasionally possible to anticipate unhelpful answers and ask for these specific responses to be elaborated. A common example is when respondents give 'convenience' as an answer to why they use a particular shop or travel by a particular type of transport. This is a common answer given to this type of question, but is frustratingly unhelpful. Where it is anticipated that this will occur, an instruction may be given to interviewers to probe for more information on the way it was convenient, and what 'convenience' means to the respondent.

Pre-coded questions

Pre-coded open questions

Frequently with interviewer-administered surveys, a list of pre-codes is provided with open questions for the interviewer's use. This may simply be a brand list on which to code the response to a question such as 'Which brand of breakfast cereal did you eat today?' or it may be used in order to categorize more complex responses (see Figure 4.2).

This requires the questionnaire writer to second-guess what the range of responses is going to be. It is usually done to save time and the cost of coding open-ended verbatim responses. This approach might also be used to try to provide some consistency of response by forcing the open responses into a limited number of options. It is important that there is always a space provided for the respondent or interviewer to write in answers that are not covered by the pre-codes. It is unlikely that the questionnaire writer will have thought of every possible response that will be given, and it is not unusual for quite large proportions of the responses to be written in as 'other answers'. However, there is still a danger that respondents or interviewers will try to force responses into one of the codes given rather than write in a response that is close to, but does not quite fit, one of the pre-codes.

FIGURE 4.2   Pre-codes used to categorize responses to open questions

Q. Why did you buy that particular brand of mayonnaise?
DO NOT PROMPT

IT'S THE ONE I ALWAYS BUY	1
THE ONLY ONE AVAILABLE	2
THE CHEAPEST	3
ON SPECIAL OFFER	4
THE FLAVOUR I WANTED	5
THE PACK SIZE I WANTED	6
OTHER ANSWER (WRITE IN)	7

The richness and illustrative power of the verbatim answer is lost by providing pre-codes, as are any subtle distinctions between responses, but the processing time and cost will be reduced. Consistency with other surveys may also be increased. The code list may be based on qualitative research that has suggested the range of answers that could be expected or on the results of previous studies.

Pre-coded closed questions

Closed questions will tend to be pre-coded. Either a prompt list of possible answers is used or there is a known and finite number of responses that can be given. These are provided on a code list for the interviewer or the respondent to select. There is little point in not providing such a list and requiring the answers to be written in, with the consequent cost and time of having to code the responses.

Dichotomous questions

The simplest of closed questions are dichotomous questions, which have only two possible answers:

'Have you drunk any beer in the last 24 hours?'

Yes

No

Dichotomous questions such as this are easy to write and easy to ask.

Multiple choice

Closed questions with more than one possible answer are known as multiple choice (or multi-chotomous) questions. Such a question might be: 'Which brand or brands of beer on this list have you drunk in the last seven days?' Clearly, there is a finite number of answers; the range of possible answers is predictable; and the question does not require respondents to say anything 'in their own words'. By defining the brands of interest the questionnaire has made this a closed question.

'Don't know' responses

Questionnaire writers are often unsure as to whether they should include a 'Don't know' response to pre-coded questions. With interviewer-administered questionnaires, it is argued, the inclusion of 'Don't know' legitimizes it as a response. If it is not on the questionnaire, the interviewer will be more likely to probe for a response that is on the pre-code list before having to write in that the respondent is unable or unwilling to answer the question.

'Don't know' can be a legitimate response to many questions where the respondent genuinely does not know the answer, and there should be no difficulty in identifying questions where a 'Don't know' code must be included:

'Which mobile phone service does your partner subscribe to?'

'When was your house last repainted?'

'From which store was the jar of coffee bought?'

With other questions, though, it is not always so clear. These tend to be questions either of opinion, where a likelihood of action is sought, or of recent behaviour, which the respondent could be expected to remember:

'Where in the house would you be most likely to use this air freshener?'

'What method of transport did you use to get here today?'

'Which brand of tomato soup did you buy most recently?'

A good reason for having a 'Don't know' code on interviewer-administered paper questionnaires is that without it the response may be left blank. The researcher cannot then be sure that the question was asked. Knowing that the respondent could not or would not answer the question gives a positive assurance to the researcher that the interview was administered correctly.

This can also provide important information about the knowledge of respondents and their ability to answer this question. Isolated responses of this type might indicate that those respondents were not recruited correctly to the desired criteria. Widespread responses of this type might indicate that the information asked is beyond the scope of this research universe (eg asking post room managers in businesses about the size of the company's stationery bill) or that the question is poorly worded and not understood by many of the respondents. This is generally information worth knowing and should encourage the inclusion of 'Don't know' codes on the questionnaire.

Bias can be introduced under certain circumstances if there is no 'Don't know' code. For example, if a brand name is asked for it is more likely that the brand leader (or best-known brand if that is different) will be the one that comes to mind first, or will be the one that respondents guess that they are most likely to have bought recently. Less-well-known brands may get under-represented, so a bias has been introduced through the lack of a 'Don't know' code.

With CAPI and CATI questionnaires it is usual to provide a 'Don't know' code for most questions, as, without being able to record that, it may not be possible to move on to the next question. With self-completion question-naires, the provision of a 'Don't know' code has to be considered question by question. Such a code on every question may indeed encourage respond-ents not to think sufficiently about their response, and if there is any uncer-tainty, to answer 'Don't know'. It is prudent, therefore, to limit the use of 'Don't know' categories to those questions where the researcher believes it to be a genuine response. With web-based self-completion question-naires there are other issues regarding not encouraging respondents to give 'Don't know' as an answer, while enabling them to continue to the next question. These issues are considered as a matter of questionnaire layout in Chapters 10 and 11.

05

Data types

Responses are measured using four types of data: nominal, ordinal, interval and ratio. It is important for the questionnaire writer to recognize which type of data is being collected for each question, as this will determine the type of analysis that can be carried out.

Nominal data

Nominal data is data that is classified into discrete categories by name, eg male, female; New York, Chicago, Los Angeles; purchaser of pizza, non-purchaser of pizza. Depending on the type of data collection system used, a number will often be assigned to each category. However, that number is purely arbitrary and implies no value that can be given to the response category; the numbers are given for identification purposes only. Thus if a sampling point is described as 'Urban' and is given a code of 1, and 'Rural' is assigned a code 2, there is no relative value implied between the two categories (see Figure 5.1). Respondents are classified into one category or another. The categories should be exhaustive (ie everybody should fit somewhere) and mutually exclusive (ie there is no overlap between them).

FIGURE 5.1 Assigning code numbers for identification purposes

Q. Which of these supermarkets in your opinion sells the best-quality fresh vegetables?

Asda	1
Morrisons	2
Safeway	3
Sainsbury's	4
Somerfield	5
Tesco	6

The responses are usually presented in an order that is the most convenient for the respondent, which may be alphabetically, or by size, or by geography. Nothing can be done with the data except to count the number of responses against each code. It is meaningless to calculate an average across the responses or to carry out any other calculation based on the value of the code.

Ordinal data

Ordinal data is usually found in questionnaires as ranking scales, otherwise known as 'comparative scales'. Respondents are asked to put nominal categories in order according to a criterion contained in the question. This is often order of preference, as in Figure 5.2.

FIGURE 5.2   Placing nominal categories in order

Q. Please put the following flavours of yoghurt in the order in which you prefer them, starting with 1 for your first choice through to 5 for your least preferred.

Blackcurrant	3
Black cherry	1
Peach	4
Raspberry	5
Strawberry	2

Other questions might include ranking by order of:

- a product characteristic – sweetness, consistency, strength;
- frequency of use – most used, next most used, etc;
- recency of use – last used, next to last used, etc;
- perceived price – most expensive to least expensive;
- ease of comprehension – easiest to understand to most difficult.

Ranking puts the nominal data into the appropriate order, but tells the researcher nothing about the distance between the points. In the example above, strawberry yoghurt might be liked almost as well as black cherry, with both of them liked considerably more than blackcurrant. The researcher cannot deduce this from the data. Nor can the researcher determine whether the last choice, raspberry, is actively disliked and would never be chosen by this respondent, or whether it is firmly in the repertoire of flavours. It may even be the case that the respondent actually likes none of these five flavours and the ranking is based on which flavours are least disliked.

Ranking can be used to force differences between brands, products or services, which would not be apparent with rating scales. On a five-point rating scale of sweetness, from not at all sweet to very sweet, the five flavours of yoghurt may all be rated fairly or very sweet, giving the researcher insufficient discrimination in the resulting data. By using ranking, that discrimination is forced out.

In an experiment where they assessed 13 attributes of children for desirability, Alwin and Krosnick (1985) found that there was general agreement in what were most and least important but that 12 of the attributes were rated 'extremely important' by between 24 and 40 per cent of respondents, a span of 17 percentage points giving poor discrimination between them. The same attributes ranked as one to three of the most important spanned 3 to 41 per cent giving much greater discrimination but at the loss of the knowledge that even the least important is extremely important to a quarter of the sample.

The task of ranking can become difficult for respondents where there is a large number of items. Suppose that we want to ask respondents to give their order of preference for 15 flavours of yogurt. With electronic self-completion interviews, either web-based or CAPI, the process of doing this is relatively straightforward, as respondents can be asked to drag and drop the flavour descriptions into their rank order of preference, but is still intellectually a significant task.

Ranking 15 flavours of yoghurt would be a tedious exercise. Even if they could do it, for many people it would be unrealistic, as they may have a number that they like and a number that they dislike, but have some in between that they have no feelings about. The length of the task and its unrealistic nature would be likely to lead to fatigue, with a consequent lack of care given to the responses. There may be a knock-on effect to the rest of the interview, damaging the quality of the responses thereafter. With interviewer-administered and paper questionnaires the task is even more onerous. This problem can be approached in a number of ways.

Respondents can be asked to rank their preferred flavours up to a predetermined number and their least preferred, or those that they don't like at all, if this is more appropriate. Or they may be asked to rank their preferred three and then to nominate their least preferred three, but with no order recorded for the least preferred.

In a face-to-face interview, each flavour can be presented on a card (see Figure 5.3). Respondents are asked to put their five preferred flavours (or the five sweetest flavours, or whatever is appropriate to the question) in one pile, and the five least preferred (or least sweet) in a second pile. They are then asked to rank-order the cards in each pile, from preferred to least preferred.

This type of exercise then gives a notional rank order equal to the mid-point for all of the items not ranked in the top or bottom five. This is not unrealistic, as respondents will often know what they like and what they

FIGURE 5.3   Ranking preferences

Q. SHOW CARD.

On this card are 15 different flavours of yoghurt.

a) Which one do you prefer most?

b) Which is your second preference?

c) Which next?

d) And which three do you like least?

	Preferred	Second preference	Third preference	Three liked least
Apricot	1	2	3	4
Banana	1	2	3	4
Black cherry	1	2	3	4
Blackcurrant	1	2	3	4
Gooseberry	1	2	3	4
Grapefruit	1	2	3	4
Mandarin	1	2	3	4
Passion fruit	1	2	3	4
Peach	1	2	3	4
Pear	1	2	3	4
Pineapple	1	2	3	4
Raspberry	1	2	3	4
Rhubarb	1	2	3	4
Strawberry	1	2	3	4
Tangerine	1	2	3	4

dislike, and have a group of items in between about which they have no strong views.

Interval scales

Interval scales provide for a rating of each item on a scale that has a numerically equal distance between each point, and an arbitrary, zero point. Such scales are used to determine the relative strength of relationships between items. The five flavours of yoghurt could be individually rated on a scale from 1 to 10 for how much each is liked. There is an equal interval between each point, but a score of 8 does not necessarily mean that the item is preferred twice as much as another item scored 4. The advantage of the interval scale over the ordinal scale is that the researcher can tell whether an item is liked or disliked (or thought to be sweet or not, etc) by its rating. It will, however, not always be possible to assign a rank order for the items from this information.

Figure 5.4 gives the results for two respondents asked to rate the five yoghurt flavours on a 10-point interval scale. The first respondent has given a different score to each flavour, so that not only can we rank-order that person, but we can now tell that the person likes black cherry and strawberry rather better than blackcurrant, whilst peach and raspberry are not liked. The second respondent, however, likes all five flavours and it is difficult to deduce a meaningful rank order of preference from the interval scale responses.

FIGURE 5.4   Rating on an interval scale

Please give each flavour a mark between 1 and 10 based on how much you like it.

	Respondent 1		Respondent 2	
	Rating 1 to 10	Deduced ranking	Rating 1 to 10	Deduced ranking
Blackcurrant	5	3	9	1=
Black cherry	9	1	8	3=
Peach	2	4	9	1=
Raspberry	1	5	8	3=
Strawberry	8	2	8	3=

In practice, the researcher is rarely dealing with data at an individual level but with aggregated data over the whole sample. Interval scales allow mean scores and standard deviations to be calculated across the sample for each item. Using mean scores can often appear to overcome this, as over a large sample it is rare for the mean score for two items to be identical. The analyst, though, must be careful that any two mean scores are significantly different with a desired level of confidence before concluding that across the sample one item is rated differently to another.

The distribution of the data across the scale should also be examined because the same mean score can be produced by very different distributions. Many of the scales used in measuring attitude, brand perceptions, customer satisfaction, etc are interval scales; these include the semantic differential scale and Likert scale.

Ratio scales

Ratio scales are a particular type of interval scale. The zero point has a real meaning, such that the ratio between any two scores also has a meaning. Age is a ratio scale, with a 50-year-old person being twice as old as a 25-year-old. Income is another.

This type of scale is also used to ask questions such as:

'Out of the last 10 cans of baked beans that you bought, how many were Heinz?'

'What proportion of your household income do you spend on your rent or mortgage?'

'How long ago did you buy your car?'

In some instances we might choose to record the responses directly and sometimes within categories. For these three questions the recording of the responses may be as in Figure 5.5.

Note that the response categories are not necessarily of equal length. These have been chosen to suit the purposes of the researcher or to reflect the expected distribution of the data. The proportion of income spent on rent or mortgage could have been recorded as a direct percentage and categorized at the analysis stage. The reason for putting this into bands is that most respondents will not know the answer to the exact percentage point, and if they are asked to be precise, this could lead to a higher level of non-response to this question. The length of time since respondents bought their car could be recorded as days, months or years. Few could work out the number of days, however, and only the most recent buyers would easily be able to give the time in months. The researcher here is particularly interested in differences between people who have bought their car relatively recently, so it is important to be able to distinguish between very recent purchasers (within the last three months) and less recent purchasers.

Be aware, though, that changing the scale can alter the way in which people respond. Dillman (2000) quotes an example where responses in the same category changed from 23 to 69 per cent when that category changed from being the highest response to being the lowest response on a time-based ratio scale. The category options facing most question writers will rarely be so great as to result in this scale of difference, but this emphasizes the importance of making the scale appropriate to the anticipated distribution of answers.

The fact that the recording of the data is categorized does not affect the underlying property that there is a relationship between the responses, and the researcher can identify a respondent who buys twice as many cans of Heinz beans, or spends twice as much on rent or mortgage, or bought a car twice as long ago as another. The accuracy of this calculation is restricted only by the size of the categories used to collect the data.

FIGURE 5.5 Recording on a ratio scale

Of the last 10 cans of baked beans that you bought, how many were Heinz?

None	☐
1	☐
2	☐
3	☐
4	☐
5	☐
6	☐
7	☐
8	☐
9	☐
10	☐

What proportion of your household income do you spend on your rent or mortgage?

0% to 5%	☐
6% to 10%	☐
11% to 15%	☐
16% to 20%	☐
21% to 25%	☐
26% to 30%	☐
31% to 40%	☐
41% to 50%	☐
51% to 60%	☐
61% to 80%	☐
81% or more	☐

How long ago did you buy your car?

Within the last month	☐
Between one month and three months ago	☐
Longer than three months and up to six months ago	☐
Longer than six months and up to one year ago	☐
Longer than one year and up to two years ago	☐
Longer than two years and up to three years ago	☐
Longer than three years and up to five years ago	☐
Longer than five years and up to ten years ago	☐
Longer ago than ten years	☐

With allocation of appropriate scores to each point, or average values to each range, we can now calculate mean values and standard deviations for the sample, and carry out statistical tests.

Rating scales

06

Attitude measurement

The measurement of attitude frequently poses more problems than does the measurement of behaviour. Respondents are able to respond relatively easily to behavioural questions, limited only by their memory of events, the amount of effort they are prepared to give to answering the questions and the degree to which they are prepared to be truthful. It is easier for respondents to say how they travelled here today, which brand of pasta sauce they last bought or which phone company they are with than it is for them to describe their attitude towards the government's transport policy, to say how they feel about the use of convenience foods or to describe their perception of the telephone company's brand image.

Respondents need to be helped to express attitudes and describe images, particularly to describe them in a format that we can analyse. The most commonly used approach to measuring attitude is the itemized rating scale.

Itemized rating scales

Itemized rating scales are used to help the researcher obtain a measure of attitudes. The researcher first develops a number of dimensions – attitude statements, product or service attributes, image dimensions, etc. Respondents are then asked to position how they feel about each one using a defined rating scale, usually an interval scale (see Chapter 5) on which respondents are asked to give their answer using a range of evenly spaced points, which are provided as prompts.

Rating scales are widely used by questionnaire writers. They provide a straightforward way of asking attitudinal information that is easy and versatile to analyse, and that provides comparability across time. However, there are many different types of rating scales, and there is skill in choosing which is most appropriate for a given task.

All of the itemized rating scales given in Figure 6.1 are from actual surveys. The wording on each scale is tailored to be appropriate to the question, and all have five points representing a gradation from positive

FIGURE 6.1   Some examples of itemized rating scales

SHOW CARD.

How likely are you to use the train for this journey in the near future?

Very likely	1
Quite likely	2
Neither likely nor unlikely	3
Quite unlikely	4
Very unlikely	5
Don't know (not on card)	6

SHOW CARD.

Using the scale on this card please indicate how effective are the management and staff in seeming well organized and systematic in carrying out their work.

Highly effective	1
Effective	2
Neither effective nor ineffective	3
Not very effective	4
Not at all effective	5

SHOW CARD.

Thinking about travelling in and around the city, which of the statements on this card best describes how you feel about using the bus?

The only method I would use	1
One of the methods I would be happy to use	2
It's not my preferred way to travel but I would consider it	3
I would only use it if there was nothing else available	4
I would never use it	5

---

to negative. The first two are balanced around a neutral mid-point with equal numbers of positive and negative statements for the respondent to choose from.

Being interval data, scores can be allocated to each of the responses to assist in the analysis of responses. The allocated scores are most likely to be from 1 to 5, from the least to the most positive, or from –2 to +2, from the most negative to the most positive with the neutral point as zero. In all of these examples the scales presented to respondents run from the most positive to the most negative or, if rotated, from the most negative to the most positive for half of the respondents. It is usual to present the responses in this way for clarity and to assist the respondent to find the most appropriate answer.

FIGURE 6.2   An alternative order for responses

Based on everything you saw or heard in this ad, how likely will you be to purchase this product in the future?

Please select one.

Much more likely to buy it	1
Somewhat more likely to buy it	2
Somewhat less likely to buy it	3
Much less likely to buy it	4
The ad had no effect on my likelihood to buy it	5

However, there are occasions when there is a reason for an alternative order that overrides this. Consider Figure 6.2, which is from an Australian web-based survey: the questionnaire writer has placed the mid-scale neutral statement at the end of the list offered because of the subject matter. This is because there is a tendency for respondents to deny being influenced by advertising, or even to acknowledge to themselves that they are influenced. The neutral statement has been placed last in the list in the expectation that, by offering the four statements that acknowledge advertising influence together as a block, the visual impact will be such that respondents will be more prepared to consider that they may be influenced. The questionnaire writer has tried to bias the responses, but is doing so to offset another known bias. When scoring the responses, the researcher must remember that the mid-point score must be given to the last statement in the list.

Balanced scales

It is usual to balance scales by including equal numbers of positive and negative attitudes. If there are more positive than negative attitudes offered, then the total number of positive responses tends to be higher than would have otherwise been the case. Consider the balanced scale when asking respondents to describe the taste of a product:

Very good

Good

Average

Poor

Very poor

With two positive and two negative statements the respondents are not led in either direction. However, if the scale were as follows, the three positive dimensions would tend to be chosen more often:

Excellent

Very good

Good

Average

Poor

In most circumstances it is important to balance the scale to avoid this bias. However, there are occasions when an unbalanced scale can be justified. Where it is known that the response will be overwhelmingly in one direction, more categories may be given in that direction to achieve better discrimination.

An example is frequently found when measuring the importance of service in customer satisfaction research. When asked to state how important various aspects of customer service are, few customers say that any are unimportant – the customers will be looking for the best service that they can get. And the dimensions about which we ask are the ones that we believe are important anyway. The objective is mainly to distinguish between the most important aspects of service and the less important ones. An unbalanced scale might therefore be used, offering just one unimportant option, but several degrees of importance:

Extremely important

Very important

Important

Neither important nor unimportant

Not important

Here the questionnaire writer is trying to obtain a degree of discrimination between the levels of importance. The mid-point is 'important', and the scale implicitly assumes that this will be where the largest number of responses will be placed. Ideally the scale would have seven points extending from 'Extremely unimportant' to 'Extremely important' to preserve the balance, but there may be good reasons, such as lack of space, or a desire to reduce visual clutter, to show only the five.

Because of the difficulty that respondents have in determining what is important in driving their attitudes and the lack of discrimination in direct questions such as these, a number of techniques have been developed to derive the relative importance of attributes in decision making. It is not possible to cover those here.

Unbalanced scales should only be used for a good reason and for a specific purpose, and by experienced researchers who know what the impact is likely to be (see Figure 6.3).

FIGURE 6.3 An unbalanced scale

Seen in print

Q. SHOW CARD.

Which of these phrases best describes your overall opinion of the chances of winning a prize in this game?

VERY POOR	1
POOR	2
NEITHER FAIR NOR POOR	3
FAIR	4
GOOD	5
VERY GOOD	6
EXCELLENT	7
DON'T KNOW	8

With just two negative and four positive statements, the emphasis is clearly positive in this case. The researcher clearly knew that greater discrimination would be required between the positive scale positions.

Number of points on the scale

The illustrations in Figures 6.1 and 6.2 show five-point scales, which are probably the most commonly used. A five-point scale gives sufficient discrimination for most purposes and is easily understood by respondents. The size of the scale can be expanded to seven points if greater discrimination is to be attempted. Then the scale points can be written as:

Extremely likely
Very likely
Quite likely
Neither likely nor unlikely
Quite unlikely
Very unlikely
Extremely unlikely

or:

Excellent
Very good
Good
Neither good nor poor
Poor
Very poor
Extremely poor

There is little agreement as to the optimum number of points on a scale. The only agreement is that it is between five and 10. Seven is considered the optimal number by many researchers (Krosnick and Fabrigar, 1997) but there is a range of opinions on this issue and whether extending the number to 10 or more increases the validity of the data. More recently, Coelho and Esteves (2007) have demonstrated that a 10-point numeric scale is better than a five-point scale in that it transmits more of the available information, without encouraging response error: the definition given by Cox (1980) for assessing the optimum number of points. They hypothesize that, amongst other things, consumers may be more used these days to giving things scores out of 10 and are able to cope with them better than was the case 20 years ago.

The questionnaire writer's decision as to the number of points on the scale has to be taken with regard to the distinction that is possible between the points, the ability of respondents to discriminate between those points, and the degree of discrimination that is sought. The interview medium must also be considered. With telephone interviewing, scales with more than five points are difficult for respondents to remember. With self-completion questionnaires, the additional page space required for more points may be a factor.

'Don't knows'

In Figure 6.1, each of the scales is balanced around a neutral mid-point; this is included to allow a response for people who have no strong view either way. This is frequently the case when the subject is groceries or other everyday objects. However, this point is also frequently used by respondents who want to give a 'Don't know' response, but are not offered 'Don't know' as a response category and do not want, or are unable, to leave the response blank.

The reluctance of respondents to leave a scale blank where they genuinely cannot give an answer has always been an issue with self-completion interviews, or where these scales form a self-completion section to an otherwise interviewer-administered interview. Unpublished work from TNS BMRB shows that up to three-quarters of those who choose the mid-point may be using it as a substitute for 'Don't know', although this varies by the attribute or attitude asked about. However, electronic interviews frequently do not allow respondents to pass to the next question if any attribute is left blank. Thus for CAPI, CATI and particularly web-based interviews, distinguishing between genuine mid-point responses and 'Don't knows' can become a serious issue.

'Don't know' codes or boxes are frequently not provided, as the questionnaire writer does not wish to encourage this as a response but to encourage the respondent to provide a response that, in all likelihood, reflects an attitude unrecognized at a conscious level. Also, non-response to one scale among a battery of scales can raise issues of how to treat the data when using certain data analysis techniques. The reluctance to accept 'Don't know' as a response is understandable. The questionnaire writer must consider whether it is preferable to be able to distinguish between genuine mid-point responses and people who did not want to, or could not, answer.

Odd or even number of points

Some practitioners prefer to use a scale with an even number of points. They eliminate the neutral mid-point in an attempt to force those who would otherwise choose it to give an inclination one way or the other. The response points for a six-point agree-disagree scale could be:

Extremely likely

Very likely

Quite likely

Quite unlikely

Very unlikely

Extremely unlikely

or:

Excellent

Very good

Good

Poor

Very poor

Extremely poor

In studies where it would be expected that most people would have a view, for example about crime, it can be argued that they hold a view even if they do not recognize that they do. It is therefore legitimate, it is argued, to force a response in one direction or the other. When the subject is breakfast cereals, though, it must be recognized that many people may really have no opinion one way or the other.

It is possible to accept a neutral response if that is offered spontaneously by the respondent in an interviewer-administered survey. Studies have shown, though, that including a neutral scale position significantly increases the number of neutral responses compared to accepting them spontaneously (Kalton *et al*, 1980; Presser and Schuman, 1980). This indicates that eliminating the middle neutral point does increase the commitment of respondents to be either positive or negative. This is supported by Coelho and Esteves (2007), who found that the mid-point was used by respondents who are trying to reduce the effort, and so exaggerated the true mid-point score, and by Saris and Gallhofer (2007) who showed that not providing a neutral mid-point improves both the reliability and the validity of the data. However, mid-points continue to be widely used and the questionnaire writer must decide whether or not including one is appropriate for the particular question and subject matter. Other factors, such as precedence and comparability with other data, will often have greater import.

Attitudinal rating scales

A number of forms of rating scale have been developed specifically to address responses to a series of attitudinal dimensions. The three most commonly used are Likert scale, semantic differential scale and Stapel scale.

Likert scale

The Likert scale (frequently known as an 'agree/disagree' scale) was first published by psychologist Rensis Likert in 1932. The technique presents respondents with a series of attitude dimensions (a battery), for each of which they are asked whether, and how strongly, they agree or disagree, using one of a number of positions on a five-point scale (see Figure 6.4).

With face-to-face interviewer-administered scale batteries, the responses may be shown on a card while the interviewer reads out each of the statements in turn. With telephone interviewing, the respondent may sometimes be asked to remember what the response categories are, but preferably would be asked to write them down.

The technique is easy to administer in self-completion questionnaires, either paper or electronic, and may often be given to respondents as a self-completion section in an interviewer-administered survey. Responses using the Likert scale can be given scores for each statement, usually from 1 to 5, negative to positive, or –2 to +2. As this is interval data, means and standard deviations can be calculated for each statement.

The full application of the Likert scale is to sum the scores for each respondent to provide an overall attitudinal score for each individual. Likert's intention was that the statements would represent different aspects of the same attitude. The overall score, though, is rarely calculated in commercial research (Albaum, 1997), where the statements usually cover a range of attitudes. The responses to individual statements are of more interest in determining the specific aspects of attitude that drive behaviour and choice in a market, or summations are made over small groups of items. The data will tend to be used in principal component or factor analysis, to identify groups of attitudinal statements that have similar response patterns and that could therefore represent underlying attitudinal dimensions. Factor analysis can be used to create a factor score for each respondent on each of the underlying attitudinal dimensions, thereby reducing the data to a small number of individual scores.

FIGURE 6.4   Use of the Likert scale

Below are a number of statements regarding attitudes to shopping. Please read each one and indicate whether you agree or disagree with it by ticking one box for each statement.

	Disagree strongly	Disagree	Neither agree nor disagree	Agree	Agree strongly
Being a smart shopper is worth the extra time it takes.	❐	❐	❐	❐	❐
Which brands I buy makes little difference to me.	❐	❐	❐	❐	❐
I take advantage of special offers.	❐	❐	❐	❐	❐
I like to try new brands.	❐	❐	❐	❐	❐
I like to shop around and look at displays.	❐	❐	❐	❐	❐

There are four interrelated issues that questionnaire writers must be aware of when using Likert scales:

1 order effect;

2 acquiescence;

3 central tendency; and

4 pattern answering.

The *order effect* arises from the order in which the response codes are presented. It has been shown (Artingstall, 1978) that there is a bias to the left on a self-completion scale presented horizontally. (Order effects are returned to in Chapter 9.)

Acquiescence is the tendency for respondents to say 'yes' to questions or to agree rather than disagree with statements (Kalton and Schuman, 1982). This is also known as 'yea saying'. In Figure 6.4, the negative end of the scale is placed to the left, to be read first. With the 'Agree' response to the left, the order effect and acquiescence would compound each other. With the 'Disagree' response to the left, there is a possibility of the biases going some way to cancelling out each other. Importantly, it has been shown that acquiescence bias tends to be consistent for individual respondents. If measures can be found to assess the bias for each respondent, then corrections can be made. This, though, can be a complex and time-consuming exercise (Weijters *et al*, 2010).

Central tendency or extreme response bias is the reluctance of respondents to use extreme positions. Greenleaf (1992) showed that, like acquiescence bias, the extreme response bias is consistent within a respondent's answers. He also showed that it is related to age, income and education, but not to gender. It has been shown (Albaum, 1997) that a two-stage question elicits a higher proportion of extreme responses. This work used the question:

> For each of the statements listed below indicate first the extent of your agreement and second how strongly you feel about your agreement.
>
> 'A product's price will usually reflect its level of quality.'
>
> *Agree – Neither Agree Nor Disagree – Disagree –*
>
> How strongly do you feel about your response?
>
> *Very Strong – Not Very Strong –*

The question arises, of course, as to whether the two-stage approach is a better measure of the attitude or whether it creates its own bias towards the extreme points. Albaum *et al* (2007) explored this issue by correlating reported attitude to actual behaviour in charity giving. The results were not conclusive but suggested that the two-stage approach provides the truer reflection of attitudes.

With a large number of dimensions to be evaluated, this approach may be too time-consuming for most studies, but the questionnaire writer should be aware of this approach and of the different response patterns it is likely to give. This approach is particularly appropriate for telephone interviewing, where the complete scale cannot be shown.

Pattern answering occurs when a respondent falls into a routine of ticking boxes in a pattern, which might be straight down the page or diagonally across it. It is often a symptom of fatigue or boredom. The best way to avoid it is to keep the interview interesting for the respondent. To minimize pattern answering, both positive and negative statements should be included. The respondent then has to read them or listen to them carefully to understand the polarity and to give consistent answers. Conflicting answers from the same respondent will identify where pattern answering has occurred.

Saris *et al* (2005) argue that agree/disagree scales are flawed not just because of these issues but because the cognitive process involved for the respondent is more complex and burdensome than with a simpler question asked directly about the specific issue. Such construct-specific questions are also believed to suffer less from acquiescence bias and they found that construct-specific questions gave more reliable responses. This is supported by unpublished work by TNS BMRB, which looked at a number of constructs where the agree/disagree scale could be replaced by a construct-specific scale. Here it was found that while there were significant differences between the responses to end points on the agree/disagree scale when rotated between respondents, demonstrating order bias, the construct-specific scale showed far more consistency, indicating less bias.

It should be noted that the European Social Survey no longer uses such a scale for new questions. Nevertheless, the agree/disagree scale continues to be widely used because it is simple to administer.

Semantic differential scale

The semantic differential scale is a bipolar rating scale. It differs from the Likert scale in that opposite statements of the dimension are placed at the two ends of the scale and respondents are asked to indicate which they most agree with by placing a mark along the scale. This has the advantage that there is then no need for the scale points to be semantically identified. Any bias towards agreeing with a statement is avoided, as both ends of the scale have to be considered. The original development of this scale by Osgood (Osgood *et al*, 1957) recommended the use of seven points on the response scale, and this number continues to be the favourite of researchers (McDaniel and Gates, 1993), although both five-point and three-point scales are used for particular purposes (Oppenheim, 1992).

With semantic differential scales the statements should be kept as short and precise as possible because of the need for the respondent to read and understand fully both ends of the scale. Attitudes can be difficult to express concisely, and it is sometimes hard to find an opposite to ensure that the scale represents a linear progression from one end to the other. For these reasons semantic differential scales are usually better suited to descriptive dimensions.

Care must be taken to ensure that the two statements determine the dimension that the researcher requires. The opposite of 'modern' might be 'old-fashioned' or it might be 'traditional'. The opposite of 'sweet' might be 'savoury' or 'sour' or 'bitter'. This forces the questionnaire writer to consider exactly what the dimension is that is to be measured. This gives the semantic differential scale an advantage over the Likert scale where disagreeing with 'The brand is modern' could mean that the brand is seen as either old-fashioned or traditional, and the researcher does not know which. As with all self-completion techniques it is wise to provide an example of how to complete the grid (as in Figure 6.5).

Figure 6.6 comes from an advertising study. Note that the questionnaire writer has reversed the polarity of the statements alternately. The statements have been shown to the respondent on a card so, although this is not a self-completion questionnaire, there is still a danger of pattern answering, which needs to be minimized. Also note the difficulty that the questionnaire writer has in achieving exact opposites in the first pair of statements. The

FIGURE 6.5   Use of a semantic differential scale

Below are pairs of statements. Each one may or may not apply to the advertisement that you have just seen. Please read each pair and indicate which of the statements you agree applies to the ad by ticking one box for each pair of statements.

For example, if you agree strongly that the advertisement was 'mundane', you would tick the box closest to that statement, but if you only agreed slightly, then you should tick a box further away from the statement.

Example

Fascinating ☐   ☐   ☐   ☐   ☐   ☑   ☐   Mundane

Please complete the remaining items according to how you feel about the ad:

Boring	☐	☐	☐	☐	☐	☐	☐	Interesting
Important	☐	☐	☐	☐	☐	☐	☐	Unimportant
Relevant	☐	☐	☐	☐	☐	☐	☐	Irrelevant
Exciting	☐	☐	☐	☐	☐	☐	☐	Unexciting
Unappealing	☐	☐	☐	☐	☐	☐	☐	Appealing
Involving	☐	☐	☐	☐	☐	☐	☐	Uninvolving
Means nothing	☐	☐	☐	☐	☐	☐	☐	Means a lot to me

Scale items taken from Zaichkowsky (1999).

ad may be worth remembering because it contains useful information, but that does not necessarily mean that it is not also easily forgettable. The questionnaire writer could have included both of the pairs: 'Worth re-membering – Not worth remembering' and 'Easy to forget – Difficult to forget', but has chosen to force a decision between two statements that are not strictly opposites in order not to have to extend the number of pairs asked about.

As with the Likert scale, dimensions of similar meaning should be given with reversed polarity to minimize pattern answering and to check internal consistency of responses.

Stapel scale

With the Stapel scale, named after Jan Stapel, the dimension or descriptor is placed at the centre of a scale that ranges from –5 to +5. Respondents are asked to indicate whether they agree positively or negatively with the statement, and how strongly, by selecting one of the points on the scale (see Figure 6.7).

FIGURE 6.6   Example of a semantic differential scale

Seen in print

SHOW CARD.

Here are two opposite ways in which someone could describe this ad. For example, 'worth remembering' at this end of the scale (POINT) or 'easy to forget' (POINT) at the other end of the scale. I'd like you to tell me which number on this scale best describes what you personally feel about this ad. You can use any number from 1 to 5.

CIRCLE NUMBER.

And how would you rate the ad in the second scale? POINT TO AND READ OUT DESCRIPTORS.

REPEAT FOR REMAINING SCALES.

Worth remembering	1	2	3	4	5	Easy to forget
Difficult to relate to	1	2	3	4	5	Involving or easy to relate to
Lively, exciting or fun	1	2	3	4	5	Dull
Ordinary or boring	1	2	3	4	5	Clever or imaginative
Helps make the brand different from others	1	2	3	4	5	Does not really make the brand appear any different from the others
Makes me *less* interested in the brand	1	2	3	4	5	Makes me *more* interested in the brand

The advantage of this type of scale over semantic differential scales is that it is not necessary to find an accurate opposite to each dimension to ensure bipolarity. The data can, however, be analysed in the same way as semantic differentials, and the scale, with 10 points, has the potential to provide greater discrimination than a five-point scale. By having no centre point, these scales also avoid the issue of whether or not there should be an odd or even number of points on the scale. Stapel scales are, however, not widely used as they are thought to be confusing for respondents. They must be self-administered if the researcher is to be confident that the respondent has properly understood the task. This has limited their use in telephone interviewing and with much face-to-face interviewing. However, with imaginative layout, they could work well with online web-based interviewing.

FIGURE 6.7   Use of the Stapel scale

Please indicate how accurately you feel each of the following words and phrases describes the GingerBread Store. Select a positive number for the phrases you think describe the store accurately. The more accurately you think it describes it, the larger the number you should choose. Select a minus number for the phrases you think do not describe it accurately. The less accurately you think the phrase describes the store, the larger the negative number you should choose. You can select any number from +5 for words and phrases you think are very accurate to –5 for words and phrases you think are very inaccurate.

The GingerBread Store

+5	+5	+5
+4	+4	+4
+3	+3	+3
+2	+2	+2
+1	+1	+1
is well laid out	has helpful staff	is attractive
–1	–1	–1
–2	–2	–2
–3	–3	–3
–4	–4	–4
–5	–5	–5

Numeric scales

A simple form of scale is to ask respondents to award a score between 1 and 10, or between 0 and 10 if a mid-point is required, or even between 1 or 0 and 100. The end points of the scale should be verbally anchored. In practice whether a 10-point scale starts at 0 or 1 makes little difference to the distribution of the responses. It may be clearer to respondents that 0 is the lowest point on the scale, whereas there may be some ambiguity as to whether 1 is the top of the scale if it runs from 1 to 10. For this reason a 0 to 10 scale may be preferred.

Numeric scales are appropriate for measures such as importance, where the bottom point equates to 'Not at all important' and the top point to 'Extremely important' or similar. The researcher must remember, though, that this is an interval scale and not a ratio scale. A score of 8 out of 10 does not mean that something is twice as good or twice as important as a score of 4. These scales are not appropriate for a choice between two equally positive anchor points, such as a choice between two brands, because of the more positive associations implicit in the higher score, which would bias response towards that option.

As a technique this is more suited to self-completion questionnaires than to interviewer-administered interviews. With the self-completion survey, respondents can see their responses and reference their subsequent responses against them. A write-in box (as in Figure 6.8), where the score is recorded, also takes up less space than a semantic or graphic scale. This is one reason why this type of numeric scale has become popular with writers of web-based questionnaires, as it allows more dimensions to be accommodated on a single screen.

FIGURE 6.8   Example of a numeric scale using a write-in box

Below are some phrases that may or may not apply to any retail store. We would like you to indicate how **important** each of these is to you when choosing where to shop. Please give a score between 1 and 99, where:

01 = Not at all important
and
99 = Extremely important

Is well laid out

Has helpful staff

Is attractively decorated

Numeric write-in scales have been shown to produce different results from semantic scales despite purporting to measure the same thing and to use similar anchor points. Christian and Dillman (2004) demonstrated in a postal self-completion survey that responses were consistently higher for the numeric answer box than for a semantic differential scale and for a polar point scale.

Graphic scales

A graphic scale is one presented to the respondents visually so that they can select a position on it that best represents their desired response. In its most basic form it is a continuous bipolar scale with fixed points verbally anchored at either end. It can simply be a line between the two anchor points (see Figure 6.9). This is a form of graphic scale which has become known as a 'visual analogue scale'.

FIGURE 6.9 Graphic rating scale (visual analogue scale)

Please indicate by marking on the line how you rate the GingerBread Store for each pair of statements below:

| Well laid out | | Poorly laid out |

| Has helpful staff | | Has unhelpful staff |

| Attractive window display | | Unattractive window display |

The distance from the end points of the respondent's marks is measured to provide the score for each attitudinal dimension. Essentially this is a continuously rated semantic differential scale, which provides a greater degree of precision and avoids the issues of numbers of points on the scale. It is a simple way of measuring attitudes and image perceptions, but is impractical to use with paper questionnaires. Measuring the position marked on hundreds of paper questionnaires, with possibly dozens of scales on each one, is not viable for most commercial projects. This technique cannot be used with telephone interviewing. With CAPI interviewing, though, and to a greater degree with online web-based interviewing, the continuous graphic scale is a realistic option. Respondents can drag a cursor along the line to the exact position they want it, and that position is automatically recorded.

When the technique is being used to measure attitudes to brands or products, as in Figure 6.10, more than one cursor can be used to represent different brands, or brand logos can be used in place of cursors. Each respondent can place a number of brands along the scale, so that they are positioned relative to each other as well as to the scale ends, according to the respondent's perceptions. This is quicker for respondents than rating each brand individually, is more interesting for them when logos are used, and provides better relative measures of the attitude variation between brands.

Although the data collected is continuous, the measurements will be assigned to categories and treated as interval data for analysis purposes. It is possible to have a large number of very small intervals, but the researcher must decide at what level the apparent accuracy of the data becomes spurious. That will depend on the length of the line used, the accuracy with which respondents are able to place the cursor, and the degree of accuracy with which respondents are likely to have tried to place the cursor.

FIGURE 6.10   Slider scale on electronic questionnaire

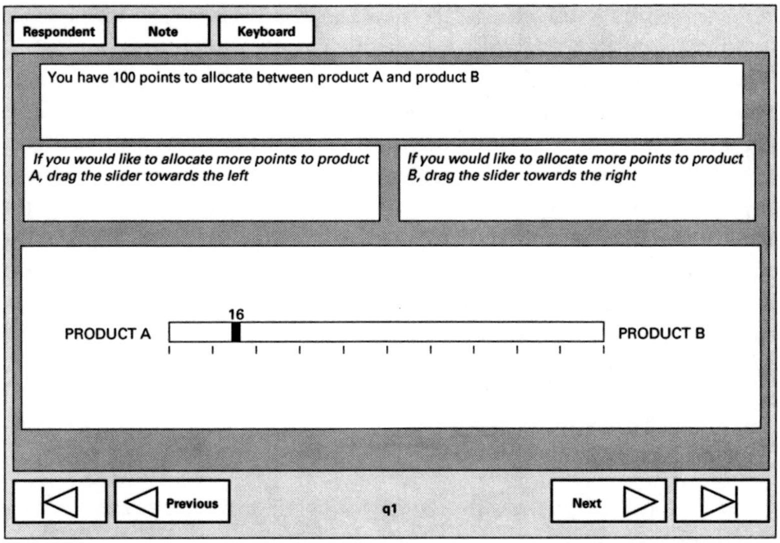

FIGURE 6.11   Graphic rating scale with labelled mid-point

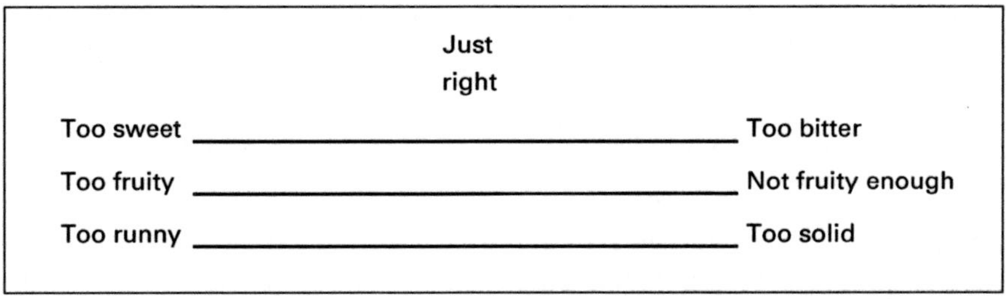

The questionnaire writer may wish to apply labels to the scale. The scale can be labelled numerically, so that one end is 0 and the other 100. The position of the cursor can then be indicated as a number between 0 and 100, which allows the respondent to place the cursor accurately. In some instances, a centre-point label might be added, for example if the technique is being used to evaluate reactions to a new product. This scale could have just the verbal descriptors (see Figure 6.11), or these could be combined with numeric values, either shown on the line or appearing with the cursor. Here a numeric scale would have a 0 point at 'Just right' extending to −50 for each of the end points, as they always represent a move away from the preferred positioning. For further differentiation the line can be divided into segments that may assist respondents to determine where their desired response should be.

If each of the five segments is verbally anchored, this becomes a graphic rating scale, equivalent to an itemized rating scale such as a Likert scale. It does, however, have the advantage that there is variation *within* each of the scale points, and that variation can be measured and recorded.

It has been shown (Thomas *et al*, 2007) that in web-based online surveys, respondents found visual analogue scales (VAS) as easy to complete as rating scales using fixed points denoted by radio buttons and that they felt that VAS scales conveyed their responses with greater accuracy than with a numeric box entry. Responses obtained from VAS and the fixed-point radio buttons were similar and the respondents found the VAS approach more interesting than the radio buttons. As maintaining the interest and involvement of respondents is one of the objectives of the questionnaire writer, the use of VAS or graphic rating scales should always be considered as an alternative to radio buttons.

Pictorial scales

In many instances, it is desirable to avoid using semantic scales in favour of pictorial representations; this may be:

- where the target population is children who are unable to relate their responses to verbal descriptors;
- where there are cultural differences between sub-groups of the target population that may mean that they interpret descriptors differently;
- with multi-country studies where translation of descriptors may alter shades of meaning;
- where there is a low level of literacy in the target population.

A common solution to this is the use of smiley or smiling face scales. A range of smiles and down-turned mouths is used to indicate that the respondent agrees with or is happy with the statement, or disagrees with or is unhappy with the statement (see Figure 6.12).

A pictorial version of the continuous rating scale is the thermometer scale. With this the respondent 'colours in' a depiction of a thermometer so that colouring to the top is positive and not colouring it is negative. As with other types of continuous scale it is difficult economically to measure and code responses, except with electronic self-completion questionnaires.

Anchor strength

With all semantic scales, the wording of the 'anchor statement' is crucial to the distribution of data that is likely to be achieved. A five-point bipolar scale that goes from 'Extremely satisfied' to 'Extremely dissatisfied' is likely to discourage respondents from using the end points and to concentrate the distribution on the middle three points. If the end points were 'Very satisfied'

FIGURE 6.12 Smiley scale

and 'Very dissatisfied', the end points would be used by more respondents and the data would be more widely distributed across the scale. This can make the data more discriminatory between items. As a general rule, the stronger the anchors, the more points are required on the scale to obtain discrimination.

Comparative scaling techniques

Paired comparisons

With paired comparisons, respondents are asked to choose between two items based on the appropriate criterion, eg that one is more important than the other or preferred to the other. This can be repeated with a number of pairs chosen from a set of items, such that every item is compared against every other item (see Figure 6.13). Summing the choices made provides an evaluation of importance or preference across all of the items. The task is often easier and quicker for respondents than being asked to rank-order a list of items, because the individual judgements to be made are simpler. By careful rotation of the pairs, some of the order bias inherent in showing lists can be avoided.

The disadvantage of this technique is that it is limited to a relatively small number of items. With just six items, 15 pairs are required if each is to be assessed against every other, and the number of pairs required increases geometrically. With 190 possible pairs from a list of 20 items, clearly no respondent can be shown all of them. A balanced design of the pairs shown to each respondent can provide sufficient information for the rank order of each item to be inferred.

Constant sum

With a constant sum technique, respondents are asked to allocate a fixed number of points between a set of options to indicate relative importance or relative preference. The number of points given to each option reflects the

FIGURE 6.13   Paired comparison

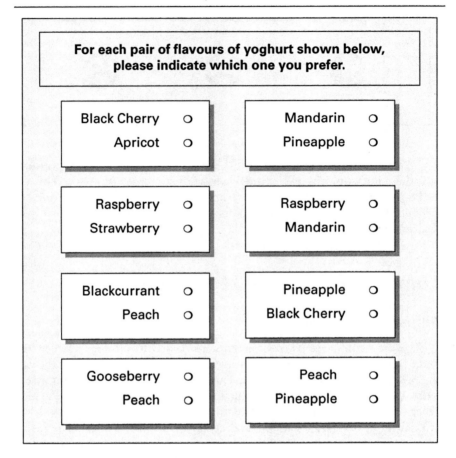

magnitude of the importance, from which we can also deduce the rank order of the options for each respondent (see Figure 6.14). Some respondents are likely to have problems with a constant sum question, as it requires some effort and mental agility on their part, both to think simultaneously across all of the items and to do the mental arithmetic.

It is easier with electronic questionnaires, where the scores allocated can be automatically summed and the respondent not allowed to move on until exactly 100 points have been allocated. The need to make simultaneous comparisons between a number of different items still remains, though. As the number of items increases, it becomes more difficult to think through and to mentally keep a running total of the scores.

Another way of asking this is to use a constant sum approach combined with paired comparisons. In Figure 6.15 the task for respondents has been reduced to making comparisons between 10 pairs of items. Dealing with

FIGURE 6.14 Constant sum technique

Following is a list of items that might or might not be important to you when choosing a new car. I would like you to take 100 points and allocate them across the five items depending on how important each one is to you when choosing a new car. So if something is very important to you, you should give it a lot of points, but if it is not important you should give it relatively few points. Remember the total number of points must add to 100.

The engine size	☐
The colour	☐
Manual or automatic gearbox	☐
Quality of the radio/CD player	☐
Country of manufacture	☐
	100

pairs is usually easier for respondents to manage. In this example respondents are asked to allocate 11 points between each pair. An odd number has been chosen so that the two items in any pair cannot be given the same number of points; this forces a distinction between them. Had the respondents been asked to allot 10 points per pair, this would have allowed items in a pair to be given equal weight of five points each. This technique can be used equally well for comparing preferences for products, when forcing even small distinctions can be important to the researcher.

Both the paired comparison and direct point allocation approaches have difficulties as the number of items increases, either because of the increased mental agility required in the direct approach or because of the increasing number of pairs that are generated.

Card sorting

When the number of objects is large, say more than 30, then a different approach is required to obtain a rank ordering or rating. One such approach is card sorting.

In face-to-face interviews each object is described on a card. The card needs to be relatively small but not so small that respondents cannot read it. Larger cards are then laid out, marked as itemized rating scales, for example from 'Very important' to 'Not at all important'. Respondents are then asked to sort the cards into piles according to the rating scale laid out in front of them. Once that task is completed each pile is returned to and the objects in the pile put into rank order.

FIGURE 6.15   Constant sum combined with paired comparisons

Following is a list of pairs of items that might or might not be important to you when choosing a new car. For each pair please allocate 11 points depending on how important each is to you. So if one is very important and the other not, you would give one 10 points and the other 1. If they are of similar importance you would give one 5 and the other 6 points.

Engine size	Colour	
❑ +	❑	=11

Manual or automatic gearbox	Quality of radio/CD player	
❑ +	❑	=11

Country of manufacture	Engine size	
❑ +	❑	=11

Colour	Manual or automatic gearbox	
❑ +	❑	=11

Quality of radio/CD player	Country of manufacture	
❑ +	❑	=11

Engine size	Manual or automatic gearbox	
❑ +	❑	=11

Colour	Quality of radio/CD player	
❑ +	❑	=11

Country of manufacture	Colour	
❑ +	❑	=11

Quality of radio/CD player	Engine size	
❑ +	❑	=11

Manual or automatic gearbox	Country of manufacture	
❑ +	❑	=11

With electronic self-completion questionnaires, respondents first go through the list of objects, rating them against the itemized rating scale. They are then presented with the objects they have placed in each category in turn and asked to rank-order them. The data obtained is thus a combination of rating and rank ordering.

This technique is relatively simple for respondents to cope with, either in face-to-face or web-based interviewing, and provides a sensitive ranking system for a large number of objects.

Q sort

A similar approach designed for larger numbers of attributes is Q sorting. This might be used where there is a very large number of objects, in the region of, say, 100.

The objects are sorted by respondents into a number of categories, usually 11 or 12, representing the degrees on the scale, such as appeal or interest in purchase. Respondents may be instructed to place a specific number of objects on each point of the scale so that they are distributed approximately according to a normal distribution. They are asked to put a few objects at the extremes of the scale, with increasing numbers towards the middle of the scale. Objects placed in the two extreme positions can then be rank-ordered by the respondent for increased discrimination.

Using just five scale points and 10 attributes, Chrzan and Golovashkina (2006) showed that the Q sort technique produced results that were better than several other techniques in terms of discrimination and prediction, and was quicker to administer than most. However, with a larger number of attributes it may be more difficult to administer and more time-consuming than other techniques.

07

Behavioural questions

Introduction

Asking about behaviour, including product ownership and descriptive data, is generally a good way to start a questionnaire. Early behavioural questions should be straightforward for the respondent to answer and allow them to ease into the subject. If for any reason they are not straightforward and cause the respondent to work hard to provide the answer, this will increase the likelihood of an early termination of the interview, so efforts should be made to make them as simple as possible.

With any questionnaire there is a danger that the order in which the questions are asked will affect how people respond. By establishing behavioural patterns early in the questionnaire there is a possibility that answers to attitudinal questions asked later will be given to justify the behaviour. Thus if a particular brand is regularly bought, in later questions the respondent is likely to say that the brand is of high quality or good value in order to justify their loyalty to it. However, the alternative is to ask attitudinal questions first, with the consequence that behaviour may be misreported to justify attitudes. A respondent may then claim to buy a brand more often than they really do because in the attitudinal questions they had said how good it is.

If the sample is defined as something other than total population, then qualifying for the sample is often related to behaviour or ownership. There is a need then for behavioural questions to appear very early in the questionnaire.

Question types

Blind response options

Wherever a question about behaviour is asked, the interest of the researcher should be disguised to avoid acquiescence bias; that is the tendency for people to say they have done or own something that may not be strictly accurate when asked a direct question. This is particularly important in screening questions to avoid the possibility of respondents trying to guess which answers they should give so as to be included or excluded as they wish. Respondents may also feel pressure to say that they have bought something when they have not, for fear of appearing mean or ungenerous, or lacking social status. The blind responses should be designed to give most people the opportunity to provide a positive answer. If the real interest is in a minority or niche product, more popular products should also be included to allow as many as possible to give a positive answer and remove pressure from them to overclaim purchase or ownership of the minority product.

It is not good practice to ask, for example, 'Have you bought a wide-screen television in the last six months?', as respondents' reasons for answering 'yes' or 'no' may have little to do with whether they actually have bought one or not. A less biased version of the question, containing a number of blind responses, is given in Figure 7.1.

FIGURE 7.1 Screening questions

SCREENING QUESTIONS

SHOW LIST. (On card, screen or paper, or read out, depending on inter-view medium.)

Which, if any, of the items on this card (list which I am going to read out) have you bought in the last six months, either for yourself or for anybody else?
TELEPHONE
TELEVISION
DIGITAL RADIO
DVD PLAYER
MICROWAVE OVEN
NONE OF THESE

IF BOUGHT TELEVISION IN PAST SIX MONTHS, SHOW LIST.

Which of these describes the television that you bought?
PLASMA SCREEN
HIGH DEFINITION
FLAT SCREEN
WIDE SCREEN
SURROUND SOUND
DOLBY SOUND

RESPONDENT IS ELIGIBLE FOR INTERVIEW IF BOUGHT WIDE-SCREEN TELEVISION IN PAST SIX MONTHS.

Funnelling questions

The screening questions in Figure 7.1 provide a simple form of funnelling. Much more complex pieces of information can often be broken down into a series of disguised choice questions that funnel respondents to the precise information sought.

If we are screening to find people who have bought packs of four cherry yogurts in the last seven days, it would be dangerous to ask: 'Have you bought any four-packs of cherry flavoured yogurt in the last seven days?' The cognitive task being asked of respondents is too great, as they are asked to process four pieces of information:

1 product type;
2 pack type;
3 flavour; and
4 time period.

Many respondents simply won't bother, while amongst others the risk of acquiescence bias is high. The resulting sample is unlikely to be an accurate reflection of the desired research population. This should be broken into a series of smaller tasks, with the researcher's interest disguised at each stage, as shown in Figure 7.2. In a face-to-face interview each of the response options would be presented on a show card; online they would appear on screen.

The cognitive process for the respondent is broken down into simple steps rather than having to cope with several pieces of information in the one question. Additional information is also picked up along the way. When the questioning is through a single question, we can only determine the penetration of the defined group. By breaking the questions down we can also determine the penetration of past seven-day yogurt purchasers. This is information that could be checked against other sources to establish the accuracy of the sample, or it may be new information.

Dichotomous questions

Another way of simplifying the task for respondents is to reduce it to a series of dichotomous questions.

The question: 'Have you bought a guitar in the last 12 months as a present for a child in your family that cost over £100?' again presents a large cognitive task for the respondent. Following an initial disguised choice question to hide the topic of interest, this can be broken into a simple multiple choice question followed by a series of dichotomous questions, as shown in Figure 7.3. Again the task has been reduced to steps that funnel the respondent through a series of dichotomous options to provide the precise information that we are seeking without bias.

FIGURE 7.2   Funnelling questions

Which, if any, of these items have you bought in the last seven days?

CRÈME FRAICHE
PLAIN YOGHURT
FLAVOURED YOGHURT
SOURED CREAM
COTTAGE CHEESE
NONE OF THESE

(IF FLAVOURED YOGHURT BOUGHT)

What types of pack were the flavoured yoghurts in?

INDIVIDUAL POTS
PACK OF FOUR
PACK OF SIX
OTHER

(IF PACK OF FOUR)

What flavour were they?

MIXED FLAVOURS
BANANA
CHERRY
CHOCOLATE
MANGO
PEACH
RASPBERRY
RHUBARB
STRAWBERRY
STRAWBERRY AND RASPBERRY
GARDEN FRUITS
FRUIT (OTHER/UNSPECIFIED)
OTHER
DON'T KNOW/CAN'T REMEMBER

However, care must be taken that the questions really are dichotomous. Consider the question: 'Will you buy a new bicycle in the next six months?' This may appear to be dichotomous, capable of being answered 'yes' or 'no'. But if they were the only answers offered it would result in a high proportion of 'Don't know' answers because future behaviour is unpredictable. Some respondents will be certain that they will not buy a bicycle in the next six months, some will be certain that they will. Others, though, will not be sure. They may think that there is a possibility that they will, but have not been given this option as an answer.

The real question here is about current expectations or intentions. It could therefore be asked as: 'At the moment, do you intend (or expect) to

FIGURE 7.3   Dichotomous questions

Which, if any, of these have you bought in the last six months:

PIANO (ACOUSTIC)
PIANO (ELECTRONIC)
ELECTRONIC KEYBOARD
ELECTRIC GUITAR
ACOUSTIC GUITAR
DRUMS OR DRUMKIT
BRASS INSTRUMENT
NONE OF THESE

(IF ELECTRIC GUITAR): 'Was it for your own use or for someone else's?'

(IF SOMEONE ELSE'S): 'Was that other person a child or an adult?'

(IF A CHILD): 'Is that child a member of your family or of someone else's family?'

(IF MEMBER OF THE FAMILY): 'Did it cost £100 or more, or less than £100?'

buy a new bicycle in the next six months?' This could now be treated as a dichotomous question, but is still probably better asked as a scale, from 'Definitely will buy' to 'Definitely will not', encompassing less certain positions along the way. This would allow respondents to express better their true uncertainty regarding their future behaviour (see Chapter 4). Note the potential ambiguity in the question with the use of the word 'new'. How will respondents interpret the word 'new'? Does this mean 'brand new' or new to them, ie second hand? This needs clarification in the question.

Asking recalled behaviour

Many of the questions that we ask about behaviour rely on the ability and willingness of the respondent to recall accurately what has occurred, often some time ago. Memory, though, is notoriously unreliable regarding past behaviour. It is invariably more accurate for respondents to record their behaviour as it happens, using a diary or similar technique. However, the cost or feasibility of that type of approach often rules it out, and the behavioural data collected in most studies is behaviour as reported by memory.

The accuracy of recall will depend on many factors, including the recency, size and significance to the individual of the behaviour in question. Most people will be able to name the bank they use, but will be less reliable about which brand of tinned sardines they last bought. They could probably describe in some detail the process of buying a car undertaken some months previously, but struggle to tell which brand of mustard they bought last week. Frequently what is reported is an impression of behaviour, the respondents' beliefs about what they do, rather than an accurate recording of what they have done. Tourangeau *et al* (2000) list the following reasons for memory failure by respondents to surveys:

- Respondents may not have taken in the critical information in the first place.
- They may be unwilling to go through the work of retrieving it.
- Even if they do try, they may be unable to retrieve the event itself, but only generic information about events of that type.
- They may retrieve only partial information about the event and, as a result, fail to report it.
- They may recall erroneous information about the event, including incorrect inferences incorporated into the representation of the event.

Researchers are generally aware that recall information can be unreliable. However, what is sometimes overlooked is the bias introduced into the responses by the third of the sources of memory failure listed above. When respondents generalize about types of events they will tend to report not only what they believe that they do, but also what they believe that they do most of the time. Even if what they say is accurate, minority behaviour will tend to be unreported.

Inaccuracy of memory regarding time periods (telescoping)

Particularly notorious is the accuracy of memory related to time. Respondents will tend to report that an event occurred more recently than it actually did. Researchers and psychologists have long been aware of this phenomenon. The first important theory of telescoping was proposed by Sudman and Bradburn (1973) who wrote: 'There are two kinds of memory error that sometimes operate in opposite directions. The first is forgetting an episode entirely ... The second kind of error is compression (telescoping) where the event is remembered as occurring more recently than it did.'

Thus, asked to recall events that occurred in the last three months, respondents will tend to include events that occurred in what feels like the last three months but is usually a longer period. Additional events are therefore 'imported' into that period and mistakenly reported (forward telescoping). In contrast, other events are forgotten or thought to have occurred longer ago than they really did (backward telescoping) and are therefore not reported. The extent to which telescoping occurs will depend on the importance of the event to the respondent and the time period asked about.

A technique suggested to help respondents (Tourangeau *et al*, 2000) in interviewer-administered surveys is to extend the number of words in the question beyond what is absolutely necessary in order to give the respondent more time to think before he or she feels obliged to provide an answer. This may be particularly the case with telephone interviewing, where silences can be awkward and the respondent may avoid them by answering before he or she has fully thought it through.

Another technique is 'bounding, where the respondent is given clear landmarks to which they find it easier to relate time periods. Public holidays and birthdays often provide such landmarks. A survey in the middle of the year that is concerned with behaviour in the previous six months might ask what the respondent has done 'in the last six months, that is since Christmas. Respondents find it easier to fix the date on which they did something as before or after Christmas than whether it was within the last six months. Unfortunately there are few landmark dates common to everybody that suit the reference period for the questionnaire writer, but if one can be found it will improve the accuracy of the data collected.

In the following, the question writer has used a convenient recent event to bind the time period in an attempt to minimize telescoping:

> Q. Have you bought any new prescription glasses, or lenses to fit your existing frames, within the last three months? That is since mid-August, after the Olympic Games?

Last week or typical week

When asking respondents to recall behaviour the question writer has to decide whether to ask what was done in the last week, or other appropriate time period, or what was done in a typical week.

It might be expected that what the respondent did in the last week would be more accurate than for a typical week. Answering for a typical week is cognitively more complex because the respondent has to determine what is a typical week, whether such a thing exists and, if not, how to construct something that is typical by taking into account behaviour over a longer time (Chang and Krosnick, 2003). Thus the typical week response may stretch back over a longer time period than a week, which we know is likely to be less accurate. In fact Chang and Krosnick (2003) found that predictive validity of typical week data was greater than last week, but concluded that that may have been because they were asking about media usage, which tends to be regular.

Another difference between the two measures is that a 'typical week' will tend to underestimate minority behaviours. Thus if most weeks you shop at Sainsbury's several times, but last week you shopped at Waitrose, your 'typical week' response will be Sainsbury's. In aggregate you may get the correct picture, if all stores are used as regular and occasional shops in roughly the same proportions. But if most people in the sample only use Waitrose occasionally, then usage of that store will be underestimated by this question. If your objective is to determine levels of usage of different brands, asking about behaviour in the last week is likely to provide more accurate data than asking about a typical week. However, if your objective is to use this information for analysis purposes to determine brand loyalty or brand perceptions, you may to want to know the respondent's majority behaviour, and the typical week question will give you that.

A more detailed approach to gaining the individual level of brand behaviour is to ask about the last 10 purchases of or visits to brands or products in the category. This tells us about both the respondents' majority and minority behaviour and has been shown to provide accurate data that mirrors brand shares in most categories. Care must be taken, though, to ensure that it is reasonable to expect respondents to be able to remember the last 10 occasions. Where a purchase is made only once a fortnight, such as is typical for car fuel purchases, then the last 10 may stretch back nearly six months and will not be accurately recalled. Conversely, where a behaviour is frequent, the last 10 may not be sufficient to adequately represent all the minority behaviour where that represents less than 10 per cent of occasions. The questionnaire writer must take into account these considerations and arrive at the optimum question for the market/product concerned.

Recording values

When recording answers that are values, the level of detail needs to be as precise as is necessary to meet the research objectives without demanding more detail than respondents can accurately give. Sometimes it is possible to record precise values (eg the number of times the respondent has visited a pub or bar in the past week), but frequently we do not want to record that level of detail, and nor can respondents be expected to provide it. Then the answers will be recorded in value bands.

In Figure 7.4, the questionnaire writer has determined that bands of £200 are sufficiently accurate to meet the demands of the study. Bands of £50 would have given the researcher greater accuracy in calculating the average cost of a holiday and in making comparisons between sub-groups, but might have been difficult for respondents to recall precisely. This could have led to an increase in the proportion of 'Don't know' responses. In this example the response categories are exclusive. If someone had paid exactly £400, it is clear where the answer should be coded.

The pre-coded response categories must be meaningful to both respondent and researcher if the first is to be able to answer and the second to interpret. Precise wording is important in achieving clarity. Words such as 'often', 'frequently' and 'occasionally' are best avoided, as their interpretation varies between situations and between people.

Constructing ranges

Wherever possible, values should be recorded as absolute numbers. However, it is not always realistic to expect respondents to remember exact values. Then we can present respondents with ranges of values within which they

FIGURE 7.4   Determining the level of detail

Q. Into which of these ranges did the cost of your holiday fall, per person?
SHOW CARD.

UP TO £200	1
£201 TO £400	2
£401 TO £600	3
£601 TO £800	4
£801 TO £1,000	5
£1,001 OR MORE	6

are more likely to be able to provide a response. When constructing the ranges ensure that they are mutually exclusive and do not overlap, as in the example in Figure 7.5, which is a common error.

The ranges should usually be constructed such that the most popular values occur in the middle of the ranges. For example, if the question is 'How much did you pay for the paperback novel that you are currently reading?', we know that most answers, if accurately given, will be £x.99. However, it would not be unusual to see the following ranges given for this question:

Under £4.99

£5 to £5.99

£6 to £6.99

£7 to £7.99

£8 to £8.99

£9 or more

This can cause loss of accuracy. A book costing £6.99 would be reported as costing precisely that by some respondents. Other respondents will round it up to £7, and the response will be recorded in the category above the one it should be in. Other respondents may say 'about £7', leaving the interviewer unsure as to where it should be coded. As important, in the analysis of this data we may want to produce an average price paid. Having collected the data in these ranges, we would normally allocate the value of the mid-point of each range to calculate the average. However, if nearly all of the actual values are at the top end of each range, the calculated average price paid will be around 50 pence below what it should be.

Other markets where prices tend to cluster around price points, such as televisions which tend to have prices around £299, £399 and so on, can suffer from this effect. The average price could then be around £50 below what they should be if the wrong banding is used. You may be left scouring

FIGURE 7.5   Duplications in the values

Seen in print

Q. And, on average, how much do you pay for these text alerts, per text?

INTERVIEWER, IF DON'T KNOW, PROBE FOR AN ESTIMATE BEFORE CODING DK.

FREE OF CHARGE	1
1–5 PENCE	2
5–10 PENCE	3
11–15 PENCE	4
16–20 PENCE	5
21–25 PENCE	6
26–30 PENCE	7
31–35 PENCE	8
36–40 PENCE	9
41–45 PENCE	10
46–50 PENCE	11
50–75 PENCE	12
75 PENCE – £1	13
MORE THAN £1	14
DON'T KNOW	15

In this case, the duplications at 5, 50 and 75 pence were all spotted by the agency's checking procedures before the questionnaire went live. It is because this type of error is so easy to make that most agencies have strict checking procedures.

---

retailer websites to try to work out a more realistic average for each price band to apply to calculations.

Don't know

In the context of behavioural questions 'don't know' is frequently a legitimate answer if a respondent cannot remember or is unsure. Sometimes respondents can be encouraged to provide an approximate answer if they can't remember an amount or a period of time, which is sufficient for the purpose of the researcher. Showing ranges, as discussed above, means that the respondent does not have to be precise and it is less effort to recall the approximate range than the exact amount, so reducing the likelihood of them giving a 'don't know' response. But for any questions where the respondent might genuinely not know the answer, and to which 'don't know' is a response, that must be accepted, as already discussed in Chapter 4.

Offering a 'don't know' option can be contentious, particularly with online surveys, where it can be thought to provide an easy option for lazy respondents; this issue is returned to in Chapter 11. With behavioural questions there is likely to be less cognitive effort in retrieving the answer than in attitudinal questions and it is therefore less likely that a 'don't know' answer will be selected to avoid having to make that effort. Without a 'don't know' option, there is the danger of forcing respondents to select answers that do not accurately reflect their behaviour, which can cause inconsistencies and difficulties in analysis.

Attitude and image measurement

08

In this chapter we look at some question techniques for measuring satisfaction, image perceptions and attitudes. By their nature, these can be more difficult to capture than behavioural data, because respondents often have never thought about or articulated the attitudes and emotions that we wish to capture. For many topics, the survey will be the first time that they have expressed how they feel, be it about the service they received on a train, their perceived images of brands of tomato ketchup or attitudes to their country's overseas aid policy. To capture these we use a range of techniques including scales, indirect questions and pictorial techniques.

Customer satisfaction research

Using scales

Rating scales are commonly used in customer satisfaction research interviews for very good reasons. They provide a relatively easy way in which a customer can assess the service on a number of different items that allows comparisons to be made between them. The interval nature of the data makes it appropriate for the production of mean scores, and for carrying out correlation or regression analyses using other data such as overall satisfaction or behavioural data.

Scales such as these are commonly found on questionnaires left in hotel rooms, and Figure 8.1 shows the first part of one of these. The questionnaire continued with 53 attributes in total to be rated on this scale and 12 other questions. It contained no instructions other than to define the points of the scale.

FIGURE 8.1   Part of hotel guest satisfaction questionnaire

Seen in print				
1 = Excellent 2 = Very Good 3 = Good 4 = Fair 5 = Poor				
Cleanliness of your guest room upon entering	1	2	3	4	5
Cleanliness and servicing of your room during your stay	1	2	3	4	5
Overall cleanliness of bathroom	1	2	3	4	5
Cleanliness of bathtub and tiles	1	2	3	4	5
Condition of duvet cover	1	2	3	4	5
Overall guest room quality	1	2	3	4	5
Overall maintenance and upkeep	1	2	3	4	5
Condition of grounds	1	2	3	4	5
Condition of the lobby area	1	2	3	4	5
Condition of the lounge and restaurants	1	2	3	4	5
Functionality of guest room	1	2	3	4	5

In today's climate of customer service, you may be asked to complete a customer satisfaction survey in a hotel, restaurant or following any number of other activities. You may be asked to complete one if you:

- use a bank;
- subscribe to a telephone company;
- take out an insurance policy;
- book a holiday;
- travel by train or air;
- buy computer software;
- buy a car;
- have a car serviced;
- shop online;
- visit a theme park.

Customer satisfaction questionnaires abound, from short one-sided cards left for the client to complete, to many-paged very detailed studies conducted by telephone or online. And most of them use rating scales. It is very common for 10- or 11-point numeric scales to be used, particularly when measuring likelihood to recommend the service or product in the future.

There are a number of different ways in which customer satisfaction research can be approached. As well as deciding whether the importance of the attributes to the customer needs to be measured, the researcher needs to decide the appropriate scale from:

- performance;
- expectations;
- needs.

Should it be a rating of absolute performance, as in Figure 8.1? This is sufficient to allow us to track any changes over time, but how does the reported performance relate to expectations? A rating of 'very good' may be wonderful news for a two star hotel but a poor score for a five star hotel where everything is expected to be 'excellent'. Do customers bear that in mind when completing customer satisfaction questionnaires? Would the same level of service be rated as 'excellent' in the two star hotel but 'poor' in the five star hotel because expectations are different? Nor can it be assumed that these factors will remain constant over time. The ratings may start to decline despite the level of service remaining constant because a new competitor has entered the market with an improved service that has changed customers' expectations.

The questionnaire writer therefore needs to consider other scales as well. A scale may be devised to monitor performance relative to expectations. One such scale might be:

- much better than I expected;
- better than expected;
- as expected;
- worse than expected;
- much worse than expected.

Achieving a high score on this scale would demonstrate both that customers are delighted with the level of service, which they did not expect, and that there is possible over-delivery that could be cut back.

In some circumstances meeting customers' needs rather than their expectations may be more appropriate. For instance:

The level of service was:

- a lot more than I needed;
- a little more than I needed;
- exactly what was needed;

- a little less than I needed;
- a lot less than I needed.

The provision of hotel services – the swimming pool, the trouser press, the range of restaurants, for example – may have been excellent, and may have been what was expected from a five star hotel, but more than was needed by the client, who will go elsewhere next time where he or she can get what he or she needs for a lower price.

In the example in Figure 8.2, adapted from a well-known British bank, the questionnaire writer has chosen to assess the absolute performance of the internet banking website but, with the second attribute in the first block, has included an attribute relating to the needs of the customer, rather than assessing the individual items in relation to needs. Note that this uses an agree-disagree scale to assess the first three attributes and a scale running from excellent to poor for the next four. Because these are both five-point scales, the temptation for the researcher would be to make direct comparisons between the two blocks of attributes. That, however, assumes that an answer saying 'strongly agree that the design of the site is clear and appealing' equates to the design and clarity of the site being excellent. This may not always be the case and must be considered at the time of writing the questionnaire.

FIGURE 8.2   Assessing the absolute performance of an internet banking website

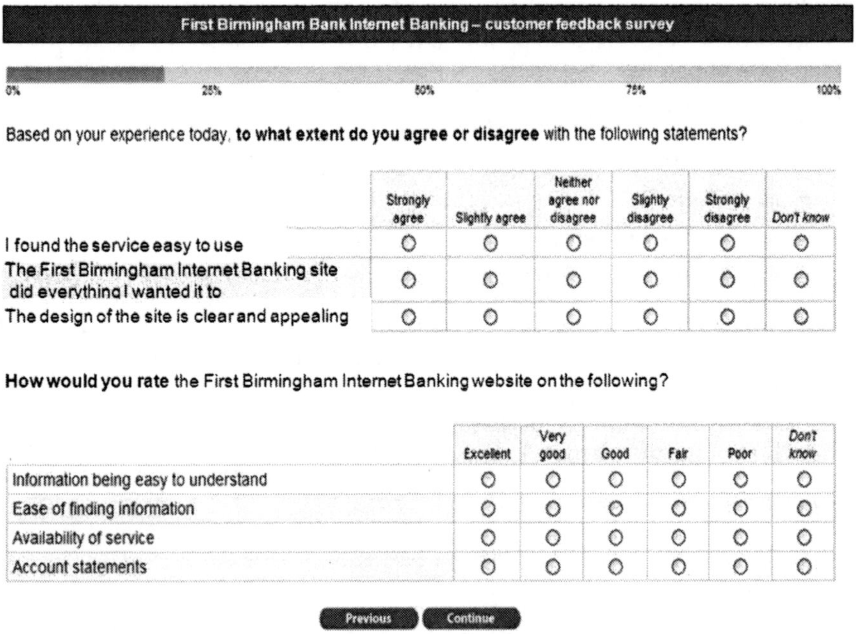

First Birmingham Bank Internet Banking – customer feedback survey

| 0% | 25% | 50% | 75% | 100% |

Based on your experience today, **to what extent do you agree or disagree** with the following statements?

	Strongly agree	Slightly agree	Neither agree nor disagree	Slightly disagree	Strongly disagree	Don't know
I found the service easy to use	O	O	O	O	O	O
The First Birmingham Internet Banking site did everything I wanted it to	O	O	O	O	O	O
The design of the site is clear and appealing	O	O	O	O	O	O

How would you rate the First Birmingham Internet Banking website on the following?

	Excellent	Very good	Good	Fair	Poor	Don't know
Information being easy to understand	O	O	O	O	O	O
Ease of finding information	O	O	O	O	O	O
Availability of service	O	O	O	O	O	O
Account statements	O	O	O	O	O	O

Previous   Continue

As we saw in Chapter 5, replacing the agree-disagree scale with an item specific question would be likely to improve the reliability of the data. Such a question might be:

How did you find using the service today:

Very easy

Easy

Neither easy nor difficult

Difficult

Very difficult.

Clearly, however, replacing each item with an individual question such as this will take up more space, in this case more screens, and may raise issues regarding the comparability of responses to the items if the individual response scales are not carefully matched. This is an issue that the question-naire writer has to consider and find the appropriate balance.

A further task for the questionnaire writer is to determine the number and level of detail of the items to be assessed. In customer satisfaction research the items are frequently defined by operational factors, such as the cleanliness of a room, or a call centre operator's ability to answer questions, or clarity of use of the website. These are usually capable of being expressed in a straightforward and succinct way. They should be:

- of a reasonable number such that the respondent is prepared to answer them;
- to a level of detail that it is reasonable for the respondent to be able to assess, usually after the event;
- expressed in terms that are clear and unambiguous.

The full version of the abbreviated questionnaire shown in Figure 8.1 contained 53 items at a very detailed level, probably in more detail than respondents are able or willing to respond to. Further, it is not always clear to what the item refers. What does 'Functionality of guest room' actually mean? Different respondents are likely to interpret it differently, with consequently meaningless data. This appears to be a list of items compiled by someone involved in the hotel's operations with no reference to a researcher.

Measuring brand image

A common objective with brand and communication studies is to measure brand image: that is, the perceptions that people hold of the main brands, how they compare and how they might occupy different positions in customers' minds, either as having functional differences or differences in emotional positioning. Two ways to measure brand image are the use of rating scales and brand-image association.

Scalar approaches

With a rating scale approach, each brand is evaluated on a number of dimensions defined as the key dimensions that discriminate between brands. Each brand is evaluated monadically, with the sequence of evaluating rotated between respondents. The rotation of the sequence order is important here as the way in which respondents rate one brand can affect the way they rate any following brands. How they rate the first brand on, say, 'quality' sets a benchmark for all subsequent brands. A slightly generous rating for the first brand, even though respondents think it might only be of average quality, requires increasingly positive ratings for any subsequent brands thought to be of better quality. Respondents are only asked to evaluate brands that they are aware of from a preceding or earlier prompted (aided) brand-awareness question.

Figure 8.3 is typical of the self-completion question to evaluate brand image using an agree-disagree scale. Note that this is technically not a Likert scale. As we are not measuring attitude but perception, there is no necessarily positive or negative position for each dimension, only different brand positionings. The individual respondent scores cannot be summed to provide an overall attitude score.

FIGURE 8.3   Self-completion question to evaluate brand image

Below are a number of statements that have been made about Crianlarich whisky. For each statement please indicate how much you agree or disagree that it applies to Crianlarich whisky.

	Disagree strongly	Disagree slightly	Neither agree nor disagree	Agree slightly	Agree strongly
High quality	☐	☐	☐	☐	☐
Traditional	☐	☐	☐	☐	☐
For younger people	☐	☐	☐	☐	☐
For older people	☐	☐	☐	☐	☐
A fun brand	☐	☐	☐	☐	☐
A modern brand	☐	☐	☐	☐	☐
To be taken seriously	☐	☐	☐	☐	☐

The questions in Figure 8.3 could equally have been posed as a bi-polar semantic differential scale. Care then has to be taken in defining the pairs of statements so that they have truly opposite meanings. For example is 'traditional' the opposite of 'modern', or should it be 'old fashioned'?

The scalar approaches to measuring brand image provide strong interval data that can be used in a variety of ways, including the calculation of mean scores and standard deviations and the analytical techniques such as correlation, regression and factor analyses. They do, though, suffer from two drawbacks. First, because they are completed monadically it is difficult for respondents to reference brands against each other. As discussed earlier, respondents may rate a brand for a particular attribute, only to find that for following brands they have not left themselves sufficient space on the scale to properly express the differences that they perceive between them.

The second disadvantage is that they can take a long time for respondents to complete. A list of 20 attributes for each of six brands requires respondents to complete 120 scales if they are aware of all six brands. At an estimated 15 seconds for each attribute for the first brand, and 10 seconds for subsequent brands, this can take over 20 minutes to complete. This adds to the potential fatigue and boredom of the respondents, the length of the interview and the cost of the study.

Attribute association

An alternative approach is the brand-attribute association grid (also known as the 'pick-any' or 'check all' technique). Here respondents are shown a list of brands and asked to say which brand or brands they associate with each of a series of image attributes. The image attributes are either read out by an interviewer or appear on the questionnaire or screen for self-completion. This is quicker because respondents only have to go through the list of attributes once. They also do not have to make such complex decisions about how well each brand performs on each attribute, only that it applies or that it does not.

Brands of which they are not aware will usually not be nominated as possessing any of the characteristics. Some respondents may nominate brands that they have previously said they are unaware of to have certain characteristics (particularly for attributes such as 'not well known') but these can be identified at the analysis stage. If respondents really are responding with an image of a brand they are hearing of for the first time, that can tell the researcher a great deal about the image attributes of the name alone. Another advantage is that respondents can assess the full set of brands together. This makes it easier for them to make comparisons between brands, and determine that an attribute is or is not associated with one brand rather than another.

One possible issue with this technique is that it is relatively easy for respondents to go through the question quickly without giving full consideration to every brand presented. It has been shown (Smyth *et al*, 2006; Stern *et al*, 2012) that compared with a forced choice question where the respondent has to say for each attribute whether or not he or she associates each brand with it, as would be necessary in telephone interview, this technique gives fewer positive associations for each brand.

A further disadvantage of attributing image statements in this way is the loss of the degree of discrimination that would have been obtained had scales been used. It may be found, for example, that most respondents think that all brands possess certain attributes, whereas a scalar approach would have shown variation in the strength with which each brand is seen to possess them.

The level of discrimination can be increased by including opposite expressions of an attribute. Both 'high quality' and 'poor quality' could be asked; 'for younger people' and 'not for younger people'. ('For older people' is not necessarily the opposite of 'For younger people' as the brand could be seen to be for both.) This doubles the number of attribute statements that need to be included, although it probably does not double the time taken to administer them. It effectively creates a three-point scale, with each brand nominated either for the point at each end of the scale, or not mentioned at all, which can be taken as the mid-point of the scale. The relationship of the association between the two end points is sometimes referred to as the 'quality of the brand image' and the extent to which the brand is associated at all with the dimension, 'the strength of the brand image'.

An alternative way to increase discrimination is to ask which brand or brands respondents would choose if they were looking for one that possessed the successive image attributes. Respondents then tend to nominate only brands that are strongly associated in their minds with the attribute. This reduces the number of brands associated with each attribute, and demonstrates 'ownership' of attributes more clearly.

Another way of improving the technique is to reduce the cognitive workload on respondents by only including brands of which they are aware, which is determined at a previous question or, possibly, only brands that appear in their consideration set.

Figure 8.4 is taken from an interviewer-administered questionnaire from which the data has to be manually entered, but the arrangement of the layout could equally be from a self-administered questionnaire. The coding numbers here have been arranged vertically rather than horizontally. This is for two reasons. First, there is no suggestion of an order of priority amongst the brands. A horizontal arrangement would have Brand A always as code 1 and Brand F as code 6. Where coding is shown on self-completion questionnaires this can be a potential source of bias. Second, it helps the researcher to think in terms of brand image profiles for each brand, and the data-processing spec-writer to write tables to produce that. It is more likely to be of value to the analyst to be able to see the image attributes associated with each brand rather than the brands associated with each image attribute. It also makes it easier to be able to analyse by respondents who have heard

FIGURE 8.4 Brand-attribute association grid

	Brand A	Brand B	Brand C	Brand D	Brand E	None of them
I am now going to read out a number of words and phrases that have been used to describe different brands of whisky. For each one I would like you to tell me to which, if any, of the brands on this card (SHOW CARD) you think it applies. Each phrase could apply to any number of the brands, all of them or none of them. READ OUT						
High quality	1	1	1	1	1	1
Traditional	2	2	2	2	2	2
For younger people	3	3	3	3	3	3
For older people	4	4	4	4	4	4
A fun brand	5	5	5	5	5	5
A modern brand	6	6	6	6	6	6
To be taken seriously	7	7	7	7	7	7

of the brand, brand users and non-users, those aware of the advertising, and so on.

A disadvantage of the technique is that the levels of association are dependent on the brand set shown. This acts as the reference set against which each brand is judged. The choice of which and how many brands are included is thus an important decision that can affect apparent brand positionings. Should the number of brands or choice set change over time, on repeat studies or tracking studies, there is a danger that comparability will be lost. A study may, for example, ask respondents to associate brands from a set of five airlines. If the number of airlines was to be increased to six in a later study, then we should expect to see the levels of association for all brands decrease. This is because the average number of brands associated with each attribute tends to remain reasonably constant, so that with more brands the average number per brand decreases.

Had one of the attributes been 'innovative' and the new brand introduced been Virgin Atlantic, a brand known for its innovation, then a substantial change in association for the remaining brands should be expected on this attribute. The frame of reference on this attribute will have changed, and brands that were previously thought to be innovative, in the context of the set asked about, will now appear to be less so. A similar change on this attribute would have been expected had Virgin Atlantic been substituted for another brand in the set, so that the total number remained the same. The levels of association recorded are not absolute, but are relative to both the number of brands asked about and the actual brands in the set.

When deciding upon the brands to use, it can be important to relate them to the attributes to be asked about. Thus, an attribute should not be included without very good reason if the brand set does not include the brand that has the strongest associations with the attribute. The false conclusion that a brand performs strongly on that attribute could easily be arrived at, because it only does so in the context of worse performing brands. The data generated by this approach allows correspondence mapping, as well as correlation analysis and, with some transformation, regression analysis.

A task for the questionnaire writer is to determine the attributes that are to be measured. Product attributes are often very specific and easily identified (eg modern, value for money, effective). Brand positioning or image attributes may be less tangible, but are often well defined within the brand positioning statement. This is a key area for the questionnaire writer to agree with the client or owner of the brand.

Binary measurement

Whilst the brand-attribute association or 'pick-any' technique remains the most popular and common way to assess brand image in commercial research, doubts have been raised as to the stability of the data. Experience with commercial research studies shows that in aggregate the data is sufficiently stable over time in tracking studies to be usable, but experimental work has shown that individual respondents change their responses between interviews and there is little replication (Rungie et al, 2005). Dolnicar et al (2012) showed that fewer than half of the brand-attribute associations made in a survey were repeated by the same respondents in as second survey four weeks later. This may raise doubts about the accuracy of any analyses that link these findings to individual respondent characteristics, such as demographic or product usage data.

Far greater stability was found by using a binary technique where the respondent was required to say for each brand whether it was thought to possess the attribute or not. This is, in effect, a two-point scale, but in an online survey it is likely to take little more time to administer than the pick-any technique.

It has been shown (Dolnicar et al, 2011) that binary questions can be substituted for multi-category scales and:

- be answered more quickly;
- be seen as less onerous;
- provide equal reliability;
- lead to the same conclusions.

Some shades of intermediate opinion are inevitably lost, but these are frequently ignored in the analysis. Others (Anderson *et al*, 2011) have shown that in street interviewing with pictorial prompts, binary questions took over a second more to answer than did a 0 to 10 scale. Clearly the context of the interview and the nature of the alternatives both need to be taken into account, but unless the shades of opinion are specifically required for analysis, binary questions should be considered as an alternative to multi-category scales.

Measuring attitudes

Attitudes are distinct from brand perceptions in that we are trying here to measure what and how people think about issues. The subject of the research can range from ready meals to punishment regimes for crimes. They can be attitudes that are clearly held and expressed or ones that individuals are barely conscious of. The questionnaire writer's task is to uncover and measure all these different types of attitudes.

Probably the most common way to measure attitudes is to use rating scales, whether it is to measure attitudes to brands, products, social issues or lifestyles. Formulating the attributes or dimensions and statements used to measure attitudes can be a difficult task. In comparison, brand, product or service attributes in customer satisfaction research are frequently easier to arrive at than are the appropriate set of attitude and lifestyle dimensions.

Measuring less tangible attitudes presents a number of considerations that the questionnaire writer must take into account. Respondents may never have considered the issues that they are being asked about. They may therefore be more open to influence from the question wording or the inferences that they draw from the statements. Some of the issues that must be taken into account when compiling the statements to represent the attitudinal dimensions are:

- whether or not the statement is balanced;
- whether it leads the respondent to a specific answer;
- how the addition or removal of wording may affect how respondents answer.

In addition, the question or questions that are to be asked need to be considered in relation to:

- whether acquiescence or yea-saying is likely to occur;
- whether this is an issue that the respondent has given conscious thought to before being asked about it in the questionnaire;
- the optimum method of measuring the importance of the dimensions to the respondent.

Balance in attitudinal questions is generally achieved by presenting all aspects of the dimension as being equally acceptable. This is important because there is a tendency for people to agree with any proposition that is put to them. With this type of attitudinal question it is important to avoid writing questions where the answer is simply 'yes' or 'no' and to force respondents to make a choice between a number of options.

There may be two aspects to the question: 'Do you think that voting in general elections should be made compulsory or not made compulsory?' Or there may be more than two: 'Do you think that women are better suited to bring up children than are men, or that men are better suited than women, or that both are equally suited?' The unbalanced version of these questions would be: 'Do you think that voting in general elections should be made compulsory?' and, 'Do you think that women are better suited than men to bring up children?'

These unbalanced versions are likely to lead to a higher proportion of the sample agreeing than would have chosen that option from the balanced questions. The evidence for acquiescence is strong. Schuman and Presser (1981) demonstrated it by asking the balanced and unbalanced version of the same question on the roles of men and women in politics in four separate surveys. The unbalanced version produced agreement with the proposition of between 44 and 48 per cent across the four surveys. The same proposition was chosen by between 33 and 39 per cent where the balanced question was used – the use of the unbalanced form added in the region of 10 percentage points.

Differences of such magnitude were not found with other topics, so acquiescence would seem to vary between subjects and possibly between individual items within a topic. Questionnaire writers rarely have the luxury of being able to test each topic and item to determine whether or not it is likely to be susceptible to acquiescence. It is therefore good practice to treat all questions as if they are, and to write the question in a balanced format. However, Schaeffer *et al* (2005) compared a fully balanced question with a minimally balanced question by replacing the full description of the alternative by 'is not':

Full balance:
As it conducts the war on terrorism, do you think the United States government is doing enough to protect the rights of American citizens, or do you think the government is not doing enough to protect the rights of American citizens?

Minimal balance:
As it conducts the war on terrorism, do you think the United States government is or is not doing enough to protect the rights of American citizens?

They found identical results, suggesting that repeating the proposition in its negative form is not necessary as long as a negative option is offered.

Whether or not the question is balanced, expression of the attitude must not lead the respondents to a particular point of view. A hypothetical example of such a question is:

Homeless people in our cities are a major problem and deter people from coming here. Do you think that the state should support homeless people or not?

The position of the question writer is quite clear. Only one aspect of the issue of homelessness has been highlighted, and this would be likely to lead respondents to a particular answer. The questions could as easily have been put as:

Some people find themselves without a home through no fault of their own, and then find it difficult to get back into work. Do you think the state should support homeless people or not?

The actual question is the same, but the information given to 'assist' the respondent in coming to an answer is biased in the opposite direction and is likely to lead to the opposite response from the first version.

With complex subjects such as this, the question writer has the choice of rehearsing all the pertinent issues as fairly and as equally as possible, or to ask the respondent to base their answer on what they already know about the subject:

From what you know about the issue of homelessness, are you in favour of or against the state supporting homeless people?

The extent of the wording change does not need to be as drastic as in this example in order to change the response. Schuman and Presser (1981) showed that a relatively small addition of a few words can change the response. In 1974 they asked the question:

If a situation like Vietnam were to develop in another part of the world, do you think the United States should or should not send troops?

To this question, 18 per cent answered that the United States should send troops. When the five words 'to stop a communist takeover' were added to the question, that proportion increased to 36 per cent. Similar increases were seen when the experiment was repeated in 1976 and again in 1978.

The additional words, in this case, were more than just a rhetorical flourish; they clearly led to a significant proportion of respondents assessing their position differently because they highlighted one particular aspect of the issue being asked about. It is unlikely that most market research questionnaires explore such emotive issues as the prospect of communist takeovers in the United States in the 1970s, but the example clearly serves to show how small additions to the question can change the response, and the care that must be taken with wording the question. Just a few words can alter the tenor of the question or crystallize an attitude that was previously only vaguely held. Question writers should be constantly asking themselves whether the inclusion of particular words or phrases helps the respondent, are just an embellishment, or in fact alter the basic question.

In unpublished work, TNS BMRB asked a balanced question in an experiment:

> Do you think that Scotland should remain part of the United Kingdom or do you think that it should be an independent country?

They also asked a shorter, unbalanced version:

> Do you think that Scotland should be an independent country?

The balanced version produced a significantly lower response across different test cells of around 6 percentage points for being an independent country. Here the difference may have been due in part to the suggestion in the balanced version that the alternative is to retain the status quo, which is not in the unbalanced version, and in part to remaining part of the UK being presented before the option of independence. The precise wording, and order of presentation of the options in the question, can both have an impact on the responses.

The case for piloting the questionnaire (see Chapter 13) is clear and should allow for alternative versions of attitudinal questions to be examined and tested whenever there is any uncertainty over them. The extent to which responses are changed by an additional phrase or a small change in wording may depend on whether the opinion had already been formed in the mind of the respondent prior to the question being asked, and how strongly that opinion is held.

The dimensions

Determining the attributes to measure

No matter which scale is used the crucial factor to get right is the wording of the items against which the attitude is to be measured. As with all questionnaire research, if the item is not measured it cannot be analysed, and if important attributes are not included then the analysis could be totally misleading.

If there is no existing set of attitude or attribute dimensions that have been proven to represent the issues in the market under consideration, they will need to be developed. Ideally the dimensions should be developed through a preliminary stage of qualitative research, designed specifically to determine the range of emotions, attitudes and perceptions that exist and that are relevant to the study and its objectives. The principal purpose of the preliminary study is to provide the attitude dimensions that are to be measured for strength of agreement in the quantitative survey. This stage can also be used to develop some preliminary hypotheses about attitudinal segments that might exist in the market, which the quantitative survey can then test.

If it is not possible to carry out a preliminary stage, the dimensions must be collated from elsewhere. Previous studies in the same area are the best place to start, even if they were not designed to meet precisely the same objectives. Any similar work carried out previously by the client should be examined. Sometimes, though, it comes down to experience and brainstorming, in an effort to try to generate every possible attitude, emotion or image perception that might exist and might need to be included in the questionnaire. This approach has obvious dangers:

- New attitudes that have not yet been identified may be omitted, which will tend to lead to a continuation of the existing perceptions of the market, rather than providing new insight.
- Something important may be overlooked completely.
- The wording used may not be that used by the respondents.
- In the absence of any information as to what is and is not important, there will be a tendency to produce too many dimensions in an attempt to ensure that everything is covered.

To counter this last point it is not unusual to conduct a preliminary survey that concentrates principally on the large set of attitude dimensions that have been initially generated. Most other questions are omitted from this questionnaire to make it manageable for the respondents. However, care must be taken not to alter the context of the attitude question by omitting preceding questions such as those about the respondent's behaviour in relation to the topic. Techniques such as principal component or factor analysis are then used to reduce a large battery of attitude dimensions to a smaller, more manageable set that can be included in the questionnaire. There is a danger here, though, that small differences in attitude dimensions – ones that were specifically introduced in the brainstorming because they are important – get excluded because the purpose of the factor analysis is to produce broader, underlying attitude dimensions. It is important, therefore, to follow any reduction process by a further review of the dimensions and reinstate those of particular importance, or showing particular nuances of difference, that have been removed.

There are sources such as the *Handbook of Marketing Scales* (Bearden and Netermeyer, 1999) that provide lists of dimensions for a range of different attitudinal subject areas that have been used in published studies. They are a useful starting point for someone compiling an attitude battery, or can be used when looking for standardized wording or checking that the compiler has not overlooked an important dimension. Before adopting a complete set of standardized scaling dimensions, however, users should ensure that they cover all aspects of the topic under consideration in their study.

Number of attributes

If the number of statements exceeds the respondents' boredom threshold, the likelihood of pattern responding is increased. The threshold will vary according to people's interest in the subject.

The size of the statement battery is something that the researcher should consider carefully. Clearly there must be a sufficient number of statements to address adequately all of the attitudes under consideration. If possible, there should be several statements for each attitudinal dimension to enable the researcher to cross-check responses for consistency within respondents. The number of statements before fatigue sets in will vary according to the level of interest of the respondent in the subject. However, the maximum number in one battery is rarely more than about 30 before a respondent's attention begins to wander. If questionnaire writers are unsure, they should ask themselves whether they could themselves maintain concentration throughout a battery of 200 statements about, say, greetings cards.

If, despite all attempts to reduce the number of statements, it is not possible to cover the required attitudinal dimensions without producing a formidable battery of statements, it can sometimes be possible to split the statements into two batteries that are located at different points in the questionnaire. The statements should be split so that the two batteries cover different sets of underlying attitudinal dimensions, and if possible this should be explained in the introduction to the question. Without this precaution, there is a danger that, when respondents are presented with the second battery, they will believe they are being asked the same questions again and will not take sufficient care. Nevertheless, with a battery of statements of any size it is inevitable that some respondent fatigue will set in. Statements at the beginning of the battery will be given more careful consideration than those towards the end (this issue is discussed further in Chapter 9).

Indirect techniques

The difficulty that people have in recognizing – let alone accurately articulating – their emotions and feelings about brands has led to a number of techniques that approach the issue indirectly. For example, instead of asking respondents to associate image dimensions with brands, techniques have been established that associate the brand with picture stimuli, which in turn are established as having certain emotional associations. The respondents' feelings about the brand can then be evaluated, even if they do not consciously recognize those feelings. Most of the techniques of this type, however, are proprietary and have a specified set of questions and are therefore outside the scope of this book.

Pictorial techniques

Many of the indirect techniques use pictorial stimuli either to convey a personality type or emotion with which respondents are asked to associate needs or brands, or to help the respondents to express how they feel in a way that would be difficult for them to do verbally. Great care must be taken with such techniques so that respondents do not identify with something in the picture that was not intended by the question writer. If depictions of people are used there may be unintended associations with age, gender or other personal characteristics and not what was intended.

Because of the difficulty that people have in identifying, acknowledging and articulating emotions, pictorial techniques have been developed to evaluate people's emotional response to advertising. Respondents are shown depictions of emotions and asked a series of questions, such as which best represents how they felt as they watched the advertisement. This type of approach relies on a theoretical framework that encompasses the full range of emotions, and that defines the emotions to be depicted.

One of the most successful of these techniques has been Brainjuicer's proprietary Facetrace (Wood, 2007), which uses photographs of a face to present seven key emotions, together with a neutral face. This approach uses a single, deliberately androgynous face to avoid the problems of introducing the response effects mentioned above. To successfully achieve these depictions, the appropriate questions and their interpretation requires considerable work and validation. It is difficult to achieve this in the context of writing a single questionnaire and expert advice should be sought.

FIGURE 8.5   Pictorial representations of emotions

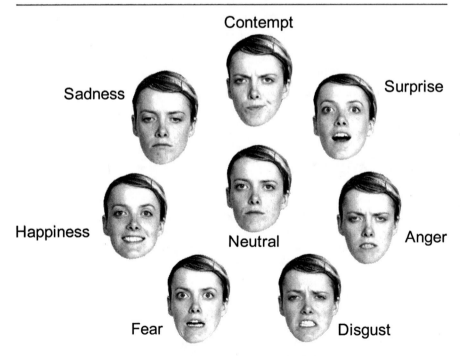

BrainJuicer © 2006

09 Writing the questionnaire

Introduction

In the previous chapters we have examined the different types of question and technique that are available to the questionnaire writer. These represent the tools in the armoury that can be used to compile a questionnaire. A number of other issues, though, need to be considered in the process of writing the questionnaire. These issues, considered in this chapter, include:

- the language and style of language in which it is written;
- ensuring that there is no ambiguity in the questions or the responses;
- whether pre-codes will be used or responses recorded verbatim;
- if pre-codes are to be used, what they should be;
- the use of prompt material and the choice between verbal and pictorial prompts;
- bias that can be caused by the order of the questions;
- bias that can be caused by the order of prompted responses.

Use of language

When writing the questionnaire it is the questionnaire writer's job to ensure that the respondents will understand the questions and that the respondents will not feel intimidated, challenged or threatened by the questions.

Writing questionnaires is about helping respondents give the best information that they can. Questions should be clear and unambiguous, and the respondent should be put at ease by the tone of the questions and not made to feel challenged by the words and phrases used. Respondents who feel challenged because they don't understand the questions will quickly become alienated from the interview process and make little effort to respond accurately. They may become fatigued earlier than they would have done and fail to complete the interview. Therefore, we must ensure that the questions are phrased in everyday language to which the respondents can relate. The interview can be seen as a conversation by proxy between the researcher and the respondent. The questionnaire should be suitably conversational in tone, while not seeking to be too familiar or condescending.

Researchers are frequently given briefs by clients that are expressed in technical terms that relate to the client's business. They may talk of 'channels of distribution' or 'above-the-line advertising'. It is the job of the questionnaire writer to turn this into phrases that will be part of the every-day speech of respondents, or at least readily understood by them.

Seen in print

In a study about aircraft noise, respondents were asked to indicate how important they thought it was that:

Cash compensation should be offered to those households that suffer a significant increase in noise to a level greater than 57 decibels but less than 63 decibels, and who therefore do not qualify for insulation.

This question falls down on two counts. First, it is difficult to understand what the question means because it is phrased in technical terms. Second, even if someone understands it, few people would be competent to answer it accurately. How many respondents understand exactly how loud 57 or 63 decibels is?

Getting rid of technical terms is not always easy. They exist because they are needed. Some sympathy must be felt for the writer of the question in the box above. How do you convey to respondents precise noise levels? But equally, how usable is any response to this question? Anyone using the data generated must be concerned about how well the question was understood.

Because technical terms are often the everyday language of the commissioners of the study, they do not always appreciate that others outside their industry or profession might not understand them, or might understand something different by them. Sometimes technical terms are used to describe something, or to differentiate between objects or services, with far greater subtlety than the non-specialist can appreciate. To most motorists a petrol pump is a petrol pump, and they would not distinguish between a 'high line fast flow' and a 'grouped hose blender'. Researchers must ask themselves if it is necessary for the respondent to be able to distinguish between them in the interview. If it is, then the differences must be clearly explained, if possible without reference to the technical terminology.

Some technical terms are words that have a different everyday use. Market researchers will use the terms 'random' and 'significance' with specific meanings that are different to the way they are used by most people.

The danger here is that researchers might think that respondents understand the terms in the same way that they do, but respondents may answer a different question to the one that the researcher thinks is being asked.

Seen in print

Q1. What do you think of Big Oil?
PROBE FULLY.

This was the opening question in the survey. The term 'Big Oil' was well understood by the questionnaire writer, who worked in the oil industry, but meant nothing to respondents.

The interview as conversation

The interview was described above as a conversation by proxy between the researcher and the respondent. However, it is not the sort of conversation that two people who know each other would have.

With interviewer-administered interviews it is not unusual for respondents to try to enter into conversation with the interviewer, to give their views and elaborate on their responses. Only when the interviewer insists on reducing this answer to one of the pre-codes on the questionnaire does the respondent appreciate that this is not really a conversation but an interaction in which they have a specific and limited role to play (Suchman and Jordan, 1990).

The lack of conversation can mask incorrect answers. Through elaboration of answers such as 'Yes, but ...' or 'I agree, except that ...' it can become clear that the true answer is 'No' or 'I disagree'. If respondents are not allowed to elaborate in this way, their true answer may not become apparent, and an incorrect answer may be recorded. With self-completion surveys we rely on respondents to think it through, to in effect elaborate to themselves, and not necessarily give their first reaction. Thus, while we conceptualize the questionnaire as the medium of conversation, we must recognize that it is not a true conversation; that this may mean that we do not acquire all of the information that respondents could give us or may wish to give us; and that it can, on occasion, lead to incorrect answers being recorded.

Schober (1999) points out two key differences between having a conversation with your aunt and carrying out an interview with a structured questionnaire, known as 'audience design' and 'grounding'. Departing from the norms of conversation can cause greater effort to formulate their answers (Holbrook and Krosnick, 2000). If, for example, the 'no' option is presented before the 'yes' this departs from the expected order, requiring more cognitive processes from the respondent than they might be prepared to make, and a consequent decrease in the validity of the data. The questionnaire writer should therefore pay attention to the norms of conversation and try to emulate them as much as possible.

Audience design

When one person who knows another asks the second person a question or makes a statement, it is framed to be heard specifically by that other person, and draws on the knowledge that each has of the other. This is known as 'audience design'. The person to whom it is said is the addressee. Addressees are likely to give different interpretations and responses to the question, 'How many hours a week do you work?' depending on whether it is asked by their aunt, their boss or someone from the tax office. Addressees will use their knowledge of the relationship to determine what type of response the questioner expects to hear.

In a survey questionnaire, the questions are not framed for specific respondents, but to have general applicability to as many people as possible. Interviewers are specifically instructed neither to deviate from the question script nor to tailor the question to the individual. In quantitative research, as hard as questionnaire writers may try, they cannot write a questionnaire to be one side of a conversation.

Grounding

Grounding occurs in a conversation when the participants establish that each has understood what one of them has said, and that it has entered their common ground. This can come from an acknowledgement of the question or statement ('uh-huh', 'ok') or a request for elaboration as to what is meant from the addressee, or clarification volunteered by the questioner if it is clear that the addressee has not understood.

Some level of grounding is available in an interview, but interviewers are deliberately restricted in the procedures that they can use in order to avoid introducing bias. Often when asked for clarification, all the interviewer can do is to repeat the question, or describe the type of response that is needed, or ask for a best estimate. Elaboration of individual words in the question is to be avoided as, apart from potentially introducing bias, the interviewers themselves may not understand precisely what is meant and present a misinterpretation of the question to respondents.

These difficulties in audience design and grounding can lead to a number of response effects from prompt material, question ordering and interpretation of questions.

Minority languages

There are many different types of question that can be asked and in many different ways. What is common to all questions, though, is that they must be worded in a way that is understood by the respondents and to which respondents can relate. This means ensuring that there are minority-language versions of the questionnaire if the sample is likely to include people who speak a language other than the majority language, or whose command of that language is unlikely to be sufficiently good to be able to complete an interview in it. By denying sections of the survey population the opportunity to participate in the study, the questionnaire writer is effectively disenfranchising them from influencing the findings.

For many studies commissioned by the public sector in many countries, it is important that the interview can be conducted in any language that is spoken by a significant number of people in the survey population to avoid the danger of disenfranchisement. In the UK many government studies require questionnaire versions in Welsh, Urdu, Hindi and other languages, and in the United States a Spanish-language version will often be required.

The relevance of minority-language speakers to the study will naturally vary by the subject of the study and the degree of accuracy required in the data. For a study of housing conditions it is likely to be important that recently arrived immigrant communities are represented in the sample in their correct proportions. If the questionnaire is not available in a language that they understand, they will be effectively excluded and hence under-represented.

For many commercial studies, the issue of minority languages can be mostly ignored in many countries, although a Spanish version of the questionnaire is frequently necessary in the United States. This is because for most commercial studies the difference that a minority of non-majority language-speaking consumers is likely to make to the findings is small, particularly in comparison to the variation caused by sampling error, non-response rates and even interviewer error.

Avoiding ambiguity in the question

Ambiguity is to be avoided at all costs. If a question is ambiguous, the respondent may be presented with the dilemma of hearing or seeing two different questions and will not know which to answer. With an interviewer-administered questionnaire the respondent may seek help from the interviewer. The interviewer may be able to assist with the knowledge of the context of the question in relation to other questions, but this may not always be the case. With self-administered questionnaires, respondents have to make their own decision as to what the question means. Either way, the researcher does not know which way the respondent has understood the question, except in the occasional instances where either the interviewer or respondent has recorded it. This rarely happens, though, except in pilot studies.

Ambiguity in the question can make it impossible for a respondent to know how to answer. Consider the following question:

Do your parents work full time?   Yes/No

There is no difficulty for the respondent if both parents work full time or if neither parent does (although a definition of what constitutes 'full-time working' would be helpful). If, however, one works full time and the other does not, what is the respondent to answer? The question would be better asked:

Do either or both of your parents work full time, that is more than 30 hours a week?
Both/One/Neither

There still remains the issue of what constitutes 'work', and whether it should include unpaid work, such as charity work, or only paid work.

While some respondents may see the ambiguity and make a decision on which way to answer, others may not see it and understand it only in the sense in which it was not intended. Then the answer given will not be the one that would have been given to the intended question and, again, the researcher is unaware of this.

If the ambiguity in the question is not spotted until the data has been collected, the researcher has no way of knowing which respondents answered the question as intended and which answered the alternative meaning. This can render the data from that question incapable of interpretation and therefore useless.

Ambiguity is obviously to be avoided in questions, but is not always easy to spot. This is because it is not always possible to anticipate every respondent's circumstances, and a question that may not be ambiguous to most respondents may, because of their circumstances, contain an ambiguity for a few. For example, 'How many bedrooms are there in this property?' is a simple question apparently incapable of more than one possible answer for most people. But what is meant by a bedroom? If someone has a study that doubles as an occasional bedroom, should that be included?

In most instances this level of ambiguity will not be a major issue. Where the number of bedrooms is collected as classification data to provide a cross-analysis of data by approximate size of house, then this degree of ambiguity may be acceptable to the researchers. Where this information is central to the data collected, then the ambiguity must be addressed. With the number of bedrooms, such ambiguity would be unacceptable in, say, a study of housing conditions. Then the question would require expanding, possibly to ask the number of rooms currently used as bedrooms, the number occasionally used as bedrooms and the number that could be used as bedrooms, or as required by the study.

Determining the pre-codes

The pre-codes that are used on the questionnaire determine what data is collected. If the pre-codes have insufficient accuracy or are incomplete, then data will be lost that may be important to answering the objectives. In many instances the responses will be obvious – yes/no, male/female – but in others care must be taken to ensure that they are:

- mutually exclusive;
- as exhaustive as possible;
- as precise as necessary;
- meaningful.

Seen in print

From a hotel customer satisfaction questionnaire:

> Level of satisfaction: Low_, Average_, High_:
> Friendly and efficient service at reception

Some of the friendliest receptionists are often the least efficient, and vice versa. How does the guest answer this question if that is the case? It is possible that the guest who wants to indicate that the service was friendly but not efficient, or that it was efficient but not friendly, will give up at this point and not complete the rest of the questionnaire.

Unless they are mutually exclusive, it will be possible to code the same response against more than one response code. This is confusing for the interviewer (or respondent with a self-completion questionnaire) and makes the output ambiguous and impossible to interpret.

The pre-codes need to be as exhaustive as they can in order to minimize the number of 'other answers' written in. If there are a lot of 'other answers' written in, the question would have been better recorded as an open-ended one.

Failure of the questionnaire to record the reply accurately or completely

The main failure of questionnaires in this respect is in not providing a comprehensive list of possible answers as pre-codes for interviewers and respondents to record the response accurately. The response to the question 'Do you like eating pizza?' sounds as if it should be a simple 'yes' or 'no', but respondents may wish to qualify the answer depending on whether it is home-made or shop-bought, the toppings or the occasion. If they are unable to do so, an answer of 'Don't know' may be recorded. Whatever is recorded is not the complete response.

It is common to see a question such as 'How often do you visit the cinema?' given the possible answers:

- More than once a week.
- Once a week.
- Once a month.
- Once every three months.
- Less often than once every three months.

Such an answer list cannot accurately record the behaviour of someone who went to the cinema twice in the last week and not at all in the three months before that. Either the respondent or the interviewer has to decide what the least inaccurate response is.

This type of questionnaire failure, leading to inaccurately recorded data, has, however, become accepted for many types of survey, principally because the alternative of allowing for all possible responses would be too complicated to process and analyse.

Using prompts

Show cards are frequently used to provide the respondents with prompted answers in face-to-face interviews. In self-completion interviews the prompts are provided with the question either on a paper questionnaire or on-screen with a web-based questionnaire. With telephone interviews the prompts are frequently read out or, if they are to be repeated as with a scale, respondents are sometimes asked to write them down.

Prompts can be scale points, attitudinal phrases, image dimensions, brands, income ranges or anything that the questionnaire writer wants to use to guide the respondents or to obtain reaction to. They can be purely verbal or they can utilize pictures, illustrations or logos. However, it is important to be clear about the different jobs that verbal and pictorial stimuli do.

Picture prompts

Pictures can be used in a number of different ways as prompts. If they are to be used, then questionnaire writers must be careful to ensure that they know exactly what role the pictures are playing.

FIGURE 9.1 Imprecise wording

Seen in print

Qa. How often do you make local telephone calls on your home line?
Qb. How often do you make national telephone calls on your home line?
Qc. How often do you make international calls on your home line?
Qd. How often do you make calls to mobile phones on your home line?

	(a) Local calls	(b) National calls	(c) International calls	(d) Calls to mobiles
VERY OFTEN	1	1	1	1
OFTEN	2	2	2	2
OCCASIONALLY	3	3	3	3
SELDOM	4	4	4	4
NEVER	5	5	5	5

Respondents may or may not have had difficulty in interpreting what each code was intended to mean, but the researcher would have had serious problems analysing the resulting data. 'Frequently' used in relation to local calls is likely to mean several calls a day to most respondents. The same word applied to international calls may well be just one or two a week. So what framework have respondents used in giving their answers? Has the frequency been judged against a common standard, with one type of call (possibly the local call, as that is asked first) being used to define what is frequent for all four types of calls, or have the response codes been interpreted independently for each type of call, so that the meaning of 'frequent' varies between types of call? The researcher cannot know. Even if the researcher did know, he or she could not know how what is considered 'frequent' varies between respondents. These answers would have been better recorded as frequency values.

Brand awareness

One use of picture prompts is to show brand logos or icons instead of a list of brand names, to measure prompted brand awareness. With CAPI and web-based interviews this is easy to do, and is often included to make the interview more interesting for the respondent. However, questionnaire writers should be aware that they might be changing the question.

Prompted awareness is a question of recognition. If a list of names is used, the respondents are being asked which of the names they recognize. If brand logos are shown, the question becomes which of the logos they recognize. The researcher infers awareness of the brand through recognition of the logo. This is likely to be higher than simple name recognition, as the logo gives more clues.

The improvement in apparent brand awareness is likely to be stronger for the smaller brands in a market. Prompted awareness of Coca-Cola does not require the use of a visual prompt to be very high amongst carbonated drink users. There is little opportunity for visual prompts to make an improvement. But for smaller brands, the opportunities for improvement offered by visual prompts are much greater. The total average number of logos recognized per respondent is usually likely to be greater than the average number of brand names from a simple list. Neither approach is necessarily incorrect, but each is likely to give a different level of response.

Likelihood to purchase

When asking about likelihood to purchase, much more information is given to respondents if a pictorial stimulus is used. Rather than show a list of brands and prices, a mocked-up shelf can be shown, as in Figure 9.2. The cues and information that are given by the pack shots mean that respondents do not have to rely on memory and recall of the brands when making their decision. Price information can easily be excluded, included or changed as required.

FIGURE 9.2   A mocked-up shelf of the brands' desired positionings

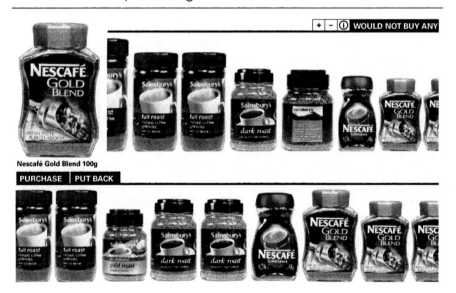

Brand image

Showing logos can also alter the responses to questions about brand image. It is normal to establish prompted brand awareness before asking about images of certain brands. If prompted brand awareness is established using a list of names, the mental picture taken into the image question is the image of the brand as it exists in isolation within the respondents' minds. The image is purely what the brand name stands for and the images that are associated with it. After prompting with a logo or pack shot, however, respondents are given clues and reminders of what the brand is trying to stand for. The logo or pack will have been designed to reflect the desired brand positioning and may well communicate something of those values to the respondents in the interview, or at least act as a reminder of them. The image question is therefore also prompted with at least a partial reminder.

Again it is not a question of one approach being incorrect. Using a brand list may be described as giving a 'purer' measure of image. This is an image, it can be argued, that the potential purchasers have in their minds before leaving home to go shopping, and it will act upon their intent to purchase the brand. But it can be equally argued that most brands are rarely seen without their logos, and that it is the image in the purchasers' minds at the point of purchase, when there are likely to be many visual cues, that is important.

The questionnaire writer should consider which is the more appropriate approach for the market in question, and decide which approach to use accordingly.

Advertising recognition

Showing advertising to establish recognition is a particular case of showing picture prompts. Except for radio advertising, it is difficult to establish advertising recognition without the use of picture prompts. These often consist of a series of stills taken from the advertisement in question, known as a storyboard. This may or may not include the script of the characters or voice-over. It also may or may not have all references to the brand removed, depending on whether being able to name the correct brand is to be asked. With CAPI and web-based interviewing, however, there is a choice between showing a storyboard and showing the actual ad as film. The two methods will generally lead to different responses, with higher awareness recorded among respondents shown the film.

For press and poster ads, copies of the actual ad can be shown. It may be necessary to use a reduced format from the actual size (particularly for posters), in which case there should be an explanation that it has been reduced.

Order bias and prompts

The order in which prompts are presented to respondents, whether on the questionnaire or screen, shown on a card or read out, can have a significant effect on the responses recorded. Such bias can occur with the presentation of:

- scalar responses;
- monadically rated batteries of attitude or image dimensions;
- lists from which responses are chosen.

The questionnaire writer must consider how to minimize the order bias for each of these.

Scalar responses

A considerable amount has been written about the effect that the order of presentation of prompted alternative answers has on responses. Artingstall (1978) showed that when respondents are given a scale from which to choose a response in face-to-face interviewing they are significantly more likely to choose the first response offered than the last. Of 72 end items that were offered in his test, 62 were given greater endorsement when offered first. This is known as 'the primacy effect'. Thus if the positive end of a scale is always presented first a more favourable result will be found than if the negative end of the scale is always first. The finding held for any length of scale, and was independent of the demographic profile of the respondents. The difference was shown to be an increase of about 8 per cent to the positive responses.

What this and other work shows is that the order of presentation has an effect. It does not say which order gives the best representation of the truth. However, it underlines the need to be consistent in the order in which scales are shown if comparisons are to be made between studies. One approach to dealing with the bias is to rotate the order of presentation between two halves of the sample. This does not remove the bias but at least has the effect of averaging it.

In new product development research, it is not uncommon always to have the negative response presented first on scales rating the concept or the product. This then gives the least favourable response pattern, thereby providing a tougher test for the new product and ensuring that any positive reaction to the idea of the product is not overstated.

When visual prompts are used, the primacy effect is noticed, as demonstrated by Artingstall, as respondents notice and process the possible responses in the order that they are presented. Where prompts are read out, a recency effect is more marked, as respondents remember better the last option or last few options they have been given. This effect has been demonstrated by Schwarz *et al* (1991). With telephone interviewing, therefore, a recency effect should be expected, unless respondents are asked to write down the scale for reference before answering the question.

Batteries of statements

Fatigue effect

Where there is a large battery of either image or attitude statements, each of which is to be answered according to a scale, there is a real danger of respondent fatigue. This can occur both with self-completion batteries and where the interviewer reads them out. As discussed earlier, the precise point at which respondent fatigue is likely to set in will vary with the level of interest that each respondent has in the subject. However, it should be anticipated that, where there are more than about 30 statements, later statements are likely to suffer from inattention and pattern responding. To alleviate this type of bias, the presentation of the statement should be rotated between respondents. With electronic questionnaires, statements can often be presented in random order, or in rotation in a number of different sequences.

With paper questionnaires, rotating the order requires producing a number of different versions for self-completion, or careful instruction to interviewers if they are to read them out. In the latter case it is common for the starting point on the battery for each respondent to be ticked or checked at the time of printing the questionnaires or before they are sent out to the interviewers. Ideally, the start point can be rotated between questionnaires so that the reading out starts at each statement an equal number of times. However, this may not always be possible to do automatically; it requires as many different versions of the page to be printed as there are statements in the battery. With possibly up to 30 statements the potential for error is considerable. Printing the questionnaire with no marked start points and marking each questionnaire by hand can be time-consuming where there are thousands of questionnaires. An alternative, which is usually acceptable, is to have a limited number of start points, and these can be printed using different versions of the page. Thus if there are 30 statements, six different start points can be used, spread throughout the battery. The statements are still reasonably well rotated and, with only six versions of the page to be printed, the scope for error is much reduced.

Where the battery of statements is to be read out by the interviewer using a paper questionnaire, it is important that every interviewer understands the process of rotating start points. In particular, interviewers must understand that every statement must be read out. It has been known for interviewers to read out only the statements from the designated start point to the end of the battery, and not to return to the beginning of the battery for the remaining statements. This is more likely to occur where the battery is on more than one page and the start point is not on the first page.

Statement clarification

The order in which statements are presented to respondents can sometimes be used to clarify their meanings. If there is a degree of ambiguity in a statement that would require a complex explanation, a preceding statement that deals with the alternative meaning can clarify what the questionnaire writer is seeking. For example:

How would you rate the station for:
The facilities and services at the station

On its own, it could be unclear to respondents whether car parking should be considered as one of the facilities or services at the station. If, however, this statement is preceded by one about car parking:

Facilities for car parking
The facilities and services at the station

or, even better:

Facilities for car parking
Other facilities and services at the station

Respondents can safely assume that the facilities and services are not meant to include car parking as that has already been asked about.

Where random presentation of statements is used, care must be taken to ensure that such explanatory pairs of statements always appear together and in the same order.

Response lists

Showing a list of alternative responses is a common form of prompting to make respondents choose from a fixed set of options; see the example in Figure 9.3.

FIGURE 9.3   List of alternative responses

Thinking about the advertisement that you have just seen, which of the phrases on this card would you say describes it? You can mention as many or as few phrases as you wish.	
A	It was difficult to understand
B	It made me more interested in visiting the store
C	I found it irritating
D	It's not right for this type of product
E	I quickly got bored with it
F	I did not like the people in it
G	It said something relevant to me
H	I will remember it
I	It improved my opinion of the store
J	It told me something new about the store
K	It was aimed at me
L	I enjoyed watching it
M	None of these

The respondent is expected to read through all of the options and select those that apply. In this question, respondents can choose as many statements as they feel are appropriate. In other questions, they may be asked to choose one option or any other specified number.

Primacy and recency effects

Similar primacy effects should be expected with response lists. The effects have been demonstrated by Schwarz *et al* (1991), even where there are a small number of possible responses, down to three or even two if they are sufficiently complex to dissuade respondents from making an effort to process the possible answers in full. In a longer list of 13 items, Krosnick and Alwin (1987) demonstrated increased selection of the first three. Duffy (2003) confirms the existence of primacy effects and adds that a significant minority read the list from the bottom. This would suggest that a recency effect can also be expected. Recency effects should also be expected in telephone surveys.

Indeed, both primacy and recency effects have been demonstrated by Ring (1975). He showed that with a list of 18 items there is a bias in favour of choosing responses in the first six and the last four positions (Table 9.1). The implication is that those in the middle of the list either are not read at all by some respondents or are not processed as possible responses to the same extent.

Where a list is of such a size, then reversing the order and presenting one order to half of the sample and the reverse order to the other half does not adequately address the problem. Ring's experiments showed that with a list of 18 items the first 14 should be reversed and the last four reversed. The items that were fourteenth and fifteenth in the initial list then become first and last in the alternative list. This asymmetrical split better balances the bias across the items than simply reversing them. For further reduction in order bias Ring suggests additional splits after the seventh and sixteenth items, but for most research purposes these are not necessary.

In practice, many, if not most, researchers satisfy themselves with two or at most four rotations. With electronic questionnaires, statements can often be presented in random order, or in rotation in a larger number of different sequences. This does not eliminate bias but spreads it across the statements more evenly.

Satisficing

Some people when buying items such as a washing machine, stereo system or car will spend a great deal of time researching which of the available models best meets their needs and requirements. Other people will buy one that satisfactorily meets their minimum needs and requirements, and are not prepared to invest the time in researching all of the available models to determine whether there is one that is marginally better. The latter approach is known as 'satisficing', and occurs when choosing attitude statements from a list.

TABLE 9.1 Asymmetrical rotation of positions on the list

Item	Two-way split Position in:		Four-way split Position in:			
	List 1	List 2	List 1	List 2	List 3	List 4
A	1	14	1	14	7	8
B	2	13	2	13	6	9
C	3	12	3	12	5	10
D	4	11	4	11	4	11
E	5	10	5	10	3	12
F	6	9	6	9	2	13
G	7	8	7	8	1	14
H	8	7	8	7	14	1
I	9	6	9	6	13	2
J	10	5	10	5	12	3
K	11	4	11	4	11	4
L	12	3	12	3	10	5
M	13	2	13	2	9	6
N	14	1	14	1	8	7
O	15	18	15	18	16	17
P	16	17	16	17	15	18
Q	17	16	17	16	18	15
R	18	15	18	15	17	16

After Ring (1975)

When presented with a list of statements from which to choose a response, satisficers will read it until they find an adequate answer that they feel reasonably reflects their view, or that they think will be acceptable to the interviewer, rather than reading or listening to all of the statements to find the answer that best reflects their view. This is another source of order bias, which will tend to reinforce the primacy effect.

Satisficing is likely to increase with interview fatigue as respondents stop making the effort to answer to the best of their ability. It is also likely to be more prevalent with telephone than with face-to-face interviewing (Holbrook *et al*, 2003). There is also evidence that it is more prevalent amongst people of lower educational achievement or who are less articulate (Krosnick and Alwin, 1987). These people appear less willing to make the cognitive effort to find the most appropriate response. This also leads them to be more susceptible to primacy effects. Researchers using online panels should also be aware that Toepoel *et al* (2008) found that experienced respondents, as are found on access panels, tend to be subject to satisficing more than are inexperienced respondents, probably as part of a strategy to complete the survey as quickly as possible.

Question order

There are certain rules regarding the ordering of questions that must always be borne in mind. These have been covered in Chapter 3 and include:

- There must be no prompting of any information before spontaneous questions on the same subject.
- The interview should normally start with the more general questions relating to the topic and work through to the more specific or detailed subject matter.
- Behavioural questions should be asked before attitudinal questions on the same topic.

These issues should have been considered when the questionnaire was planned, but still need to be thought about as the detailed questionnaire is written.

Funnelling

Funnelling sequences are used to take respondents from general questions on a topic through to questions that are more specific without allowing the earlier questions to condition or bias the responses to the later ones.

Typically in the funnelling sequence, whether respondents are asked a question depends on their response to the previous one. This means that people for whom questions are irrelevant can be routed round them. Because people are routed out without knowing what the criteria are for continuing the question sequence, we can be more confident that the response that we obtain to the final question is not biased. In the example in Figure 9.4, we would have little confidence that there was no bias had we asked the one question, 'If you have seen any advertising for Bulmer's cider on television recently, what did it say?' This question would lead to overclaiming of having seen advertising, because there is an assumption that Bulmer's cider has been advertised on television recently. Some respondents would then claim to have seen it, even though they had not.

FIGURE 9.4 Funnelling sequence

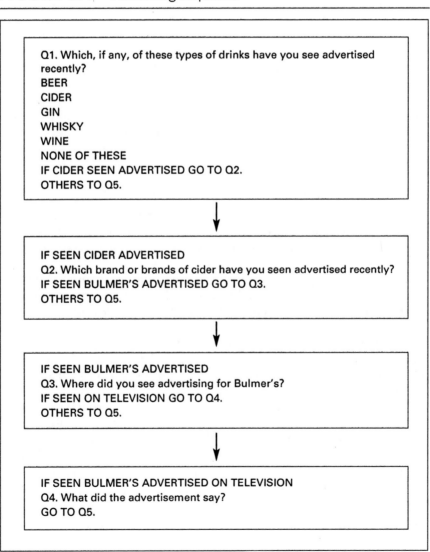

Q1. Which, if any, of these types of drinks have you see advertised recently?
BEER
CIDER
GIN
WHISKY
WINE
NONE OF THESE
IF CIDER SEEN ADVERTISED GO TO Q2.
OTHERS TO Q5.

IF SEEN CIDER ADVERTISED
Q2. Which brand or brands of cider have you seen advertised recently?
IF SEEN BULMER'S ADVERTISED GO TO Q3.
OTHERS TO Q5.

IF SEEN BULMER'S ADVERTISED
Q3. Where did you see advertising for Bulmer's?
IF SEEN ON TELEVISION GO TO Q4.
OTHERS TO Q5.

IF SEEN BULMER'S ADVERTISED ON TELEVISION
Q4. What did the advertisement say?
GO TO Q5.

Funnelling sequences can be complicated for respondents to follow on paper self-completion questionnaires because of the routeing, and are best avoided. However, they can be used with any interviewer-administered questionnaire and work very well with electronic or web-based self-completion question-naires where the routeing is hidden.

Question order bias

Priming effects

Where there is a key question to be asked, such as approval of a proposal, response to a new concept or rating of an issue, the act of asking questions about the respondent's feelings about the proposal, concept or issue prior to the key questions can have an effect on the response to it.

This can be desirable, as the researcher will want respondents to give an answer that takes into account their considered view. However, the re-searcher can suggest to respondents what they should answer. McFarland (1981) reported that asking a series of specific questions about the energy crisis led to a higher rating of the severity of the crisis than when the ques-tions were not asked. Questionnaire writers need to be aware of the influ-ence that prior questions can have, and write the questions and interpret the responses accordingly.

Consistency effect

A particular type of priming effect is the consistency effect. This can occur because respondents are led along a particular route of responses to a conclusion to which they can only answer one way if they are to appear consistent.

Consider the sequence in Figure 9.5; now compare Figure 9.6 with the sequence in Figure 9.5. It should be expected that the responses to Q2 will show significant variation between Figures 9.5 and 9.6. By using statements that reflect one side of an argument, in this case for and against the building of a new airport, respondents are led to Q2 along different paths. Most people like to appear to be consistent. If they agree with the statements in Q1, it is then very difficult not to answer 'yes' at Q2 in the first example or 'no' in the second example.

To be even-handed, the preliminary question should contain statements that relate to both or all sides of an argument. The researcher may want to put questions to respondents about the issues before asking the key ques-tion, to help them to give a considered answer to that question. However, the preliminary questions must fairly represent all the issues if they are not to bias the response to the key question.

FIGURE 9.5   The consistency effect (first sequence)

Q1. Please indicate whether you agree or disagree with each of the following statements, and how strongly, by ticking one box for each statement.

	Agree strongly	Agree	Neither agree nor disagree	Disagree	Disagree strongly
Delays at airports in this country are becoming unacceptable.	❑	❑	❑	❑	❑
There is insufficient capacity at this country's airports.	❑	❑	❑	❑	❑
Airports in this country are dangerously overcrowded.	❑	❑	❑	❑	❑
There is a shortage of jobs in this region.	❑	❑	❑	❑	❑

Q2. Do you support the government's proposal to build a new airport in this region?

YES ❑

NO ❑

DON'T KNOW ❑

FIGURE 9.6   The consistency effect (second sequence)

Q1. Please indicate whether you agree or disagree with each of the following statements, and how strongly, by ticking one box for each statement.

	Agree strongly	Agree	Neither agree nor disagree	Disagree	Disagree strongly
The countryside round here is disappearing too quickly for my liking.	❑	❑	❑	❑	❑
There is too much building on green-field sites.	❑	❑	❑	❑	❑
I would not want to see this country's plant and animal life killed off.	❑	❑	❑	❑	❑
Noise pollution is a major nuisance round here.	❑	❑	❑	❑	❑

Q2. Do you support the government's proposal to build a new airport in this region?

YES ❑

NO ❑

DON'T KNOW ❑

Standardizing questions

Where a question has been asked in a previous study it is usually to the advantage of the researcher to ensure that, unless there is a good reason otherwise, the same question should be used and the same pre-codes. Doing this allows the researcher to build up a body of knowledge about how this question is answered, and so spot any response pattern that deviates from it. It also means that results from different studies can be compared more easily.

Many major manufacturers and some research companies have standard ways of asking particular questions that allow them to build up this body of knowledge. The value of standardized questions becomes clear when we realize that even small changes in the wording of a question can change responses (Converse and Presser, 1986). For example, changing 'forbid' to 'not allow' has been shown to significantly change response patterns. Unfortunately, because language is subtle, there are no general rules about when a wording change will change responses, so the questionnaire writer must be cautious about making changes if comparison with other surveys is a priority. If there is doubt, alternative wordings should be tested before being used.

Tracking studies

Consistency of question wording is important in ongoing or tracking studies to ensure that changes in data over time are not due to wording changes.

To ensure data consistency, it is also important to maintain the order in which the questions are asked, so that any order bias that exists is itself consistent. Keeping the question order means that adding new questions can cause problems, and the positioning of them must be considered very carefully. If possible, new questions should be added to the end of the questionnaire so as not to affect responses to any of the earlier questions. For the sake of the interview flow, though, this is not always possible.

For example, in an ongoing customer satisfaction survey, respondents were asked to give a rating of their overall satisfaction with the service received on their most recent visit to the client company. This has been followed with questions rating various staff and service attributes, including one on efficiency. After a while, a competitor introduces a guarantee that all transactions will be completed within 10 minutes or customers get their money back. To measure the impact of this, the client now asks that, on the next wave of the survey, a new question is inserted between the overall satisfaction question and the service attribute ratings, on how quickly the customers perceive their transaction to have been handled and how satisfied they were with that. The introduction of these questions at this point could influence the way in which respondents rate the individual service attributes, in particular the one relating to efficiency, as the speed of transaction has been raised higher in their consciousness than in previous waves of the study. Researchers must alert the client to the potential impact of such a change in the questionnaire on the comparability of the data with previous waves, and endeavour to find an alternative solution, such as a less sensitive position.

If no alternative solution can be found and the question changes are to be included for the foreseeable future, then it may be worth considering having a split run for one wave. For this, the sample is split randomly into two. One half is asked the existing questionnaire, the other the new questionnaire with the changes incorporated. Differences in results on the affected questions between the two halves of the sample can then be attributed to the changed questionnaire. An assessment of the impact of the changes can thus be made.

Omnibus studies

An omnibus survey is a particular type of study on which clients buy space for their own questions. The questionnaire can therefore cover a number of different subject areas for a number of different clients. The cost of sampling and contacting these respondents is effectively shared between all of the clients, making this a cost-effective way of asking a limited number of questions of a large sample or one that is expensive to sample.

Several different topics are asked about, and the question writer will not know what has been previously covered. The first question should therefore include a bridging phrase or sentence to indicate that a change of subject is about to occur.

Omnibus surveys are normally charged by the number of questions; whether they are pre-coded or open-ended; whether they use prompts or not; and the proportion of the sample of which they are asked. To keep down the cost, question writers must decide what the most essential questions are that they need to cover, in order to limit the number.

The order of the questions may also be affected by the desire to keep down the cost. For example, we may be interested in asking some questions of people who have visited or considered visiting a particular resort. Normally we might ask:

Q1. SHOW CARD.
Which of the resorts on this card have you ever visited?

Q2. SHOW CARD.
And which others have you ever considered visiting?

Both questions would be asked of all respondents. However, if the number who have visited or have considered visiting is a minority, the cost can be reduced by reversing the questions:

Q1. SHOW CARD.
Which of the following resorts have you ever considered visiting, regardless of whether you have actually visited them?

Q2. SHOW CARD.
And which have you actually visited?

The first question is still asked of all respondents, but the second one is only asked of people who say that they have considered the resort in which we are interested. We can still classify all respondents into the three categories – visited, considered but not visited, and not considered – but, because the second question is only asked of a minority of the sample, we have saved money.

Laying out the questionnaire

10

Introduction

The way in which the questionnaire is laid out is very important to its success as an instrument of accurate data capture. If the layout is not clear to any of the various users, the wrong responses may be recorded or the wrong questions asked.

There are two types of user: the respondents in the case of self-completion questionnaires, and interviewers. The two user groups have different needs and requirements of a questionnaire. The two main media distinctions of paper and electronic questionnaires also present different issues to the questionnaire writer. Non-electronic questionnaire formats also have a third user group – the data entry team. They must also be considered when laying out the questionnaire in order to minimize data entry errors.

This chapter looks at the issues of laying out for interviewer-administered questionnaires and for paper self-completion questionnaires. Online questionnaires, which face a number of different issues and which have some very different solutions, are considered in the next chapter.

Interviewer-administered paper questionnaires

If a paper questionnaire is being used, the primary concern with regard to layout is that the interviewer can follow the questionnaire sequence easily, asking the correct questions for each respondent and accurately recording the answers. This is the case for both face-to-face and telephone interviews. If the interviewer has difficulty following the questionnaire or finding the correct question to ask, the flow of the interview can be lost, together with the interest and attention of the respondent. The wrong questions may be asked, which may be entirely inappropriate for the respondent and so lose the respondent's confidence that the survey is worth the time taken to complete it. And, of course, relevant data will be lost.

Most research companies adopt a set of conventions and standardized templates for questionnaire layout that are designed to help the interviewer.

Font size and formats

It may be tempting to use a small font size to fit more questions on to each page. This is particularly the case with face-to-face interviews that are relatively long. It may be thought that response rates will be harmed if the potential respondent can see that the questionnaire is the size of a small book. In practice, this is not usually the case, and a crowded layout may just lead to interviewer error.

A questionnaire in a small-sized font will be difficult for interviewers to read. They are more likely to make mistakes both in determining which questions they are supposed to ask and in recording the responses accurately. The quality of the data therefore suffers. They are also more likely to lose respondents during the course of the interview if they make mistakes and ask inappropriate questions, or if there are long pauses between questions while the next question is found. In any case, the respondent should be told the likely length of the interview as accurately as possible at the outset, so the physical size of the questionnaire should not affect the respondent's decision to cooperate.

It is usual to adopt a general font size of 10, 11 or 12 point, although larger font sizes can be used for key instructions. Bold and italic formats can also be used to draw attention to instructions and key points, or to emphasize particular words in a question where that is necessary. It is important that formatting is used consistently (eg instructions to interviewers are always in bold and underlined; anything to be read aloud is in lower case) so that interviewers can distinguish clearly between instructions, directions, etc and what is to be read out.

A question should never be allowed to go over two pages, so causing interviewers to turn the page to see all of the possible responses. This is likely to lead to errors as the interviewers turn the pages backwards and forwards trying to match the respondents' answers to the given pre-codes.

Upper and lower case

It is common to use upper and lower case to distinguish between questions that need to be read out and instructions for the interviewer that should not be. Most companies adopt the convention of upper case for instructions and lower case for items in the questionnaire that should be read out. This helps interviewers to distinguish quickly between instructions and questions and to see to whom they are meant to put a question and to whom they are not. Some agencies also make all instructions bold to help the interviewer to distinguish them. Others underline instructions for additional emphasis, or use selective underlining for important instructions.

This upper and lower case convention is often extended to the responses to pre-coded questions, which are given in upper case if they not to be read out and lower case if they are meant to be. Other agencies use lower case for all pre-coded responses. The former approach may distinguish better between what is and is not meant to be read out, so helping to avoid unintended prompting, while the latter may be easier and therefore faster for the interviewer to read and to code, so helping to maintain the flow of the interview.

Pre-coded responses

With pre-coded questions the responses are listed on the questionnaire. The order in which they are given can help (or hinder) the interviewer in finding the correct response code quickly. Usually, lists of brand names or simple categories would be given in alphabetical order. However, sometimes it is preferable to group them by categories or sub-categories, if that makes it quicker for the interviewer to find them. Note in Figure 10.1 the inclusion of an 'Other answer' code, together with an instruction that the interviewer should write in what that 'other' is. It is rare that the questionnaire writer can assume that all possible responses have been thought of and included in the pre-coded list. It is therefore generally prudent to allow for other answers to be given and recorded. Space should be left for the answer to be written in.

FIGURE 10.1   Inclusion of an 'Other answer' code

Q12. What was the main method of transport you used to get here today?

BICYCLE	1
BUS	2
CAR	3
MOTORCYCLE	4
TRAIN	5
WALKED	6
OTHER ANSWER (WRITE IN)	7

When there are a significant number of other answers, the researcher should look to see what they are. It may be that an important response has been overlooked or that there is an ambiguity in the response codes. A respondent to the question in Figure 10.1 may have travelled by tram. That this was not included in the pre-codes may have been an oversight because the researcher was unaware that the tram was an option, or it may have been that the researcher intended to include trams with buses, but failed to make this clear on the response list. If the missing response has been written in, the researcher has the option to create a new code for tram or to recode those who said tram into the bus category.

Single and multiple responses

Frequently it is clear from the question whether the anticipated response is a single answer or whether each respondent could give more than one. In the question about how the respondent travelled (Figure 10.1), the use of the term 'main method of transport' indicated to both respondent and interviewer that only one answer was expected.

Had the question been asked as in Figure 10.2, more than one answer would have been possible. An instruction to accept multiple responses has been included to ensure that the interviewers recognize that this is permissible. Wherever there is any possibility of ambiguity as to whether only one response or more than one is permissible, an instruction to the interviewer should be used to make it clear what is expected.

FIGURE 10.2　Possibility of multiple responses

Q12. Which method or methods of transport did you use to get here today?
RECORD ALL THAT APPLY.

BICYCLE	1
BUS	2
CAR	3
MOTORCYCLE	4
TRAIN	5
TRAM	6
WALKED	7
OTHER ANSWER (WRITE IN)	8

Common pre-code lists

Successive questions frequently use the same list of pre-codes. When that occurs a single set of responses can be used with the codes for each question next to each other, as in Figure 10.3. This arrangement saves space on the questionnaire, but also allows the interviewer to see what was coded for the first question and to ensure that the same answer is not coded for the second one. Clear instructions and headings are needed so that the interviewer can easily see to which question each column of code applies. Note the inclusion of a 'No others' response category for the second question.

FIGURE 10.3 Common pre-code list

Q12. What was the main method of transport you used to get here today?
SINGLE CODE ONLY.

Q13. And what other methods of transport did you use, if any? MULTIPLE
CODES ALLOWED.

	Q12 MAIN METHOD	Q13 OTHER METHODS
BICYCLE	1	1
BUS	2	2
CAR	3	3
MOTORCYCLE	4	4
TRAIN	5	5
TRAM	6	6
WALKED	7	7
OTHER ANSWER (WRITE IN)	8	8
NO OTHERS	–	9

'Don't know' responses

The example of the method of transport used does not include a 'Don't know' category in the list of possible responses. In this instance that is justified because respondents are being interviewed shortly after arriving at the place of interview and it is reasonable to assume that they will remember how they travelled there.

However, had the question been about which brands of grocery products they had bought most recently, a 'Don't know/Can't remember' category should have been included. It is not reasonable to assume that everybody will remember an event that may have taken place some time ago, particularly if it is an event that they see as being of little importance. (There is a fuller discussion of this in Chapter 4.)

'Not answered' codes

Some researchers argue that every question should include a 'Not answered' pre-code, so that, should it not be answered for any reason, there is a record that it has been asked. The argument against this is that having such a code could encourage interviewers to accept a refusal to reply too easily.

Occasionally respondents will refuse to answer or are unable to answer a question. If this occurs it is most likely to be because the question is sensitive in some way or because the response options are inadequate for the answer they wish to give. An example of the latter might be that the question asks for a single response but the answer given is a genuine multiple response. If the question asks which brand was most recently bought, but two different brands were bought at the same time, the interviewer or respondent may consider a multiple response as being contrary to instructions, and leave the question unanswered or coded 'Don't know'.

Where questions go unanswered, that is generally a shortcoming on the part of the questionnaire writer. Sensitive questions should be recognized as such and a 'Refused' category included on the list of pre-codes.

Show cards

Show cards are commonly used to prompt respondents with lists of possible responses. These can be lists of brands, time periods, behaviour, activities or attitude scales. It is important that interviewers show the correct card at the correct time. The most common practice is for cards to be identified by letters (Card A, Card B, etc) and for the instruction to show a particular card to appear at the appropriate question.

Sometimes the questionnaire writer wants to ensure that the card is removed from the respondent's sight before subsequent questions are asked. This may occur when the card contains the description of a new product concept or an advertising idea and the researcher wants to establish which parts of it have stuck in the respondent's mind. If this is the case, an instruction to remove the card from sight should be included.

Read-outs

Where an interviewer is to read out a number of response options, this should be clearly indicated as an instruction at the appropriate place.

Reading out is frequently used where respondents are asked to react to a list of attributes by associating them with brands, or to a list of attitude dimensions to which they indicate strength of agreement. The questionnaire writer should instruct interviewers as to whether or not the question should be repeated between each attribute or statement being read out. The initial question might be: 'Which of these brands do you think is ...? READ OUT.' It may be unclear to interviewers whether they should read out that question at the front of each phrase, or whether it is only necessary to read it out once. If the questionnaire writer intends that it should be read out before each phrase, then this should be made clear.

Grids

Where a large grid is used to record responses, visual aids should be included to help the interviewer or respondent to record the responses correctly. A commonly used format is to have a number of brands across the top of the grid, which appear on a card shown to the respondent, and a list of attributes down the side of the grid that the interviewers read out. It can be difficult for interviewers to read across a large grid, and they may miscode an answer on to the wrong line, particularly when standing on a doorstep or in a shopping centre. Sight lines going across the page and shading of alternate lines are simple but effective ways of helping interviewers to avoid this type of error.

Routeing

Clarity of routeing is one of the key aspects of an interviewer-administered paper questionnaire. If interviewers get lost in deciding which questions they should or should not be asking, the credibility of the survey is damaged in the eyes of the respondent and it is almost certain that questions will not be asked that should have been, so data will be lost.

Where routeing is dependent on the responses given to a question, the number of the subsequent question to be asked should be indicated alongside. In Figure 10.4, respondents who answered 'car' at Q12 are routed to Q13, whereas all others are routed to Q14. The heading at Q13 confirms to interviewers that this is the correct question to be asked of people who travelled mainly by car, and the heading at Q14 confirms that everybody should be asked this question.

FIGURE 10.4 Routeing in a questionnaire

Q12. What was the main method of transport you used to get here today?

BICYCLE	1	
BUS	2	Q14
CAR	3	Q13
MOTORCYCLE	4	
TRAIN	5	
WALKED	6	
OTHER ANSWER (WRITE IN)	7	
_____		Q14

Q13. ALL WHO TRAVELLED MAINLY BY CAR.
Were you the driver of the car or a passenger?

DRIVER	1	
PASSENGER	2	Q14

Q14. ASK ALL.
Will you mainly use the same method of transport for your return journey?

YES – USE SAME METHOD	1	
NO – WILL USE DIFFERENT METHOD	2	
DON'T KNOW/NOT DECIDED	3	Q15

Occasionally routeing can become very complex with respondents coming to a question from a variety of routes or with routes that depend upon the responses to more than one question. In these circumstances the question-naire writer should consider including the same question more than once in the questionnaire if doing so makes it less likely that routeing errors will be made.

Open-ended questions

Open-ended questions should be laid out with sufficient space for full re-sponses to be written in. Interviewers will often stop probing once they have filled the space available to record the answer. More space can mean fuller responses.

Responses to open-ended questions will be coded into a number of cate-gories depending on what answers are given and what answers are being looked for. The practices for recording these codes for data entry vary. Some companies leave a blank space for the coder to write in the appropriate code for the data enterer to use. Others print the codes on the questionnaire and the coder then circles the appropriate code in the same way as the inter-viewer records responses.

Thanking and classification questions

Interviewers rarely need reminding to thank respondents for their time and cooperation, especially if they have built up a rapport with them. However, it is good practice to include a line on the questionnaire thanking respond-ents for their time. It demonstrates that the questionnaire writer is also grateful to respondents for their help.

Some research companies record all classification details on the front page of the questionnaire even though they may not be established until the end of the interview. This is to facilitate the checking of quota controls and demographic details when the questionnaire is returned to the office. If this is the case, it is prudent to include a reminder at the end of the questionnaire for the interviewer to return to the front page and complete the classification questions. Again, few interviewers will need reminding, but it is an indica-tion of the questionnaire writer's concern to help them if it is included.

Administrative information

Each study will require an identification code if you are carrying out, or are likely to carry out, more than one similar study. Each questionnaire will require a unique identifier or serial number so as to be able to distinguish between respondents. Interviewer-administered questionnaires should also include an interviewer identification code. Interviews can then be analysed by interviewer to determine any between-interviewer effects, or to identify interviewers who may have made errors in their interviews. If there is more than one version of the questionnaire, the different versions will also usually need to be identified for analysis purposes.

Data entry

The format and layout for data entry will depend on the way in which the data is to be entered and the program that will be used to analyse them. The examples in this book generally use the column format. This has one or more columns allocated to each question, depending on the number of response codes required. Each column has 12 positions (1 to 9, 0, X, V), one of which is allocated to each response code. This is the format used by traditional analysis programs. More recent programs use different formats.

If data is to be scanned in, using optical mark reading, there will be specific instructions on the layout, depending on the type of scanning equipment used. This usually involves having fixed points on each page from which the position of the marks made by the interviewer or respondent is measured. In Figures 10.5 and 10.6 the fixed marks are the diamonds in the four corners of the page. Note that the job identification and page numbers must also be included on each page to identify the scanned data correctly.

Self-completion paper questionnaire

Much of the success of a paper-based self-completion survey depends on the appearance of the questionnaire and the ease with which respondents can use it. An unattractive questionnaire that is difficult to follow will reduce the response rate, and suggests to the respondents that you don't really care about the project, so why should they?

Making it attractive

There are many ideas about how to make a questionnaire attractive to potential respondents. However, it is almost certainly true that time, effort and money spent on improving the appearance are rarely wasted.

Printing should be of good quality and it is preferable for the paper to be a slightly heavier weight than for an interviewer-administered questionnaire. The paper should always be of sufficient quality that the printing on one side cannot be seen from the other side through the paper. Using different colours in the printing can increase the attractiveness if used sparingly. Colour can be used to distinguish instructions from questions, or to provide borders to questions. Coloured paper, though, should be used with care.

FIGURE 10.5   Questionnaire for scanning (1)

J.012345

Q11. You said that you had switched energy company recently. Which energy supply did you switch to Powerplus?

| Both gas and electricity | ☐ | Gas only | ☐ | Electricity only | ☐ |

Q12. Why have you decided to switch to Powerplus?

Tick one main reason in the first column and any other reasons in the second.

	Main	Other	
To have both gas and electricity supplied by one company	☐	☐	
They said they could offer lower prices	☐	☐	**Q13.** If Powerplus said they could offer lower prices, what were the approximate savings per year you expected?
No standing charge	☐	☐	
Moved house	☐	☐	
They offered me internet account management	☐	☐	Up to £20 per year ☐
			£21 to £40 per year ☐
I was unhappy with the customer service at the previous company	☐	☐	£41 to £60 per year ☐
			£61 to £80 per year ☐
I did not receive bills in a timely manner before	☐	☐	£81 to £100 per year ☐
I was unhappy with the accuracy of my bills	☐	☐	More than £100 per year ☐
Bills were not easy to understand before	☐	☐	Not sure ☐
Too many estimated meter readings	☐	☐	
Inaccurate estimated meter readings	☐	☐	
They offered me green energy	☐	☐	
Other (tick box and write in space below)	☐	☐	

Q14. Which supplier were you with before?

Powergen	☐
British Gas	☐
EDF Energy	☐
Npower	☐
TXU Energi	☐
Scottish Power	☐
Other	☐

FIGURE 10.6 Questionnaire for scanning (2)

J.012345

(OFFICE USE ONLY)

SERIAL NO

Dear Research Club Member

Thank you for taking the time to complete this questionnaire. Please answer all the questions by putting a cross ☒ in the appropriate box or by writing in the boxes provided.

Q1. Are you male or female?

PLEASE GIVE ONE ANSWER ONLY

Male . . . .☐

Female . . . .☐

Q2. Into which of the following groups does your age fall?

PLEASE GIVE ONE ANSWER ONLY

18–25 . . . .☐

26–29 . . . .☐

30–34 . . . .☐

35–39 . . . .☐

40–44 . . . .☐

45–49 . . . .☐

50–54 . . . .☐

55–59 . . . .☐

60–65 . . . .☐

Over 65 . . . .☐

Q3. How many times a week do you brush your teeth, if at all?

PLEASE WRITE IN BOXES – USE LEADING ZERO IF NECESSARY

Q4. What is your regular brand of toothpaste, the one you use more than any other brand nowadays?

PLEASE WRITE IN BOXES – USE 3-DIGIT CODE FROM OVERLEAF

Q5. Would you be willing to take part in surveys where we send you a tube of toothpaste to try?

PLEASE GIVE ONE ANSWER ONLY

Yes . . . .☐

No . . . .☐

Q6. If you are not the Research Club member to whom this questionnaire was addressed, please write in your name here. Otherwise leave this blank.

| First Name | | | | | | | | | | | | | | | |
| Surname | | | | | | | | | | | | | | | |

THANK YOU FOR COMPLETING THIS QUESTIONNAIRE.

PLEASE NOW RETURN IT TO US USING THE REPLY-PAID ENVELOPE PROVIDED

01

Pale or pastel colours can be used, particularly if there are different versions of a questionnaire that have to be easily distinguishable. Darker colours and gloss-finish paper, either of which makes the print difficult to read, should always be avoided.

If the budget allows, the questionnaire may be presented in the form of a booklet. This looks more professional and is easier for respondents to follow. With a questionnaire printed on both sides of the paper and stapled in one corner it is easy for respondents to miss the reverse pages, and it is possible that some later pages will become detached or inadvertently torn off. The booklet format avoids both of these potential problems. It does, however, create its own problem of forcing the number of sides to be four or a multiple of four. When the questions fit neatly on to five pages, this means that the researcher has to decide whether to use a less optimal question layout, or to drop some questions, or to accept a significantly greater printing cost.

To help make the respondents feel that the survey is worthwhile, the study should have a title, clearly displayed on the front page of the questionnaire, together with the name of the organization conducting it. The address of the organization should also be included. Even if a return envelope is provided, it may get mislaid by respondents, so an address on the questionnaire gives them an opportunity to return it.

Use of space

Little is more daunting for potential respondents than to be confronted with pages crammed full of print that they have to struggle to find their way through. Lay the questions out sparingly.

Dividing the questions into sections with a clear heading to each section helps respondents understand the flow of the questionnaire and focuses their attention on the topic of each section. It also helps give them a small sense of achievement when a section is completed, particularly if the questionnaire is long. Vertical listing of responses should be used in preference to horizontal listing, as it is easier to follow and creates a more open appearance. However, it does require more space.

Figures 10.7 and 10.8 show the same questions with responses listed horizontally and vertically, respectively. The original questionnaire used the horizontal listing. The vertical listing uses more space on the page but is easier to see, and makes the page more attractive.

Never allow questions to go over two pages, or over two columns if the page is laid out in columns. If a response list continues on another page it may not be seen. Avoid, if possible, a short question being placed at the bottom of a page, preceded by a question with a large response grid. The short question is likely to be overlooked.

In Figure 10.8 the response codes are evenly spaced vertically. If, however, one of the response codes had been so long that it had had to go on two

FIGURE 10.7   Horizontal listing

Seen in print

Q8. Do you think the property will require any of the following repairs or improvements in the next five years?

Please tick all that apply.

Additional ☐   Improved ☐   Rewiring ☐   Damp- ☐   Roof ☐   Window ☐
security   heating   proofing   repairs   repairs

Q9. Do you intend to carry out any of the following repairs or improvements in the next five years?

Additional ☐   Improved ☐   Rewiring ☐   Damp- ☐   Roof ☐   Window ☐
security   heating   proofing   repairs   repairs

FIGURE 10.8   Vertical listing

Q8. Do you think the property will require any of the following repairs or improvements in the next five years?

Please tick below all that apply.

Q9. Do you intend to carry out any of the following repairs or improvements in the next five years?

	Q8	Q9
Additional security	☐	☐
Improved heating	☐	☐
Rewiring	☐	☐
Damp-proofing	☐	☐
Roof repairs	☐	☐
Window repairs	☐	☐

lines, this would have resulted in uneven spaces between the boxes; see Figure 10.9.

It has been shown (Christian and Dillman, 2004) that uneven spacing of the category responses can significantly bias the response to the category that is visually isolated. This effect is likely to be greater for attitudinal questions than for behavioural questions, or where there is an ordinal scale. However, for all questions it is good practice to avoid the possibility of

FIGURE 10.9　Question with uneven spacing between response boxes

Q8. Do you think that the property will require any of the following repairs or improvements in the next five years?

Replacement of central heating including boiler ☐

Electrical rewiring ☐

Brickwork repointing ☐

Renewal of roof ☐

New window frames ☐

Additional security ☐

None of these ☐

this bias by ensuring that the response boxes are equally spaced, as in Figure 10.10.

Open-ended questions

Open-ended questions can be a deterrent to respondents, depending on their interest in the subject matter. If the level of interest is low then open-ended questions tend to be at best poorly completed and at worst can damage the response rate. Avoid, if possible, starting the interview with an open-ended question, as this can be a deterrent for many people even to begin. If possible, keep open-ended questions until the latter part of the interview. The questionnaire can be read through before being completed, so the respondents must be assumed to be prompted by any information that is on the questionnaire. There is thus no issue of having to ask an open-ended question before one that shows pre-codes that might prompt the open responses.

As with interviewer-administered questionnaires, the more space that can be left for respondents to write in, the fuller the response they are likely to give.

FIGURE 10.10 Question with response boxes evenly spaced

Q8. Do you think that the property will require any of the following repairs or
improvements in the next five years?

Replacement of central
heating including boiler ☐

Electrical rewiring ☐

Brickwork repointing ☐

Renewal of roof ☐

New window frames ☐

Additional security ☐

None of these ☐

Routeing instructions

Routeing should be kept to a minimum. Where they are necessary, routeing
instructions must be clear and unambiguous. If the questions can be ordered
such that any routeing only takes respondents either to the following question or to the next section, both of which are easy to find, errors of omission
are more likely to be avoided.

Often, some respondents are asked to skip one or more questions,
depending on their answer to a filtering or branching question. The routeing
instruction (which tells them where they should skip to) should be placed
after the response codes of the branching question. This makes it less likely
that respondents will read the routeing instruction before answering and
so it is less likely to affect how, or whether, they answer the branching
question. It has been shown (Christian and Dillman, 2004) that placing
the routeing instruction before the response codes (as in Version 1 in
Figure 10.11) can increase the number of non-responses to the question,
probably because respondents believe that if they meet the branching
criterion, they should skip directly to the later question without having
to answer this one. When the instruction follows the response codes
(Version 2), nearly all respondents complete the question before moving
on to the next one.

FIGURE 10.11 Location of routeing instruction

Version 1	Version 2

Q1. Have you visited the cinema at all in the last seven days?

Q1. Have you visited the cinema at all in the last seven days?

If you have not visited the cinema, skip to Q5.

Yes ☐

No ☐

Yes ☐

No ☐

If you have not visited the cinema, skip to Q5.

(Adapted from Christian and Dillman, 2004)

Covering letter

When the questionnaire is to be completed unsupervised or if it is a postal or mail survey, a covering letter and instructions will be required. The covering letter may be printed on the front page of the questionnaire if the layout allows sufficient space. There is then no danger of it becoming separated from the questionnaire. This also simplifies the production process if you wish to print a respondent identifier (eg customer type) on the questionnaire, as this can be printed on to the latter page, avoiding the need to match the letter to the questionnaire when mailing out.

Data entry

With a paper questionnaire, data entry will be required. Data entry instructions and codes should be kept as unobtrusive as possible. Where numeric codes are used to identify the responses, there is a danger of suggesting to respondents that there is a hierarchy of responses, which have been numbered from one onwards. For this reason circling of codes, in the way that is often used with interviewer-administered questionnaires, should be avoided. Ticking or checking boxes should always be preferred to avoid any such bias, and response codes should be kept as small as is possible while still compatible with accurate data entry.

Where data is read by optical scanning, data entry codes can often be completely removed or confined to the margins of the questionnaire. This has the benefit of removing some of the visual clutter from the page, so making it more attractive to the respondent. It also removes any concerns that the responses may be biased by the data entry number codes.

CAPI and CATI

Computer Aided Personal Interviews (CAPI), Computer Aided Telephone Interviews (CATI) and all forms of electronic questionnaires have a number of advantages over paper questionnaires that have already been touched on in Chapter 2. Electronic questionnaires from all of the major software suppliers can:

- cope with complex routeing;
- rotate or randomize the order in which questions are asked;
- rotate or randomize the order in which responses are displayed;
- adapt questions depending on answers to previous questions;
- adapt response lists depending on answers to previous questions.

The programs generally offer a range of standardized formats that can be customized to the research organization's conventions and layouts. This means that many of the issues of layout are predetermined and thus taken out of the hands of the questionnaire writer. However, it also means that interviewers become used to a common format, which should reduce interviewer error.

The issues that remain are not dissimilar to those encountered with paper questionnaires, namely ensuring that all of a question and its responses appear on one page or screen so that the interviewers can read questions and response codes easily, and distinguish between questions to be asked and instructions to themselves.

However, electronic questionnaires should not just be seen as paper questionnaires transferred to screen. They offer many opportunities for questionnaire writers to be more creative in the way in which they ask questions, to ask more complex questions that do not appear to be so, and with CAPI to use different types of prompt material.

'Don't know' and 'Not answered' codes

CAPI and CATI questionnaires will tend to have 'Don't know' or 'Not answered' codes for most questions. The interviewer may not be able to proceed to the following question without entering a response, and the respondent may refuse any answer other than a 'Don't know' or refusal. Where the answer is used for quota purposes or the responses are to be used for routeing, these codes may be omitted. Even then, the questionnaire writer should have a strategy for routeing the genuine 'Don't knows' from such questions.

The inclusion of a 'Not answered' category on all questions as a matter of course is a question of individual preference, but my view is that it is likely to lead to interviewers too readily accepting refusals and ambiguities in response, with a consequent increase in lost data.

Checking the questionnaire

The questionnaire layout should always be thoroughly checked from the standpoint of the interviewer, the coder, the data entry, the data processor and, if it is intended for self-completion, the respondent.

Checking for sense and usability will be repeated as part of the pilot survey (see Chapter 13). Before the pilot stage is reached, though, the questionnaire should be thoroughly proofread, and all interviewer and routeing instructions double checked. Routeing instructions in electronic questionnaires should be checked and checked again.

Online questionnaires

11

Introduction

This chapter looks specifically at web-based online questionnaires, which, as electronic self-completion questionnaires, present a number of issues but also many opportunities for creativity on the part of the questionnaire writer and involvement for respondents.

Electronic questionnaires provide the researcher with many new options, whether as CAPI or CATI or online. In CAPI and CATI questionnaires, developments have been largely aimed at helping interviewers to carry out a better interview, while retaining the structure and approach of the paper questionnaire. Some electronic self-completion techniques, such as the virtual shopping technique shown later, are equally appropriate to be used either in CAPI or online questionnaires. But it has been in web-based online interviewing that most effort has been directed in developing new techniques. These efforts have been made to:

- draw on the capabilities of the medium;
- allow the researcher to ask questions in ways that were not previously possible;
- provide as valid or better data than other techniques;
- involve and engage the respondents.

Many of the techniques described here are theoretically capable of being used as part of a self-completion section of a CAPI questionnaire. However, as most have been developed particularly for online interviewing, they are being considered here under that heading.

Replicating existing approaches

As with CAPI and CATI, electronic formatting of the questionnaire brings opportunities to replicate and improve on pen and paper approaches. Thus it is possible to:

- rotate or randomize the order in which questions are asked;
- rotate or randomize the order of response codes between respondents;
- sum numeric answers (eg to ensure that answers add to 100 per cent or to check total expenditure);
- insert responses to one question into the wording of another (eg 'Of the £105 that you spent on wine, how much was spent on *Australian* wines?' Here, both the total amount spent and one of the countries of origin of the wine bought were inserted from previous questions);
- adapt response lists according to answers to previous questions (eg the brands listed as possible responses may include only those previously given as being known to the respondent);
- ensure consistency between answers, and query apparent inconsistencies;
- require that a response be given before moving on to the next question;
- include more complex routeing between questions than would be possible with a paper questionnaire.

Questionnaire-writing programs often provide a range of standardized formats that can be customized to the research organization's conventions and layouts. However, as with CAPI and CATI online questionnaires should not just be seen as paper questionnaires transferred to screen. They offer many opportunities for questionnaire writers to be more creative in the way in which they ask questions, to ask more complex questions in completely new ways, and to use prompt material that would not otherwise be possible.

One of the most common errors that questionnaire writers make is to conceive questions as if they are to be asked by an interviewer rather than viewed on a screen. This tends to make them too long with the result that they are not read properly and lose the interest of the respondent. A good rule of thumb is that most people will decide what the question is in the first 10 or 12 words and may not read any further. Questionnaire writers should remember that they are collecting data on a website, not conducting the type of conversation that two people might have directly.

Single or multiple pages

A key layout issue for web-based surveys is whether to:

- ask one question per page or screen;
- group questions into logical sets that follow on on the same page, requiring respondents to scroll down; or
- have the complete questionnaire as a single scroll-down page.

This last format best replicates the paper questionnaire and has the advantage that respondents can see all of their answers to previous questions by scrolling up and down and be consistent in the way they respond. This is the approach recommended by Dillman (2000). However, this approach is generally only used for short, simple questionnaires. The reasons for this are that:

- If the complete questionnaire is contained in a single scroll-down page, the data is not sent to the administrator's server until and if it has been completed.
- If it is abandoned part-way through then no data is collected from that respondent, and it may not even be known whether or not the respondent started the survey.
- This approach also rules out routeing between questions and so fails to take advantage of one of the medium's key assets.
- It has been shown (Van Schaik and Ling, 2007) that respondents complete the questionnaire more quickly when there is a single question per page. They are thought to be less distracted without the text and answers of other questions on screen at the same time.

It has become general practice for most research companies to use a single page per question, although a question may include more than one part. This makes it possible to include routeing between questions and helps to make the screen appear clear and uncluttered.

An exception is where there are a series of attributes to be assessed, usually using scales, when a group of attributes may be shown on the same page. There is some evidence (Couper *et al*, 2001) that this gives greater consistency between the items than if each one is shown on a separate page.

Screen design

The layout or screen design is a crucial issue with all self-completion questionnaires, and particularly so online. The question must be clearly seen by the respondent and all of the responses offered should not only be clear, but should if possible be seen at the same time, with no emphasis given to one response over another.

Where a single question per screen is used, a need for the respondent to scroll down should be avoided. All response codes should be included on the same screen if at all possible. This may mean double or triple banking them (Figure 11.1). If it is necessary to scroll down, many respondents will not realize the need to do so. Even if they have to scroll down to progress to the next question, they will tend to use the responses that they saw initially. An exception might be for a factual question where respondents have to scroll down to find their make of car or country of residence, where they are aware that they have to keep scrolling to find the answer they need. Toepoel *et al*, (2009) tested different numbers of attributes or items on a screen, each to be answered using a five-point scale. They found that the level of item non-response increased significantly amongst some groups when respondents had to scroll down to see all items, and that the optimum number on a screen to minimize non-response was four.

FIGURE 11.1   Triple-banked screen

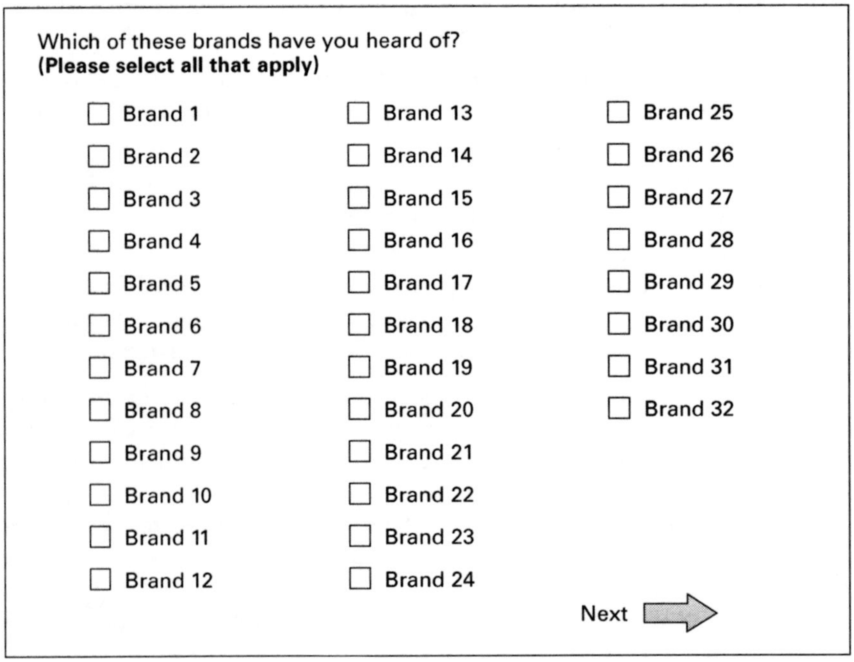

Which of these brands have you heard of?
(Please select all that apply)

☐ Brand 1	☐ Brand 13	☐ Brand 25
☐ Brand 2	☐ Brand 14	☐ Brand 26
☐ Brand 3	☐ Brand 15	☐ Brand 27
☐ Brand 4	☐ Brand 16	☐ Brand 28
☐ Brand 5	☐ Brand 17	☐ Brand 29
☐ Brand 6	☐ Brand 18	☐ Brand 30
☐ Brand 7	☐ Brand 19	☐ Brand 31
☐ Brand 8	☐ Brand 20	☐ Brand 32
☐ Brand 9	☐ Brand 21	
☐ Brand 10	☐ Brand 22	
☐ Brand 11	☐ Brand 23	
☐ Brand 12	☐ Brand 24	

Next ⇨

The need for horizontal scrolling should always be avoided. Many respondents will either not see that they should scroll across or not bother to do so. This will lead to bias against the responses that are not apparent on the initial screen.

Minimizing effort and frustration

Minimizing the number of mouse clicks a respondent has to make and the distance the cursor has to travel are also generally regarded as important as they minimize the effort required from respondents and maximize the probability of them continuing to the end.

If respondents fail to answer a question or complete it incorrectly, they may be directed back to the page on which the error occurred and asked to answer the question again. This is a source of frustration that may lead to their breaking off. Clear instructions about how to complete answers can help respondents get it right first time and avoid the annoyance of being returned to the page. Explicit instructions can be complemented by visual cues as to how the questionnaire writer wants something completed. In an experiment (Christian *et al*, 2007) it was shown that when asking for month and year of an event, providing a smaller box to enter the month and larger for the year rather than both the same size helped significantly more respondents to enter a four-digit year, as required, rather than a two-digit year, so reducing their frustration when asked to correct it.

Progress indicators

Respondents, not unreasonably, like to know how far through the questionnaire they are. One way of indicating their progress is the inclusion of question numbers. However, where there is routeing, and especially where there are question loops that are dependent on the respondents' answers, these can be misleading. For these reasons, question numbering is rarely used with online questionnaires. An alternative indicator is a progress bar that lets respondents see how far through the questionnaire they are.

Experiments have shown that telling respondents how far through the questionnaire they are affects how difficult they expect the task to be and whether or not they continue or break off (Conrad *et al*, 2005). If respondents believe early on in the questionnaire that they are making good progress, they are more likely to persevere than if they think progress is slow. The inference from this is that progress bars may be positive with shorter questionnaires, but discourage continuation with long questionnaires, and their inclusion must be considered carefully. An alternative is to provide occasional progress information, or to provide this information only later in the questionnaire once significant progress has been made. If the questionnaire contains routeing such that time taken to complete it varies greatly between respondents, then a meaningful progress bar is difficult to achieve.

Open-ended questions

For open-ended questions respondents are usually asked to type the answer into a box provided. The response box should not be too small, as the size of the box supplied will affect the amount of response given. It has also been shown (Couper *et al*, 2001) that altering the size of the box for a numeric answer can change the distribution of responses.

One of the uses for open-ended questions in online questionnaires that is not found in any other survey medium is for recording spontaneous awareness, particularly for brands. With interviewer-administered questionnaires this is usually recorded using a pre-coded list that is not seen by the respondent, while with postal questionnaires it is not a question that is possible to ask if any brand is mentioned anywhere in the questionnaire. In an online questionnaire, though, it can be asked as an open-ended question.

Frequently, when questioning spontaneous awareness, the researcher wishes to know which was the first brand that came to mind, known as 'top of mind awareness'. The online questionnaire writer has the choice of asking this as two questions: 'Which is the first brand of shaving cream that comes to mind?', 'Which other brands of shaving cream can you think of?' The alternative is to ask one question: 'Which brands of shaving cream can you think of?' and to record responses in a series of boxes that can be labelled 'First brand', 'Second brand' and so on (as in Figure 11.2). This is generally preferable as the respondent has only one screen to read and complete rather than two. It also does not highlight the first brand, which may affect later responses. It has been shown that the two approaches give comparable results (Cape *et al*, 2007) so there is no benefit in the longer approach.

FIGURE 11.2   Open ended response box; entry in box 1 can be taken as 'top of mind' awareness

Thinking about **jams and preserves** for spreading on bread and toast, what brands of jams and preserves can you think of?

Please type in as many brands as you can think of in the boxes below. Please type in brand names only. There is no need to include flavours.

1		7	
2		8	
3		9	
4		10	
5		11	
6		12	

Next ⇨

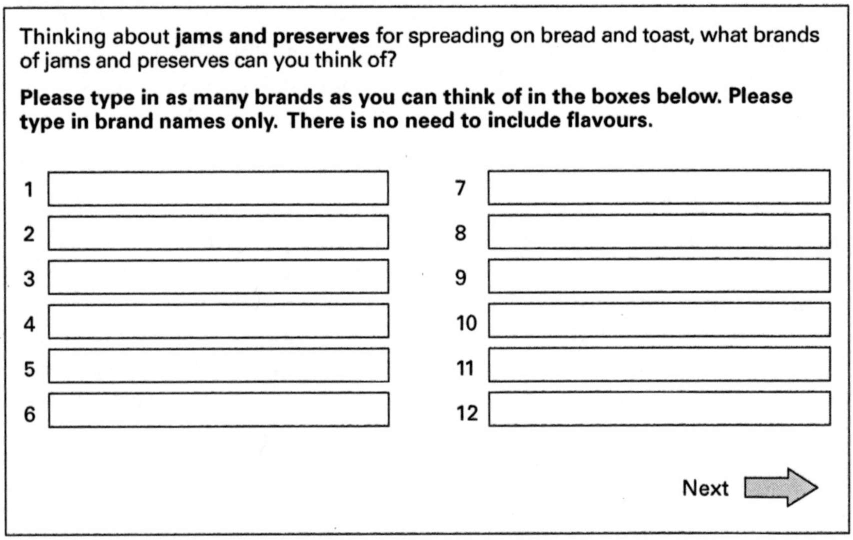

Scales and grids

Electronic questionnaires, either online web-based or self-completion CAPI, provide alternative means of presenting scales and recording responses to those available on paper questionnaires. A simple version is the single question with a scalar response presented as radio buttons (see Figure 11.3).

For more complex grids of statements and responses there are a number of options. One is to replicate the layout of paper questionnaires, with statements displayed down one side (or both sides if bi-polar) with the response options given as radio buttons across the page (see Figure 11.4). This is a familiar layout to most questionnaire writers.

FIGURE 11.3 Single question scalar response

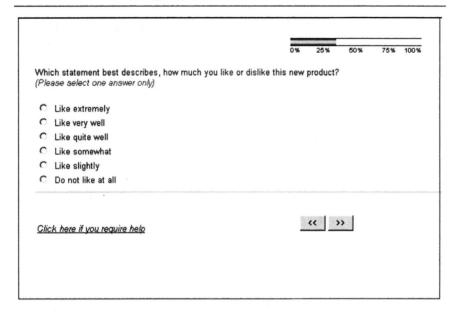

FIGURE 11.4 Scale grid using radio buttons

How much would you agree that the following brands taste good?					
(Select one answer per row)	Agree Strongly	Agree Slightly	Neither Agree Nor Disagree	Disagree Slightly	Disagree Strongly
Cadbury's Dairy Milk	○	○	○	○	○
Smarties	○	○	○	○	○
Toblerone	○	○	○	○	○

Online, the number of attitude dimensions or brand attributes shown per screen should be limited so that the task does not appear too daunting. Puleston and Sleep (2008) found that grid questions, either as scales or brand association grids, resulted in more drop outs from the survey than any other type of question. Confronted with a screen full of text and boxes, many respondents just give up.

One way of reducing the impact is to spread the attributes over more than one screen. Many research companies adopt conventions such as having no more than 10 or 12 statements to a screen to avoid scrolling down with this type of question. This then presents the researcher with issues of how to group the attributes and which to show on the same screen. It is usual to group them by topic, and possibly label them as such, but this needs to be considered alongside other requirements that may demand separating similar attributes.

For scalar questions, there are adaptations of paper questionnaire techniques available and some new techniques: slider scales, write-in boxes and drop-down boxes. The use of different types of slider scales (see Figure 11.5), visual analogue scales or graphic rating scales in electronic questionnaires has been discussed in Chapter 6, but we should note again here that it has been shown that while most respondents prefer a scale with defined points, such as radio buttons, because they believe that it is more difficult to give consistent answers with a slider scale, both slider scales and scales with defined responses give similar data distributions (Van Schaik and Ling, 2007).

FIGURE 11.5   Slider scale (courtesy of Kantar)

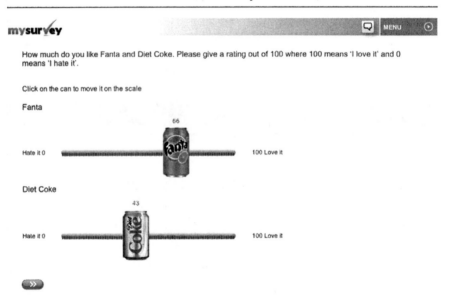

With write-in boxes, respondents are asked to write in a number, say from one to five, to represent their response on a scale where the end points have been defined for them. This is a technique often avoided with paper questionnaires where the likelihood of error in misreading many different styles of handwriting is a deterrent. However, with electronic questionnaires, it is straightforward and accurately recorded. There is more effort involved for the respondents than with radio buttons, which only require them to move a mouse and click on the button. The space saved means that more items can be included on the same page, and brands can be rated more easily alongside each other.

An option only available with electronic questionnaires is the drop-down box (see Figure 11.6). A drop-down box following the statement can contain the full scale. Respondents only have to click on their choice of response for it to be displayed and recorded. Again, a little more effort is required than with radio buttons. There might also be concerns that the direction in which the scale is displayed, with either the positive or negative end of the scale at the top of the drop-down box, will introduce a bias. This bias could be expected to be greater than that associated with the direction of the scale when using radio buttons, as respondents may not read all the way down the scale.

FIGURE 11.6 Scale using drop-down box

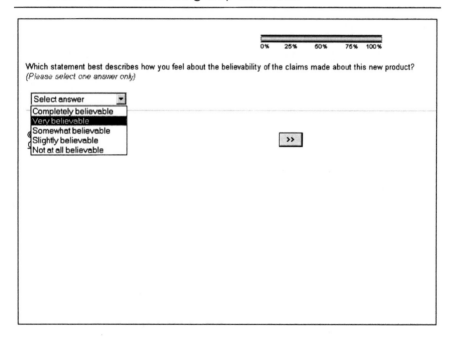

However, work carried out by Hogg and Masztal (2001) has demonstrated that this is not the case. Their study, which compared radio buttons with write-in boxes and drop-downs, showed that both write-in and drop-down boxes gave greater dispersion of responses across a five-point scale than did radio buttons. With radio buttons there was a greater likelihood for respondents to use one point of the scale repeatedly (a type of pattern responding known as 'flat-lining'). This suggests that both of the other two methods may result in respondents giving more consideration to each response. The more deliberate process of choosing a response option with these methods could mean that more consideration is given to what that response should be.

The results for the two versions of the drop-down, one with the positive end of the scale at the top of the box, the other with the negative end at the top, were almost identical, indicating that order is not a crucial issue, at least for five-point scales. However, it may become more so for longer scales, and as a precaution the order should be rotated between respondents to balance any potential bias. It is important when using drop-down boxes that the default option, which shows prior to it being answered, is not one of the responses but a neutral statement such as 'Select answer'.

There may be a concern that the additional time taken to complete the questionnaire could result in an increased rate of drop out. Hogg and Masztal (2001) found that although there was a small increase in the time taken, confirmed by Van Schaik and Ling (2007), there was no evidence of any increased drop out as a result.

An advantage of both the drop-down and the write-in box is that more responses can be accommodated on one page. However, the questionnaire designer must take care not to make the page look overly complicated or daunting (Figure 11.7).

FIGURE 11.7   Drop-down boxes: the temptation to put too many on one page

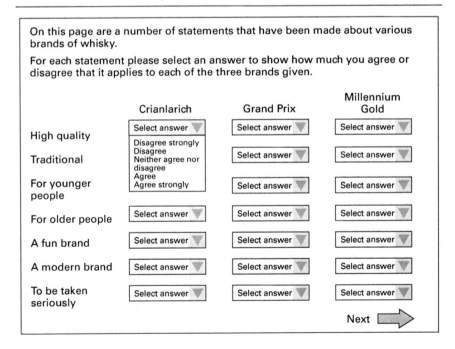

Dynamic grids are perhaps the most interesting of all recent developments in this area (Figure 11.8). This technique presents one statement or attribute at a time in a horizontally scrolling format, with the response scale static. The respondent has to consider and respond to a statement which then automatically scrolls on to the next one, clearing the response to the previous statement, eliminating any advantage to the respondent in flat-lining. While this technique can be used in many ways in the online questionnaire, its main use is to present attributes for scale rating in a quick and dynamic way.

FIGURE 11.8 Dynamic grid (courtesy of Kantar)

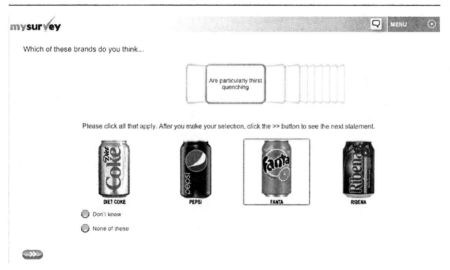

Puleston and Sleep (2008) tested slider scale, drag and drop (See Figure 11.9), horizontal dynamic grids, and vertically scrolling versions, against the standard grid presentation for a bank of attitude statements answered with a five-point scale. They found that the drag-and-drop and dynamic grid options all reduced the amount of pattern answering, or flat-lining, but slider scales showed no improvement, consistent with Van Schaik and Ling (2007) referred to above. They also found that respondents liked best the horizontally scrolling dynamic grid.

Avoiding grids

Dynamic grid and drag and drop techniques can be used for attitudinal and image questions, but behavioural questions also frequently involve having response grids on screen that do not encourage respondents to give full consideration to their answers. Asking for frequency of use of a series of brands can be presented as a grid with brands across the top and the responses vertically to the side. Or a dynamic grid can be used as shown in Figure 11.10, with each brand being considered individually. This is almost

FIGURE 11.9   Drag and drop used for brand attributes (courtesy of Kantar)

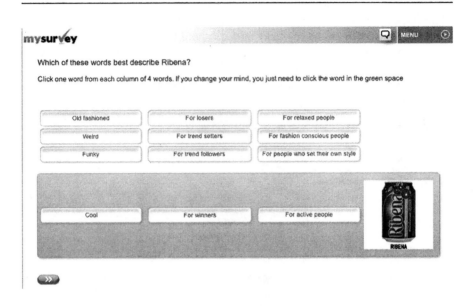

FIGURE 11.10   Dynamic grid used for behavioural question (courtesy of Kantar)

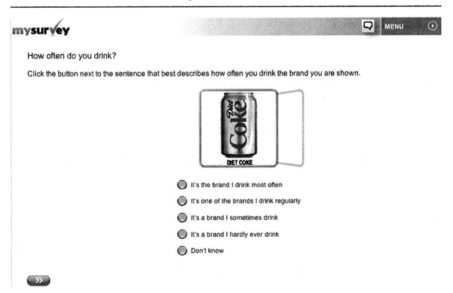

certain to give better quality data, removing the temptation to flat-line, even on a behavioural question.

'Don't know' and 'Not answered' codes

As discussed in Chapter 4, with any self-completion questionnaire there is the issue of whether or not the inclusion of a 'Don't know' code encourages 'Don't know' responses, which the researcher usually wants to keep to a minimum. Such a response option is therefore often not provided.

Similarly, with online questionnaires the issue arises as to whether the respondent should be allowed to continue to the next question if no answer is recorded at all. To allow this would be to allow respondents to simply skip questions that they did not want or felt unable to answer. For this reason, many web-based surveys do not permit the respondent to continue to the next question until an answer has been provided. The absence of a 'Don't know' code and a requirement to enter a response before being able to proceed thus forces the respondent to give an answer. Several companies have carried out their own investigations that show that very few respondents terminate an interview because of the lack of a 'Prefer not to answer' (or 'No opinion') or 'Don't know' code, nor does this significantly alter the distribution of responses. Against this it can be argued that there is an ethical issue that respondents should be allowed not to answer a question without having to terminate the interview or provide a random answer. There is also the question as to the value of an answer that a respondent has been forced to give unwillingly and that may simply be a random choice.

In a parallel test, Cape *et al* (2007) asked about brand ownership, using one sample with a 'Don't know' code provided and one without. For the version with a 'Don't know' code, 10 per cent selected that as their answer. In the version without that code, the 'Other answers' response was 9 percentage points higher. Without a 'Don't know' code these respondents were selecting 'Other answer' as the closest they could get. But if 'Other answer' had not been provided, where would they have gone? Similarly Albaum *et al* (2011) found that when a 'Prefer not to answer' code was offered, a significant proportion of respondents used it, so when it was not there, how would these people have answered and what would their answers have meant?

An alternative to having a 'Don't know' response, which is adopted by some companies, is to have a screen or a pop-up that appears if a respondent tries to continue without having answered a question. This screen points out that they have not answered the previous question and gives the opportunity to return and complete it. The respondent must actively click to say that they do not want to or cannot answer the question before being allowed to continue to the next one. This approach, although it requires more complex programming, provides the researcher with full information about respondents' abilities to answer questions and avoids them inventing answers just to proceed. Questions that demand a response to route the respondent to

FIGURE 11.11   Two presentations of 'Don't know' and 'No opinion' codes

Version 1	Version 2
☐ Far too much	☐ Far too much
☐ Too much	☐ Too much
☐ About the right amount	☐ About the right amount
☐ Too little	☐ Too little
☐ Far too little	☐ Far too little
☐ Don't know	☐ Don't know
☐ No opinion	☐ No opinion

the next question would normally treat a 'Not answered' as a 'Don't know' and route accordingly.

If 'Don't know' and 'No opinion' codes are to be included, the questionnaire writer must be aware that the positioning of them on the screen can affect the responses to other codes. If they are added to the end of a list of codes with no visual break between them, this can alter the way in which the respondent regards the list, by altering the perceived mid-point of the responses. This is particularly important if the response is in the form of a scale. In an experiment (Tourangeau *et al*, 2004) it was shown that when 'Don't know' and 'No opinion' codes were simply added to the end of a five-point scale presented vertically, a higher proportion of responses were given to the bottom two codes of the scale than when the 'Don't know' and 'No opinion' responses were separated from the scale responses by a dotted line (see Figure 11.11). Without the dotted line, the two codes at the bottom of the scale were visually closer to the middle of the response options. The questionnaire writer needs to make it visually clear that the 'Don't know' and 'No opinion' options are not part of the scale.

Enhancing the experience

Some of the advances offered by web-based questionnaires are the enhancements that can be made to the ways in which the questions are asked, material displayed and responses recorded. Such enhancements include:

- drag and drop;
- page turning;
- magnifying;
- highlighting;
- virtual shopping.

It has been shown that online questionnaires that utilize techniques such as these, that enhance the experience for respondents and engage them better, lead to fewer breakings off during the survey for reasons unrelated to speed of download, and a greater willingness to participate in future surveys (Reid *et al*, 2007). Thus such enhancements are to the benefit of both the respondent and the researcher.

Drag and drop

With drag and drop, items can be organized by the respondent into response boxes. This makes the technique suitable for a range of questions, including associating brands with image dimensions, grouping of similarly perceived attributes, and rating brands, products or statements on a scale.

Reid *et al* (2007) compared responses to a series of attitude statements asked as five-point scales shown as radio buttons with a drag and drop technique, where each statement on a 'card' was dragged by the respondent into one of the five response areas; see Figure 11.12. They found that the drag and drop technique resulted in fewer mid-point or neutral answers, mainly with an increase in negative answers, and less flat-lining. Using drag and drop for this type of question would therefore appear to improve both the respondents' experience, so maintaining their engagement better, and the quality of the data.

For an example of improving the respondent experience we shall look again at the question in Figure 5.1, where respondents were asked to rank order their three preferred yoghurt flavours and the three least liked from a list of 15. Translated directly on to the screen using radio buttons the question looks something like Figure 11.13.

The screen is a mass of radio buttons and does not look at all enticing. With drag and drop, however, the question can be asked similarly to Figure 11.14. The screen is now more attractive and the engagement of the respondent improved by making the task simpler. Card sorting as a data collection technique has long been used in face-to-face interviews, but drag and drop programs make them simple to execute. The Q sort technique described in Chapter 6 is one that transfers readily to online questionnaires, as are other specialist sorting techniques such as repertory grid sorting.

In Figure 11.15, drag and drop has been used to enable respondents to place brands on a scale. This enables the respondent to see the relative position of each brand in a simple way. Note that the brand image turns to a label once placed on the scale, so that they can be placed close together if required.

FIGURE 11.12   Drag and drop

online MR II services

When visiting the cinema, please let us know how often you would consider buying each of the following.
Please drag the images from the left to the appropriate tray on the right.

| Would always buy | Would sometimes buy | Would never buy |

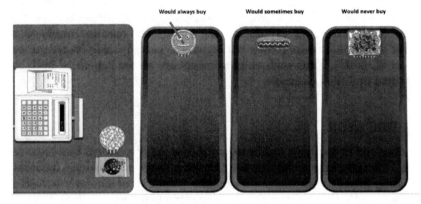

FIGURE 11.13   Ranking question translated from the paper questionnaire

Below are fifteen different flavours of yoghurt. Please indicate the three that you like best in order of preference and the three that you like least.

	Preferred	2nd preference	3rd preference	Three liked least
Apricot	O	O	O	O
Banana	O	O	O	O
Black cherry	O	O	O	O
Blackcurrant	O	O	O	O
Gooseberry	O	O	O	O
Grapefruit	O	O	O	O
Mandarin	O	O	O	O
Passion fruit	O	O	O	O
Peach	O	O	O	O
Pear	O	O	O	O
Pineapple	O	O	O	O
Raspberry	O	O	O	O
Rhubarb	O	O	O	O
Strawberry	O	O	O	O
Tangerine	O	O	O	O

FIGURE 11.14   Ranking question using drag and drop (courtesy of Kantar)

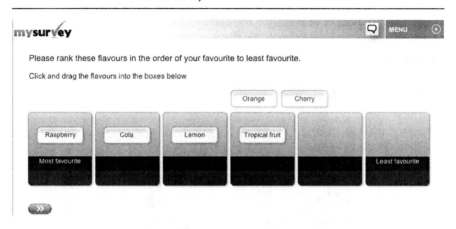

FIGURE 11.15   Combining drag and drop and scale question

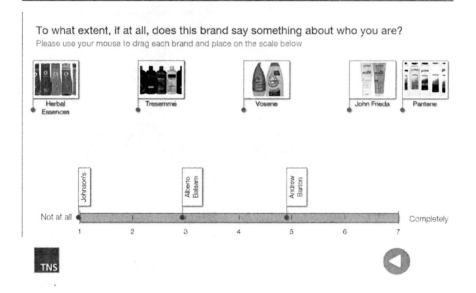

Page turning

Some of the techniques can be used to increase the sense of reality for the respondent, or at least to decrease the artificiality of the interview. One such technique is the page turner, which many leading agencies include in their tool kit. This enables 'pages' to be turned forward and back by 'grabbing' one of the corners with the cursor and folding it over, simulating page turning in a magazine or newspaper. Figure 11.16, from Ipsos MORI, shows a simulated magazine that the respondent has been asked to look through.

In the illustration the right-hand page is in the process of being turned as if the reader is progressing through the magazine. If the respondent wants to turn back to look again at a previous page, the technique works equally well. The purpose is to improve the verisimilitude of the experience to help respondents react more closely to the way that they would if it were a real magazine.

FIGURE 11.16   Page turner

Magnifier

When respondents look at magazines or press ads on screen the text is frequently too small to be easily readable. A common technique is to use a magnifier to help respondents; Figure 11.17 shows an example of this. Here the respondent has moved the magnifying glass over the particular piece of text of interest to be able to read it better. These types of techniques have come to be expected by respondents who see them being used elsewhere.

Highlighter

Some of the techniques allow us to ask questions in new ways that were previously either not possible or impractical.

Using highlighter pens to indicate text or visuals within an ad has always been possible in qualitative research, but the difficulty of both collecting and analysing this data from large numbers of respondents has prohibited

FIGURE 11.17   Example of magnifier in use

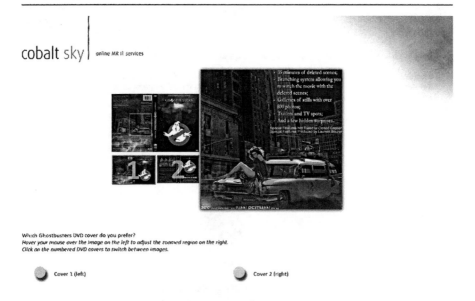

its use in quantitative research. On screen, though, respondents can be asked to highlight sections of text or graphics relatively easily. The number of times a section of text or a graphic is highlighted can then be counted. So it is now possible to use highlighting to count the frequency for each part of the text or graphic for any designated response, such as what particularly catches the respondents' eye, or delights them or annoys them, or whatever the questionnaire writer asks.

Figure 11.18 shows a page containing a press ad where respondents are being asked to highlight parts of it depending on whether they feel positive about it, negative or neutral. In this example clicking once turns the text green to indicate a positive response, and clicking twice turns it red to show negativity. This technique allows heat maps to be displayed, responding to the frequency with which each section has been selected for each purpose asked about.

Highlighting need not be restricted to questions about advertisements. It can also be used, for example, with maps to determine where respondents would or would not want to live, or where they went on holiday, or where they live and work. This is a technique that really is open to the creativity of the questionnaire writer.

Brand prompts

It is relatively straightforward with electronic questionnaires to incorporate logos or pack shots as stimuli for brand recognition or brand image questions. The use of these as prompts has already been discussed in Chapter 9.

FIGURE 11.18   Press ad for highlighting (courtesy of Kantar)

However, it is worth reiterating here that different visual prompts will produce different responses, because electronic questionnaires present the opportunity to use graphical and pictorial displays far more easily and readily than is possible with paper questionnaires.

Adding brand logos or pack shots can be a good way of obtaining greater respondent involvement. However, including such displays will often change the data that is collected. Brand awareness data may change because:

- Respondents are better able to distinguish between similar brands or brand variants.
- They do not recognize the pack from the picture used.
- It reminds them of another brand with a similar looking pack.

The larger the pack shot appears on the screen, the less likelihood there is for confusion. However, the larger the pack shots, the greater likelihood there is that the respondent will have to scroll to see them all. It is better to avoid scrolling with this type of question. The aim should be to have all brands visible to the respondent at the same time to allow them to discriminate properly between them (see Figure 11.19).

With image questions, data will also often change between questions asked using a verbal descriptor and those asked using logos or pack shots.

FIGURE 11.19 Pack shots on screen

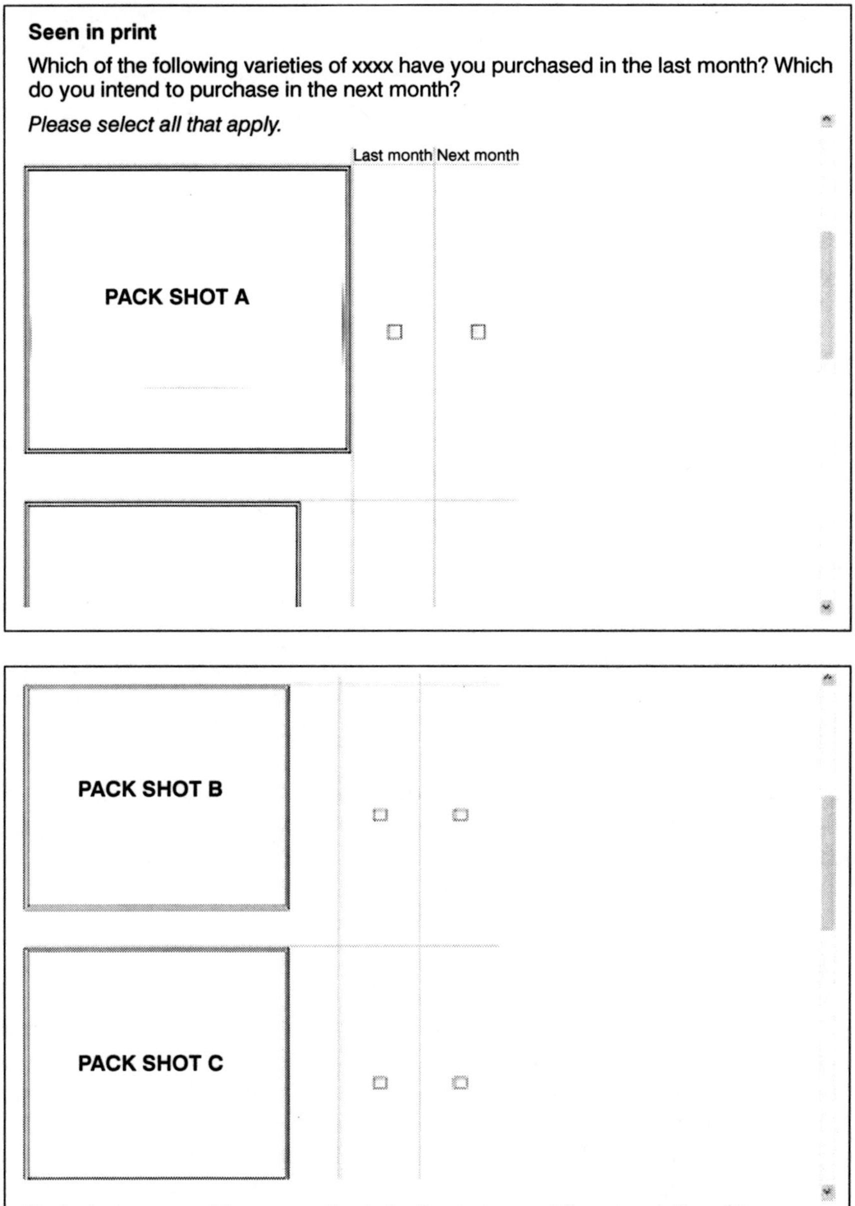

Seen in print

Which of the following varieties of xxxx have you purchased in the last month? Which do you intend to purchase in the next month?

Please select all that apply.

Last month | Next month

PACK SHOT A

☐ ☐

PACK SHOT B

☐ ☐

PACK SHOT C

☐ ☐

Pack shots are used to ensure discrimination between different varieties of the same brand. This means that the question scrolls down over several screens.

But the labels for the two response categories are only at the top and have to be remembered by the respondent.

This should not be surprising as much effort will have gone into the logo or pack design to ensure that it conveys messages and brand cues to the viewer, and these are prompting the respondent on these attributes. It can be hypothesized that for a grocery product, the brand image collected using only verbal prompts represents the image that exists in the respondents' minds in the absence of any prompts, that is at home, before going shopping, whereas the image obtained using pack shots is that which the respondent has when seeing it on the supermarket shelf.

In an experiment I carried out, in a brand image association question, 36 out of 85 brand-image association scores changed significantly when pack shots were used instead of brand names.

Colour cues

Another temptation with electronic questionnaires, particularly online, is to use colour to enhance the appearance of the page and make it more attractive to respondents.

Great care, though, must be taken with the use of colour. The highlighting of particular answer codes must always be avoided. Also different colours can have different subconscious associations, which may themselves vary depending on the context. Thus blue can suggest 'cold' and red 'warmth', but red coupled with green can mean 'stop' with green meaning 'go'.

That colour can affect how people respond to a question has been demonstrated by, for example, Tourangeau *et al* (2007). In experiments they showed that the use of colour in scales had a noticeable impact on responses in the absence of verbal or numerical cues, and hypothesized that, in this context, colour provides cues to respondents. Toepoel and Dillman (2010) found that positive responses were given more often when they were shaded green, but that this effect could be reduced by using fully labelled scales. The implication is clear: the use of colour must be treated with care.

Simulated shopping

One technique that combines a new way of collecting data with offering respondents a task that is interesting for them to complete is the simulated shopping technique. Originally developed for use with CAPI, this approach is now widely used online.

In this technique, supermarket shelves are simulated and packs displayed. This creates opportunities to simulate a presentation, as it would appear in a store, with different numbers of facings for different products, as an attempt to better reproduce the actual in-store choice situation. Respondents can be asked to simulate their choice process. Or they can be asked to find a particular product with the time taken to find it automatically recorded. Three-dimensional pack simulations can be shown and rotated by the respondent, while questions are asked about them.

Illustrated in Figures 11.20 to 11.26 is the 4^D Research Simulation from Advanced Simulations LLC of Atlanta, Georgia. This shows a series of screen shots from a program that allows respondents to simulate a shopping trip on the computer screen. The respondent can enter the store, approach the aisles, scan the shelves, pick up items, turn them to read the labels for nutritional or other information, and decide whether or not to purchase. The predominant colouring of the store can be changed to simulate each respondent's regular supermarket.

FIGURE 11.20   Entering simulated store

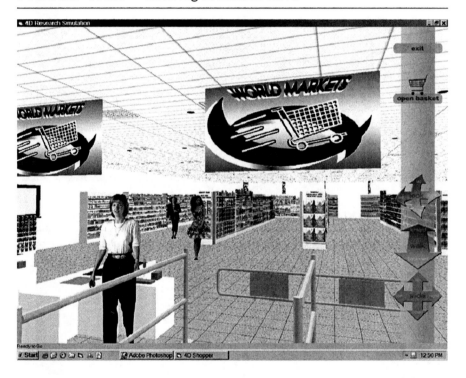

FIGURE 11.21 Approaching the aisles

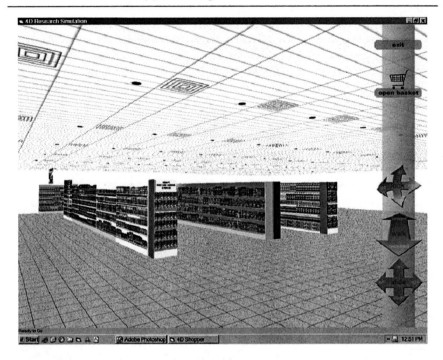

FIGURE 11.22 Entering the aisle

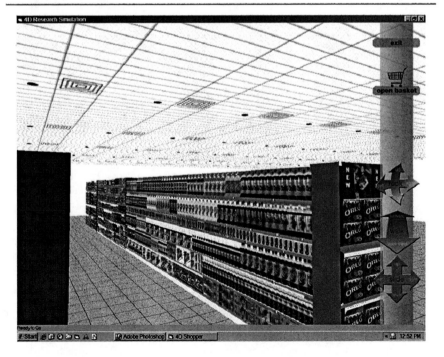

FIGURE 11.23 Picking up a product

FIGURE 11.24 Rotating product to read labels

FIGURE 11.25   Selecting and viewing a further product

FIGURE 11.26   Items in the trolley

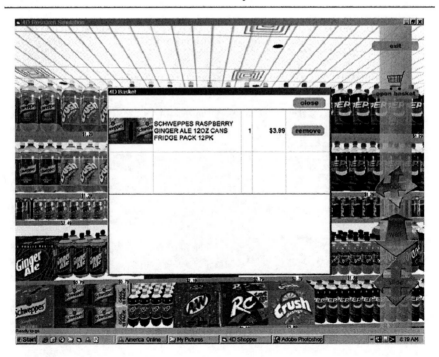

Electronic, particularly web-based online questionnaires provide the possibility of showing improved stimuli, of offering new ways of measuring consumer response, and making the process more interesting and involving for the respondent. The appropriateness of both the enhancement techniques and the way in which the questionnaire is presented should, though, be considered in relation to the subject and the target audience. A questionnaire linked to a website for teenage girls would be different from one intended for an older target group; something intended as entertainment would look different from a scientific investigation (Couper, 2000).

Keeping respondents on-side

With a self-completion questionnaire it is much easier for a respondent to stop answering and drop out of the survey than where there is an interviewer who will try to ensure that the interview is completed. It is therefore important to avoid frustrating respondents, as that is likely to increase the probability of their discontinuing or breaking off.

One such frustration is slow loading times between pages. This can occur because the questionnaire contains too many advanced features for the download speed available to the respondent's computer. This is particularly the case where the respondent is connected to the internet via a dial-up modem, or has a slow computer or uncommon configuration (Reid *et al*, 2007). Thus you need to be aware of the probable mix of respondents' connection types and hardware before deciding which features you include in the questionnaire.

Another consequence of different hardware and software configurations is that what respondents see on their screens may not match what the researcher sees when writing the questionnaire. The researcher or script writer is likely to have up-to-date equipment, probably more advanced than the majority of the respondents if they are individual consumers (business respondents are more likely to have similar equipment to the researcher). It is frustrating for these respondents if the formatting of the questionnaire they see is wrong, with text and response boxes out of line, or screens difficult to read. The researcher must again ensure that the questionnaire as written will appear intelligible to all respondents or it will be another cause of breaking off.

As well as some of the more interactive techniques described here, simply making the questionnaire more visually attractive can improve the experience for the respondents, reduce errors, retain the respondents through to the end of the questionnaire, and help make sure that they are happy to complete further questionnaires in the future. In Figure 11.27 what could have been presented as a mundane radio button question has been enhanced by putting some thought into what it looks like.

FIGURE 11.27   Enhanced visual appearance

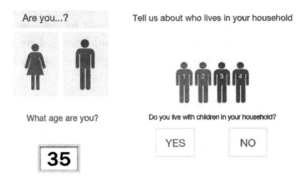

Questionnaires on mobile phones

Increasingly people access the internet via their mobile or cell phone. Indeed in many parts of the world mobile phones are the main, or sometimes only, form of internet access. That the initial contact might be on a mobile phone is something that we have to take into account when we design an online questionnaire.

Clearly the mobile phone imposes considerable limitations on what can be asked, the length of the interview and the use of many of the techniques previously discussed for online surveys. The size of the screen restricts what can be shown and the circumstances under which the survey is likely to be taken are likely to constrain the amount of time that the respondent is to be prepared to spend on it.

If it is intended, or expected, that the majority of respondents will take the survey on their phone then the rule must be to keep the questionnaire simple and short. Each question and its responses should be capable of being viewed without scrolling or with a minimum of scrolling. If scrolling has to be used it should be up and down and not from side to side. This rules out questions involving grids, for example. Drag and drop is excluded from the armoury of techniques because of the size of the screen.

Designing for mobile phones could also be important where the survey is to be carried out 'in the moment' of the experience. This could include situations where the objective is to:

- obtain reaction to an event such as airline check-in, where a phone number is known and sending the survey invitation can be triggered by the event;
- get responses to a TV programme where a sample has been primed to watch it and respond via their phones in real time (Johnson and Swinton, 2011)
- follow people's behaviour over time, such as having people reporting on what they drink as they drink it as an evening out unfolds.

Where online access panels are used to source the sample, then it will probably be a condition of membership of such a panel that the member has access to a PC or laptop. However, they may respond to an e-mail invitation from their mobile phone. An option in this case is to ask on what type of device they are taking the survey and ask them to not take it until they have access to it on a PC. However, this may lose the respondent who will never come back to complete this survey. Someone accessing e-mails on their tablet on the sofa may well not be prepared to go to another part of the house to log on to a PC (Johnson and Rolfe, 2011). Another option, therefore, is to offer a simplified version of the questionnaire that is suitable for mobile phones. This is technically more complex, more costly and may raise issues about comparability of data between that collected on mobile phones and that collected via PCs. However, it may be sufficient to inform the researcher that respondents with particular characteristics are under- (or over-) represented in the PC-based responses, and so increase their knowledge of the limitations of the sample.

Where the respondent does not have a smartphone we are limited to SMS text surveys, but as the smartphone becomes more ubiquitous then accessing questionnaires through internet links or applications becomes not only more important but also increasingly a viable route to conducting complete surveys. As more and more people around the world access the internet via their phone or tablet, so the PC is likely to become increasingly a minority tool for communication. This has the capability of changing the way in which we conduct online surveys and design the questionnaires. This is a rapidly changing area that could present research with 'its biggest opportunity and its biggest challenge' (Johnson and Rolfe, 2011) and make us rethink the amount and depth of information that we can obtain from surveys. Questionnaire writers contemplating a mobile phone-based questionnaire should take advice from technical specialists as to what is possible and what is advisable at the time, because the pace of change in this area is currently so fast (Figure 11.28).

FIGURE 11.28 The continuum of devices on which online questionnaires can be accessed

The range of devices and questionnaire delivery mechanisms

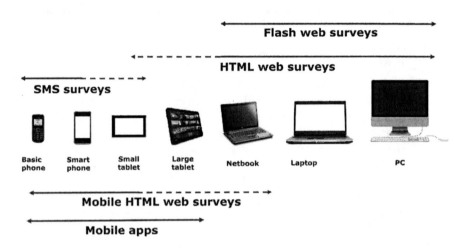

(Courtesy of Kantar)

Engaging the respondent online

12

Introduction

A problem that researchers frequently encounter is the quality of the data provided by the respondent. We have already seen that respondents consciously or subconsciously use a number of strategies to minimize the task that is asked of them. In Chapter 9 we saw that satisficing is one such technique and it is necessary for the questionnaire writer to develop approaches to minimize this. We also know that the amount of effort the respondent is prepared to make varies according to the circumstances of the interview: a spontaneous brand awareness question will elicit more brands if asked as part of an in-home interview than in the street.

These are effects which the questionnaire writer must recognize and deal with either by adopting an appropriate strategy or by recognizing the effect when interpreting the resulting data. However, there is a major effect that can seriously damage the quality of the data and which the questionnaire writer can often remedy by applying some care and thought to the questionnaire design – boredom, losing the attention and engagement of the respondents. Once that occurs little thought is given to the answers and extreme strategies such as flat-lining are adopted just to get the task of answering the questions done as quickly as possible. The data provided consequently becomes of increasingly dubious value.

Maintaining respondent engagement

When the interview is conducted by interviewers, one of their roles is to maintain the engagement of the respondent, and they will adopt a range of techniques to do this. They will frequently empathize with respondents over how boring or repetitive the interview is. That may not just be a technique:

they may well really think that! They will explain questions and, occasionally, even paraphrase them or edit them if they feel that the question wording is too long or is repetitive. Of course they are trained not to alter the wording, but where they feel that the interview is slipping away from them and no thought is being given to the answers, or, indeed that the respondent is about to terminate the interview because he or she is bored, then it is understandable that this can happen. Their objective is to complete the interview with a reasonable amount of consideration going to the answers by the respondent.

With self-completion questionnaires such strategies cannot be adopted. The questionnaire must do all the work itself to keep the respondent interested and engaged. With paper self-completion questionnaires this may not be too much of a problem. By their nature they tend to be quite short and the respondent can see exactly how big the task ahead is. With online questionnaires, though, the respondent cannot always see the size of the task they are faced with. A progress bar can provide an indication but because of routeing and optional questions they are rarely accurate and may not be trusted (see Chapter 11).

The questionnaire writer needs to remember that the respondent's reference set for online questionnaires is not a face-to-face or telephone questionnaire, which may be the comparison for the researcher, but other websites that collect information. And that information is often collected in an efficient and entertaining way. These websites can do this because generally the information they are collecting is simpler and more straightforward than in a research survey. Nevertheless, the respondent's reference point is likely to be contact details or product preferences on an e-commerce site or an interaction with friends on a social site. There is thus a different expectation of what an online questionnaire should be like.

Using questionnaire design to engage

Puleston and Eggers (2012) reported that 85 per cent of respondents in their experiments over 11 countries showed evidence of speeding at some stage of their online survey, and concluded that the only weapon we have to combat that is effective questionnaire design. Keeping the questionnaire short is also key: Cooke (2010) reports a six-fold increase in 'bad survey behaviour' between a 15-minute and a 30-minute questionnaire.

In Chapter 11 we looked at response techniques that can be used to break up the questionnaire, involve the respondent more and minimize some of the effort-avoidance techniques that lead to unreliable data, as well as techniques to obtain otherwise unavailable data. These included:

- drag and drop;
- page turning;
- slider scales;

- dynamic grids;
- magnifying;
- highlighting; and
- virtual shopping.

But to get the best out of an online questionnaire, and to really engage and involve respondents, it is necessary to think differently about how the questions themselves are asked. There are three ways in which we should be thinking differently:

1 Making the questions more accessible by keeping down the number of words, laying out the page well, avoiding repetition, etc.

2 Changing what is asked to make the questions more directly related to the respondent and more entertaining.

3 Asking respondents to play games and have fun while providing the data.

Making the questionnaire accessible

There is a simple technique that the questionnaire writer can use to greatly improve the quality of the questionnaire and that is to think about how the question appears on screen and word it appropriately.

One of the key causes of disengagement with online interviews is that the questions and the screens simply contain too many words. Large blocks of text are daunting and will not be read. There is evidence that most people have made up their minds what the question is about by the time they have read about 10 words (Tourangeau *et al,* 2000). They don't read beyond that and go straight into answering the question they think is being asked.

However, many people write questions as if they are to be asked by an interviewer. That is the way in which we may articulate the question to ourselves. But when this goes on to the screen as an online question, it does not work. Often it is far too wordy, so that not only does the respondent not read all of it, but it creates a visual impression of making the questionnaire appear a chore and a tedious task.

With an interview-led questionnaire the interviewers have strategies to maintain interest. A question asked by an interviewer may also have the function of helping the interviewer to build rapport with the respondent or to avoid embarrassment, and be deliberately longer than it strictly needs to be for these purposes. Online, we are asking respondents to do all the work and a wordy questionnaire simply presents a task to the respondents that many will not bother with.

To obtain a person's age it may be asked in a face-to-face interview as: 'Would you mind telling me how old you are?' or, 'In which of the categories on this card does your age fall?' Online it needs to be as follows.

> Your age:
>
>   16 to 34   _
>   35 to 54   _
>   55 or older   _

If the screen is headed 'Some details about yourself' or something similar, then even the word 'Your' may be omitted. This format is what respondents are used to online and is the least visually oppressive.

Using response codes to frame the question

Long explanations are sometimes thought necessary in face-to-face interviews. These are rarely so necessary with online interviews, where instructions and supplementary information can be provided outside of the question itself. Often the response list provides the entire context that is required. A face-to-face question:

'Please read the following list of statements and indicate which you agree with'

can be replaced with:

'Which of the following do you agree with?' or 'Which of these do you agree with?'

In Figure 12.1 it is clear from the scale itself that the answer is required on a scale from 0 to 10 and what the end point anchors, and does not need to be repeated in the question. The heart of the question gets relegated to the end of a long sentence. The question length is halved if written as:

How likely would you be to recommend Joe Bloggs's Internet Banking Service based on today's experience?

Frequently in interviewer-led questionnaires we read out the response codes to define the question to the respondents, who are then able to reply straight away with their answer. Online, this just clutters the screen with unnecessary words. The response codes can be made to do the work of the question (Figures 12.2 and 12.3).

There is no need to provide lengthy explanations when it is clear what is required. Nor are the pleasantries required, which just add words to the screen.

Breaking up the text

Arriving on a page that is busy and cluttered with text is likely to produce dismay in the respondent who is then less likely to read the questions and all

FIGURE 12.1 Unnecessarily detailed question

Seen on screen

Based on your experience today, on a scale of 0 to 10 where 0 is not at all likely and 10 is extremely likely, how likely is it that you would recommend Joe Bloggs's Internet Banking service to a friend or colleague?

☐ 10 Extremely likely

☐ 9

☐ 8

☐ 7

☐ 6

☐ 5

☐ 4

☐ 3

☐ 2

☐ 1

☐ 0 Not at all likely

☐ Don't know

FIGURE 12.2 Keep down the number of words

Seen on screen

Did you know who was advertising when you first saw it, or did showing the ad remind you, or did you previously not know who the ad was for at all?

☐ Knew who was advertising when first seen

☐ Showing the ad reminded me

☐ Previously didn't know who the ad was for

(LET THE RESPONSE PRE-CODES DO THE WORK. DON'T REPEAT THEM IN THE QUESTION.)

When you first saw the ad did you:

☐ Immediately know who it was for

☐ Was reminded who it was for

☐ Didn't previously know who it was for

FIGURE 12.3   Reducing wordage

Seen on screen

Now please look at the names of some companies that provide telephone services into the home. For each company, please click on one statement that best describes how you feel about it for telephone services. Just click on the one that best applies in each case.

Company A

☐ The only company I would ever use

☐ One of a number of companies I would prefer to use

☐ From what I've heard I might try that company in the future

☐ I'd use this company in certain circumstances

☐ I've heard of this company but didn't know they provided this service

☐ I've never heard of it

☐ I would never use this company

Only a third of the words are required in the question if it is online:

Here are some providers of home telephone services. How do you feel about each of them?

Company B

☐ The only company I would ever use

☐ One of a number I would prefer to use

☐ From what I've heard I might try them in the future

☐ I'd use them in certain circumstances

☐ I've heard of them but didn't know they provided this service

☐ I've never heard of them

☐ I would never use them

If we do not need to emphasize the service provision context, then even more words could be saved online:

How do you feel about each of these providers of home telephone services?

---

the text; be less likely to understand what is being asked; and to answer at random rather than give a considered or accurate response. Separating the core question from instructions or supporting information can help to reduce the blocks of text and keep the screen uncluttered.

An interviewer-administered question might be:

'Have you travelled from London to Birmingham in the last three months by public transport, that is by train, coach, aeroplane or taxi, but not by private car?'

For an online questionnaire there is too much text presented in a single sentence. On the screen this is less daunting as:

'Have you travelled from London to Birmingham in the last three months by public transport?'

The additional information can be added a couple of lines below:

'Public transport includes train, coach, aeroplane and taxi, but not private cars.'

Personalizing the questions

A way of increasing respondent involvement is to make the questions more personal and expressed in more conversational language. Researchers tend to write questions in terms of the information that they want to collect, rather than in terms that the respondent is more familiar and comfortable with. This can make the questions very formal and sometimes difficult for respondents as it requires them to work harder to understand the task they are being set. The point has been made earlier that the questionnaire should facilitate a conversation between researcher and respondent. Too often questionnaires are designed simply to extract information without sufficient thought given to how well it works as a conversation. For example, a frequently asked question is:

'Please select the three items from the list below that are the most important to you.'

This has been written from the researcher's point of view, who has formulated the question in terms of importance, the language of the research brief. This question could be written as:

'If you could only have three of these items, which would they be?'

This changes the question from an abstract notion of 'importance', which may be something that respondents have never considered before and so requires some cognitive processing, to a more personal and easier to answer construct that relates to their behaviour. If the data changes as a result, then it may well better reflect the respondents' real notions of importance.

Starting at the beginning

Engaging the respondent begins with the first screen they see. From the start the survey should be seen as something interesting and fun to do (see Figures 12.4 and 12.5). We want respondents to want to continue and complete the survey, not just because they are going to be rewarded with points from their panel but because it is interesting to do. 'Another tedious survey' is not the reaction that we want. Some of the ways of achieving this are:

- Including some questions they find fun to complete. These may not be directly relevant to the subject of the main survey, although equally they should not be completely dissonant. They must not influence or bias responses to later questions, so need to be carefully constructed.

- Starting with a short quiz. Most people enjoy quizzes and like to see how well they score. A relevant quiz with feedback on the respondent's performance can be engaging and fun, as well as getting the respondent into the mind set for the following questions. This approach will be returned to later.

- Constructing the questionnaire as a fun website rather than a boring survey. With customer satisfaction surveys, for example, where the client is apparent to the respondent, it can be constructed as the client's feedback site, with appropriate characters and animation.

Including animation, particularly at the beginning of the questionnaire, has been shown to increase the involvement of respondents and cause them to spend more time on the following questions (Puleston and Sleep, 2008).

FIGURE 12.4   Introducing the survey in a more interesting way

We're a market research agency and we're going to ask you how you feel about some everyday products you may buy and use at home.
We'll tell you more about our client and why we're doing this research at the end of the survey.

Adding fun

In Chapter 11 we saw how slider scales and other techniques can be used to vary the task and make it easier. To make it more fun and involving, this can be taken further by, for example, making the slider scales look like a mixing desk, or turning the radio button on a scale into a series of facial expressions. By doing this, Malinoff and Puleston (2011) found that respondents enjoyed the experience more and the quality of the data improved in that flat-lining was reduced or eliminated. However, they also found that the distribution of responses was different, and that it could be varied in particular by changing the face used to depict the facial expressions. Thus introducing pictorial images has an effect and they must be used with caution.

FIGURE 12.5   Using graphics to add interest

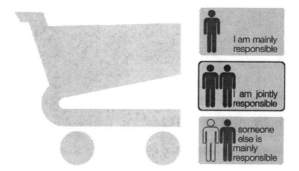

In Figure 12.6, the size and number of hearts increases the higher the score that is given to the brand using the slider scale.

In Figure 12.7 the depiction of how you feel changes for different points on the scale. Clearly great care has to be taken with this so as not to bias responses.

Gamification

Some of the engagement techniques already described are steps towards full gamification of questionnaires; that is making the questionnaire as much as possible a fun, interactive experience that can enhance the fullness and value of the responses obtained. There are a number of ways of achieving this, and for this section I make no apologies for drawing heavily on the work carried out by Jon Puleston and Deborah Sleep. The techniques described below are more than simply adding badges and avatars to the questionnaire, but require real thought being applied by the questionnaire writer to involve and engage the respondents.

FIGURE 12.6   Graphics make it more fun

Move the slider to indicate how you feel about yourself and each of these brands

FIGURE 12.7   Different depictions appear for different points on the scale

Which of these emotional states most closely reflects how you feel when you buy shampoo!

They never quite sell the type of product I am looking for   I find it really difficult deciding what to buy   I take a while thinking about it   It's simple I always buy the same product

Challenging the respondent

Presenting the question as a challenge has been found to increase respondent involvement and to increase the number of responses significantly. Puleston and Sleep (2011) found that asking for advertising recall in this way increased the number of brands mentioned threefold. They also found that adding the words 'can you guess' to a question increased the time spent on considering the response from around 10 seconds to up to 2 minutes. Clearly these fairly small changes had increased the engagement of respondents. For example, asking:

'We challenge you to name as many brands of (product) as you can that you have seen advertised recently'

instead of:

'Which brands of (product) have you seen advertised recently?'

is likely to give a longer list of responses, which may be important where the brand of interest is not the most salient in the category.

Of course, they may not always be appropriate. If it is a quick, front of mind response that you are seeking, then you may not want respondents to give it too much consideration. Then, you might change the question to:

'As quickly as you can, name one/two/three brands that ...'

or

'You have 10 seconds to name as many brands as you can that ...'

In Figure 12.8, the respondent is challenged to match the brands with the ads. The serious purpose is to obtain brand association with the ads, but presented in this way respondents find it much more fun. The counter in the top right corner shows how many seconds they have left, so the respondent is competing against the clock. This encourages respondents to be spontaneous in their answers, more closely matching the associations they would normally make without the benefit of unlimited time to consider it. The following screen (Figure 12.9) tells them how many they got right, their score, arrived at by summing the seconds left when the response is made, and a comparison against the average. This turns it into a game, where respondents can assess their performance against that of others.

Arbitrary rules

Adding arbitrary rules to a question can turn it from a task into a game. Many sports would be no more than a task if there were no rules, and teaching children is often made easier and more engaging by turning it into a game.

One type of rule is a time limit, as used in the example above. Another type of rule is to ask respondents to use an exact number of words to describe something. Puleston and Sleep (2011) tested the two questions:

FIGURE 12.8   Challenge the respondents – they find it fun

Here are five pictures from adverts for different brands, but 8 brands. Your goal is to find the brand that goes with each picture by dragging the brand's logo into the picture. See how many you can get right; and see if you can find the odd ones out.

| Alberto Balsam | Dove | Head & Shoulders | Herbal Essences | L'Oréal | Pantene | Timotei | Tresemmé |

FIGURE 12.9   Comparing scores turns it into a game

You got = 3 correct

These are the real ads

'How would you describe yourself?' and 'In exactly seven words how would your friends describe you?' With the standard question 18 per cent failed to respond and those that did gave an average of 2.4 descriptors. With the rule added, only 2 per cent failed to respond and the average number of descriptors given rose to 4.5.

Framework

Putting questions into an imaginary framework is another way in interesting and involving respondents. We have already seen the simple version of this with the question, 'If you could only have three of these items which would they be?' This idea can be extended to create an imaginary situation, into which respondents are drawn. Puleston and Sleep (2011) tested various variations of this idea; see Table 12.1.

TABLE 12.1   Tapping into the respondent's imagination

Standard wording	Question using imaginary framework
What is your favourite meal?	Imagine you are on death row and had to choose your favourite meal. What would it be?
How much do you like each of the following recording artists?	Imagine you were in charge of your own private radio station. From the following list of artists we want you to build up a play-list by deciding how much each artist should be played.
What did you think of the advertising?	Imagine you work for an advertising agency. One of your key client's rival brands has just released a new ad, and you are about to see a sneak preview before anyone else. You have to report back to the agency what you thought of it.
Please name your favourite foods.	You have an opportunity to go to a supermarket with unlimited budget, and buy all your favourite foods. The catch is, you only have 2 minutes.

Adapted from Puleston and Sleep (2011)

In each case, the respondents spent longer on the questions posed in the imaginary framework than the standard question. For the question describing the advertising the average number of words in the answers rose from 14 in the standard question to 53 for the imaginary framework question. This demonstrates that the respondents were more engaged, and importantly gives the researcher a far more detailed evaluation of their response to the ad. For the last question the average number of foods given increased from 6 per respondent to 35. This may be more than the researcher needs, but to increase discrimination the analysis can look only at the first 10 or 15 given, for example. Note that this question also introduced an arbitrary rule by limiting the answer to 2 minutes. All of these questions appear to violate the rule of keeping the number of words to a minimum. What they are doing, though, is intriguing the respondent within the first few words, which maintains the attention and ensures that they read them through fully.

There are many types of games that may have application to enhance questions and keep respondents engaged. Findlay and Alberts (2011) list 47 different game mechanisms from games company SCVNGR, many of which could be used to create engaging ways of asking questions.

It is important to ensure that gamifying the survey improves respondents' experience and does not add to their burden or increase the amount of cognitive processing that is necessary. Baker and Downes-Le-Guin (2011) created a game that ran throughout the questionnaire with avatars and weapons purchased in a fantasy world. Having the game run throughout the survey did not improve any of the measures of data quality. This approach, though, is different to the approach of Puleston and Sleep (2011), which is to gamify individual questions.

At the time of writing the gamification of questions and questionnaires is not universally accepted or used, and many of the major research providers are still experimenting and validating the approaches for commercial use. This includes the cost implications of the script-writing involved in many of these techniques, although that will decrease with experience. Importantly, though, these techniques require thought, time and creativity from the questionnaire writer to find the most appropriate technique for the task in hand.

Piloting the questionnaire

13

Introduction

It is always advisable to pilot the questionnaire before the survey goes live. Whether it is a new questionnaire written to meet a set of specific objectives or a set of questions that have been used before and adapted or arranged for a new study, testing it out is an essential precaution. Questionnaires are rarely the best that they could be at the first attempt. They need revising and testing until all concerned, researcher and client, are happy that they have the best questionnaire they can get. Piloting the questionnaire should be an integral part of that process.

Unfortunately, it is very common with commercial studies for piloting time not to be built into the project schedule. This stage in the process is often seen as expendable in the light of the pressure for information to be delivered as fast as possible. The experience of the researcher is relied upon to get it right first time, but even the most experienced researchers cannot be expected to do that every time. Failure to pilot the questionnaire is a serious risk to the success of the project.

Why pilot questionnaires?

There are two key tests for a questionnaire: reliability and validity. A questionnaire is reliable if it provides a consistent distribution of responses from the same survey universe every time. The validity of the questionnaire is whether or not it is measuring what we want it to measure. In addition the questionnaire must be error free.

Testing a questionnaire directly for reliability is very difficult. It can be administered twice to the same sample of test respondents to determine whether or not they give consistent answers. However, the time between the two interviews cannot usually be very long, both because the respondent's answers may in fact change over time and because, to be of value to the researcher, the results are usually required fairly quickly. The short period causes further problems in that respondents may have learnt from the first interview and so may alter their responses in the second one. Conversely, they may realize that they are being asked the same questions and deliberately try to be consistent with their answers. In testing for reliability we are therefore often asking whether respondents understand the questions and can answer them meaningfully.

Testing a questionnaire for validity requires that we ask whether the questions posed adequately address the objectives of the study. This should include whether or not the manner in which answers are recorded is appropriate. In addition, questionnaires should be tested to ensure that there are no errors in them. With timescales to produce questionnaires sometimes very tight, there is often a real danger of errors. Piloting the questionnaire can thus be divided into three areas: reliability, validity and error testing.

Reliability

- Do the questions sound right? It is surprising how often a question looks acceptable when written on paper but sounds false, stilted or simply silly when read out. It can be a salutary experience for questionnaire writers to conduct interviews themselves. They should note how often they want to paraphrase a question that they have written to make it sound more natural.

- Do the interviewers understand the questions? Complicated wording in a question can make it incomprehensible even to the interviewers. If they cannot understand it there is little chance that respondents will.

- Do respondents understand the questions? It is easy for technical terminology and jargon to creep into questions, so we need to ensure that it is eliminated. Have we included any ambiguous questions, double-barrelled questions, loaded or leading questions?

- Does the interview retain the attention and interest of respondents throughout? If attention is lost or wavers, the quality of the data may be in doubt. Changes may be required to retain the respondents' interest.

- Can the interviewers or respondents understand the routeing instructions in the questionnaire? Particularly with paper questionnaires, we should check that the routeing instructions can be understood by the interviewers, or if self-completion, by respondents.

- Does the interview flow properly? The questionnaire should be conducting a conversation with the respondent. A questionnaire that unfolds in a logical sequence, with a minimum of jumps between apparently unrelated topics, helps to achieve that.

Validity

- Can respondents answer the questions? We must ensure that we ask questions to which they are capable of providing answers.

- Are the response codes provided sufficient? Missing response codes can lead to answers being forced to fit into the codes provided, or to large numbers of 'other' answers.

- Do the response codes provide sufficient discrimination? If most respondents give the same answer, then the pre-codes provided may need to be reviewed to see how discrimination can be improved, and if that cannot be achieved, queries should be raised regarding the value of including the question.

- Do the questions and the responses answer the brief? We should by this time be reasonably certain that the questions we think we are asking meet the brief, but we need to ensure that the answers respondents give to those questions are the responses to the questions that we think we are asking.

Error testing

- Have mistakes been made? Despite all the procedures that most research companies have in place to check questionnaires before they go live, mistakes do occasionally still get through. It is often the small mistakes that go unnoticed, but these may have a dramatic effect on the meaning of a question or on the routeing between questions.

- Does the routeing work? Although this should have been comprehensively checked, illogical routeing sequences sometimes only become apparent with live interviews.

- Does the technology work? If unusual or untried technology is being used, perhaps as an interactive element or for displaying prompts, this should be checked in the field. It may work perfectly well in the office but field conditions are sometimes different, and a hiatus in the interview caused by slow working or malfunctioning technology can lose respondents.

- How long does the interview take? Most surveys will be budgeted for the interview to take a certain length of time. The number of interviewers allocated to the project will be calculated partly on the length of the interview, and they will be paid accordingly. Assumptions will also have been made about respondent cooperation based on the time taken to complete the interview. The study can run into serious timing and budgetary difficulties and may be impossible to complete if the interview is longer than allowed for. Being shorter than allowed for does not usually present such problems, but may lead to wasteful use of interviewer resources.

Types of pilot surveys

There are various types of pilot surveys that may be carried out according to the perceived need for piloting, time available and budget. These are:

- informal pilots carried out with a small number of colleagues;
- cognitive interviewing in which the questionnaire is tested amongst respondents;
- accompanied interviewing, which may be used principally to test for interviewer and routeing errors;
- large-scale pilot studies where a larger number of interviews can be used to test for completeness of brand lists or incidence of sub-groups;
- dynamic pilots, where question wording is changed between interviews to test alternatives based on responses received.

Informal pilot

An informal pilot represents the minimum that any questionnaire should undergo. In the informal pilot, the questionnaire writer should carry out the interview with a number of colleagues. This will at least give an indication of the length of time taken to complete the interview. It must be remembered though that an interview undertaken in the calm conditions of an office will usually take less time than one in the field when the respondent may be subject to a number of distractions and interruptions. Because colleagues are familiar with the conventions of questionnaires and they know it is not a 'real' interview, they will also tend to answer more quickly and without the same pauses for thought that occur with respondents.

Ideally, the colleagues interviewed should meet the eligibility criteria for the study, so that they can answer as respondents. This may highlight incomplete sets of pre-codes when a colleague's responses don't fit those provided, or an inadequacy in the routeing or in the questions when key information is not elicited.

If colleagues do not fit the eligibility criteria, they must be asked to pretend to. This is less likely to identify problems such as incomplete code lists, as the pretend respondent, who may not know the market well, will tend to give the same sorts of responses that the questionnaire writer has already anticipated. Nevertheless, this type of interview may well identify issues of timing, wording and routeing errors.

It is often worthwhile asking a colleague to pretend to be someone in the market with particular characteristics or a particular minority pattern of behaviour. If there is complex routeing in the questionnaire, this approach can be used to test it. If the colleague can be as obstructive as possible, challenging questions and providing the most difficult responses that he or she can think of, this will give the questionnaire a further test. Remember that the questionnaire has to work not just for most respondents but for *all* respondents.

The questionnaire writer should conduct these interviews, and it may be that no more than two or three such interviews are required. The questionnaire writer is the best person to understand the intent of each question and therefore to identify if it is misunderstood. However, if possible, a colleague who has not been involved in the questionnaire design can also be used as an interviewer. This will give the questionnaire some degree of testing as a tool to be used by someone not familiar with it.

Colleagues may not be thought to be the ideal sample for testing questionnaires, but it has been shown that people with a knowledge of questionnaire design are more likely to pick up errors in questions than are people who are not (Diamantopolous *et al*, 1994), so they are a good place to start.

Self-completion questionnaires should be given to a small number of colleagues to complete. These colleagues should be asked to make notes about any questions or routeing instructions with which they have difficulty.

Cognitive testing

Testing a questionnaire amongst colleagues may identify some issues with it, but cannot properly replicate what will happen in the field with real respondents, their understanding of the questions or their thought processes when answering. To test these requires specific pre-test interviews to be carried out with a number of respondents who fall into the survey population, usually in one-to-one interviews. These interviews can be carried out by the researchers themselves, who have a good knowledge of the subject and the questionnaire; cognitive psychologists, who have a good understanding of the processes of cognition; or specially trained senior interviewers who have expertise in this area. For online questionnaires the interviewer sits with respondents as they complete the survey. As these interviews proceed, the interviewer talks to the respondents to find out what they understood by certain questions or why they responded as they did. The researchers should make notes throughout the interview of points they want to return to.

It is also possible to ask the respondents to 'think out loud' as they answer the questions, and so give a running commentary on their thought processes. What the interviewer is aiming to achieve, based on models put forward by Tourangeau (1984) and Eisenhower *et al* (1991), is determining whether respondents:

- have a memory of what is being asked about and hence the ability to answer the question (encoding in memory);
- understand the question (comprehension);
- can access the relevant information in their memory (retrieval);

- can assess the relevance to the question of what they retrieve (judgement);
- can provide answers that meet the categories provided, and decide whether they want to provide an answer, or whether they want to provide a socially acceptable answer (communication/response).

A question always worth asking is whether the respondents felt that the questionnaire allowed them to say all that they wanted to say on the subject. It is not uncommon to find that one of the main things that respondents wanted to say was not asked about. It may not have arisen because it was not seen as relevant to the objectives of the study. Nevertheless, the impression left with the respondent is that the study was incomplete and that decisions would be made without full knowledge of the facts. This perception can be damaging to the image and reputation of market research, and could affect the willingness of the respondent to take part in future surveys. If there is an issue that consistently comes through as important to respondents but that is not asked about, consideration should be given to including it in the interview regardless of its apparent relevance to the study objectives.

Using cognitive testing of this nature can reveal a range of difficulties with the questionnaire. In a cognitive test of a questionnaire associated with the US Current Population Survey (McKay and de la Puente, 1996) problems were identified with:

- sensitive questions that respondents were uncomfortable answering;
- abstract questions that respondents found difficult to understand and to answer;
- vocabulary problems where the questionnaire writers had used terms unfamiliar to some of the respondents;
- order effects in which responses changed depending on the order in which questions were asked.

After the questionnaire had been revised, further testing identified other confusing and redundant questions.

Respondents should be chosen to represent a broad range of the types of people to be included in the main study. Any particular sub-groups whose members might experience some difficulties with the questionnaire should be represented. Questionnaire writers should also conduct some interviews themselves so as to be able to understand any difficulties that the interviewers might have with following the questionnaire instructions or in reading out the words of the questions as they have been written.

This type of pilot survey should allow the researcher to amend the questionnaire so that there can be confidence that it works in asking respondents questions that they can understand and can cope with the answers that they give.

Accompanied interviewing

A further stage of piloting face-to-face or telephone interviews is for the researcher to accompany or listen in to interviews carried out by regular members of the interviewing force. The questionnaire writer should be listening for:

- mistakes by the interviewer in reading the questions;
- mistakes by the interviewer in following routeing instructions;
- errors in the routeing instructions that take the respondent to the wrong question.

If it has not been possible to carry out a proper cognitive test, this approach can be combined with interviewing the respondents to test the question. However, this can sometimes cause conflict in the approach of the researcher due to the multiple objectives of testing both the way in which the interviewer handles the questionnaire and the way in which the respondents understand and answer the questions.

Large-scale pilot survey

With completion of the small-scale pilot survey, it may be possible to move to a larger-scale exercise. The objective here is to extend the pilot exercise to a larger number and broader range of respondents, and for there to be a sufficient number of respondents for some analysis to be carried out to confirm that the questions asked are delivering the data required to answer the project objectives.

Some commentators suggest that for interviewer-administered surveys the interviewers used should be the most experienced interviewers available, who are capable of determining ambiguities and other errors in the questions. Others suggest that a mix of interviewer ability is more appropriate, as it reflects the ability range of interviewers likely to be used on the main study. The principal purpose of the pilot study should be determined and the type of interviewers chosen accordingly. Thus if the focus of the pilot is more on the wording of the questions, more experienced interviewers may be appropriate. If the focus is equally on how well the interviewers can cope with a complex questionnaire, then a range of abilities would appear to answer the needs better.

This type of large-scale pilot is only likely to be carried out with large-scale studies, where the cost of failure is high if the study is unable to meet its objectives. Upwards of 50 interviews may be carried out in this pilot, which should be designed to cover different sections of the market and possibly different geographical regions. With online surveys the number can be higher with marginal increase in cost. It is at this stage that small regional brands may be discovered that should be added to brand lists, or unanticipated minority behaviour that had not been catered for. It is also at this stage that unusually high numbers of 'Don't know' or 'Not answered' responses may indicate an issue with a question.

The questionnaire writer is unlikely to be able to be present at all of the interviews. Indeed, doing so could be counterproductive, as it would be difficult not to give guidance to an interviewer consistently making an error. Interviewers should therefore be asked to write notes on each interview. They should be provided with note sheets on which to record comments – their own and the respondents' – as they go through the interview, which can be referred to later.

A debriefing of the interviewers should be held if possible, where they are brought to a central location to discuss their experiences with the questionnaire. The questionnaire writer should have seen all of the completed questionnaires before the debrief so as to have determined where there might still be issues with some questions, including issues that the interviewers themselves might not be aware of. If, for example, they all consistently misinterpret a question, they are unlikely to identify that as a problem. It will require the questionnaire writer to do so. Should significant changes be made to the questionnaire as a result of the pilot testing, then, of course, another round of pilot testing should be carried out.

Although not part of the questionnaire development process, a further use to which the large-scale pilot survey can be put is to give an indication of the incidence of minority groups within the research universe. If it is intended that the study should be capable of analysing specific sub-groups, the incidence of which is unknown, the pilot sample can give a first indication of this and so suggest whether the intended sample size of the main study is sufficient for this analysis. This may lead to revision of the sample size or sample structure for the main survey.

Dynamic pilot

The dynamic pilot can be very useful where a questionnaire is experimental. It is similar in scale to the small pilot survey. However, instead of the questionnaire writer listening in to a number of interviews and then deciding what is and is not working, the questionnaire is reviewed after each interview and rewritten to try to improve it. The client and researcher will often do this together. The improved questionnaire is then used for the next interview, after which it is reviewed again.

This is a time-consuming and possibly costly process, particularly if a central location has to be hired to accommodate it. However, where there is real concern about the sequence of questions or the precise wording of questions, it can be the quickest way to achieve a questionnaire that works, particularly if the client is part of the dynamic decision-making process.

An example of where this might be appropriate is if we wish to test the reaction to a complex government policy proposal. In this situation, it may be important to ensure that respondents understand some of the detail of the policy. A key component of the questionnaire design would be how to explain a number of different elements of the policy and gain reactions to each one. So we may need to test the wording of the descriptions of the different elements to judge how clearly it correctly conveys the policy; and to assess any order effects dependent on the sequence in which the components are revealed. By observing the reaction of the pilot respondents and where necessary asking them questions on what they understand from the descriptions, the questionnaire writer can adjust the wording and the order of the questions between interviews until a satisfactory conclusion is reached.

It is rare for all of these techniques to be used in a project. However, it is important that at least one type of questionnaire testing should always be carried out.

14 Ethical issues

Introduction

The ability of the market research industry to continue to use sample surveys as sources of primary data depends upon the willingness of members of the public to give their time and cooperation to answer our questions. There is frequently little, if any, obvious reward for them (although we regularly employ the argument that research helps to improve products and services on the market), and they are rarely paid. To be able to continue, market research needs to maintain this goodwill.

The level of goodwill and cooperation has declined in most countries over the past 30 years. Possible reasons include:

- Direct marketing has increased, which makes potential respondents distrustful that market researchers are not trying to sell them something.

- Potential respondents do not distinguish between market research and activities such as database marketing. Indeed in one study three-quarters of respondents said that they could not distinguish between them (Brace *et al*, 1999).

- Many people lead busier lives than they used to or than their parents used to. Many genuinely have less time for non-rewarding activities such as market research.

- There are more market research studies than there used to be, and many people are asked to participate in research surveys more often. Some markets are very over-researched, particularly business-to-business and medical markets.

- Our demands on respondents have increased. Interviews have got longer and more tedious as demands for information from client management have increased. Many potential respondents have been bored by a market research interview once before, or know someone who has been, and are not prepared to go through the same tedium again.

There is little that the questionnaire writer can do to free up more time in people's lives or to prevent markets becoming over-researched. However, by treating respondents honestly, openly and respectfully when writing the questionnaire, the questionnaire writer can help to distinguish genuine market research from direct marketing. And by creating involving and interesting interviews, he or she can improve the standing of market research interviews. Potential respondents may then be more willing to participate in surveys in the future.

This is one of the reasons codes of conduct exist. There are three main codes: those of the Market Research Society (MRS) in the UK, the Council of American Survey Research Organizations (CASRO) in the United States, and the European Society for Opinion and Marketing Research (ESOMAR). All market researchers should make themselves familiar with the code that is appropriate to them. The codes can be found on the organizations' websites: **www.mrs.org.uk, www.casro.org** and **www.esomar.org**. Membership of any of these bodies requires adherence to their code. In addition to their code, which provides an overall set of principles to be followed, some organizations provide more detailed guidelines on specific aspects of research. As an adjunct to its code, the MRS has produced 'Questionnaire design guidelines', which are regularly updated and can be found at **www.mrs.org.uk/ standards/guidelines**.

Many countries now have laws, usually in the form of data protection laws, which define certain points of information that questionnaire writers are required to give to respondents. These laws take precedence over codes of conduct, should there be any conflict. In the UK, the relevant law is the Data Protection Act 1998. There is variation in these laws between countries with, for example, the laws of Germany and the UK being more prescriptive than the corresponding laws in many other countries. Again, it is the responsibility of questionnaire writers to ensure that they comply with the laws of the country in which they work, as well as with the laws of the country or countries in which they are carrying out the survey, if they are different.

Responsibilities to respondents

The introduction

What is said in the introduction to an interview is crucial in securing the cooperation of respondents. This is true for both interviewer-administered surveys and self-completion studies. From an ethical standpoint the introduction should include:

- the name of the organization conducting the study;*
- the broad subject area;
- whether the subject area is particularly sensitive;

- whether the data collected will be held confidentially or used at a personally identifiable level for other purposes such as database building or direct marketing, and if so by whom and for what purposes;*
- the likely length of the interview;
- any cost to the respondent;
- whether the interview is to be recorded, either using audio or video, other than for the purposes of quality control.*

*These items are required by the Data Protection Act 1998 in the UK.

This gives respondents or potential respondents the information they require to be able to make an informed decision about whether or not they are prepared to cooperate in the study. Sometimes it is not easy to comply with these requirements, but the questionnaire writer should make every effort to do so.

Name of the research organization

The name of the organization carrying out the study would usually be the research company that is responsible for writing the questionnaire if that is the same as the company that will be responsible for analysis of the results. (In UK Data Protection Act terms, this is the Data Controller.) If part or all of the fieldwork is to be subcontracted, then the name of the subcontracting agency need not be mentioned, provided it is passing on completed interviews to the main agency for processing, and it is possible to identify individual interviewers in case of a complaint being made.

Subject matter

The broad subject area should be given so that the respondent has a reasonable idea of the area of questioning that is to follow. Frequently we do not wish to reveal the precise subject matter too early as this will bias responses, particularly during the screening questions. However, every effort should be made to give a general indication. For example, a survey about holidays could be described as being about leisure activities, although such a description may be inadequate for a survey about drinking habits. 'Leisure activities' would certainly be an inadequate description for a survey about sexual activity, which is regarded as a sensitive subject.

Sensitive questions

In the UK sensitive subjects are defined as including:

- sexual orientation;
- racial origin;

- political opinions;
- religious or similar beliefs;
- physical or mental health;
- implication in criminal activity;
- trade union membership.

This list, though, is not exhaustive in terms of what respondents may find sensitive, and the questionnaire writer should examine the study for any possible sensitive content. Anyone working in areas dealing with drugs and medication, or illness, or conducting studies on financial topics should be particularly alert to this issue.

If you need to determine the ethnicity of respondents, then The Market Research Society suggests using the question found in the Census and recommended by The Equality and Human Rights Commission, shown in Figure 14.1. This question is only applicable to the UK, as it reflects the ethnic makeup of that country. For other countries different categories will be required both to reflect the prevalence of different ethnic groupings and to reflect any different use of acceptable terminologies. Within the UK it may be necessary to amend the categories for localities where a more detailed description is required, or to distinguish between English, Scottish, Welsh and Northern Irish.

Sexual orientation is not an issue that requires to be asked about frequently in market research but there are occasions when it might be necessary. It can be a very personal and private issue, and it is important to get the correct wording so as not to offend, and to encourage as many people as possible to answer. Stonewall, the pressure group (**www.stonewall.org.uk**), recommend the question shown in Figure 14.2 for asking about sexual orientation. An alternative is to provide one category for lesbian/gay and cross-analyse by gender if necessary. It is, of course, important to include a 'Prefer not to say' option for all sensitive questions.

Gender identity is also an issue that is only rarely asked about in commercial research, but that may be relevant for certain social research issues or social advertising research. The question in Figure 14.3 is recommended by Press For Change (**www.pfc.org.uk**). It recommends the use of these descriptive questions rather than questions that rely on terminologies or labels which could offend.

Like all sensitive issues, race, sexual orientation and gender identity should never be asked about unless it is absolutely necessary for the purposes of the study.

Confidentiality

One of the key distinctions between market research surveys and surveys carried out for direct marketing or database building is that the data is held confidentially and for analysis purposes only. No direct sales or marketing

FIGURE 14.1   Recommended question for recording ethnicity

What is your ethnic group?

Choose one from A to E then tick the appropriate box to indicate your cultural background.

A   White

☐   British

☐   Irish

☐   Any other White background (write in)

B   Mixed

☐   White and Black Caribbean

☐   White and Black African

☐   White and Asian

☐   Any other Mixed background (write in)

C   Asian or Asian British

☐   Indian

☐   Pakistani

☐   Bangladeshi

☐   Any other Asian background (write in)

D   Black or Black British

☐   Caribbean

☐   African

☐   Any other Black background (write in)

E   Chinese or other ethnic group

☐   Chinese

☐   Any other (write in)

Question recommended by The Equality and Human Rights Commission for the Census.

FIGURE 14.2   Question for recording sexual orientation

What is your sexual orientation?

☐ Bisexual

☐ Gay man

☐ Gay woman/lesbian

☐ Heterosexual/straight

☐ Other

☐ Prefer not to say

Sexual orientation question recommended by Stonewall.

FIGURE 14.3   Question for recording gender identity

Is your gender identity the same as the gender you were assigned at birth?

☐ Yes   ☐ No

or

Do you live and work full time in the gender role opposite to that assigned at birth?

☐ Yes   ☐ No

Gender Identity questions recommended by Press For Change.

activity will take place as a result of the respondent having taken part in the study. If this is the case, this should be stated in the introduction on the questionnaire or in the covering letter in the case of a postal survey. It is then the responsibility of the research organization to ensure that it is treated solely in this way.

This may not be the case because, for example, the survey is a customer satisfaction survey intended to utilize individual-level data to enhance the client company's customer database or to allow selective marketing to customers, depending on their recorded level of satisfaction. Nor is it likely to be the case if it is to be used to identify respondents who show an interest in a new product or service that the client can follow up with marketing activity. (This may occur in small business-to-business markets.) Such studies are not confidential research and the questionnaire must not represent them as such. Respondents must be told which organizations are going to see their data and how they are going to use it, and given the opportunity to opt out. In most European countries this is a legal requirement under data protection legislation.

Apart from it being against the law in these countries to represent such studies as confidential research, it is morally wrong to mislead respondents. It is also bad for the image of market research if respondents are wrongly led into thinking that nothing will occur to them as result of participating in the study. It can only damage response rates for future surveys if respondents become disillusioned about the reassurances they are given.

Interview length

How long the interview is likely to take is another area where a respondent once misled is unlikely to trust future assurances. One of the most common causes of complaints received by the Market Research Society from members of the public is that the interview in which they participated took significantly longer than they were initially told. Sometimes they were not told how long the interview would take, and wrongly assumed that it would be only a few minutes. On other occasions, though, they were told the likely duration of the interview, which was then significantly exceeded.

Sometimes it is straightforward to estimate the length of the interview. When the study has a questionnaire with a simple flow path and little routeing, the pilot survey will have demonstrated how long it will take, and that is likely to be about the same for all respondents. However, the time required to complete the interview can vary considerably between respondents as the questionnaire becomes more complex. It can depend on the speed with which respondents answer the questions and the amount of consideration they give to each. It can also vary significantly depending on the answers that they give. The questionnaire may contain sections that are asked only if the respondent displays a particular behaviour, knowledge or attitude at an earlier question. The time taken to complete the interview can increase or decrease considerably, depending on whether or not such sections are asked. The eligibility of any individual respondent for these sections cannot be predicted at the outset of the interview, with the consequence that the interview length could vary between, say, 15 minutes and 45 minutes for different respondents.

If there is likely to be a significant variation in interview length between respondents, the questionnaire writer should try to reflect this in the introduction. The introduction must never deliberately understate the likely time required. It is better to be vague about the interview length than deliberately to mislead.

Source of name

Respondents have a right to know how they were sampled or where the research organization obtained their name and contact details. For surveys using non-pre-selected samples, this does not usually present any difficulties, although explaining how random digit dialling works to someone who is ex-directory can sometimes be difficult.

Where the names have been supplied from a database, this can sometimes present more of a problem. With customer satisfaction surveys, we often want to say in the introduction that respondents have been contacted because they are customers of the organization. Frequently, clients will see the customer satisfaction survey as a way of demonstrating to their customers that the organization cares about the relationship between them. It is not uncommon for the introduction to state this and for postal or web-based satisfaction questionnaires to include client identification and logos.

However, sometimes we do not want to reveal the source at the beginning of the interview because that may bias responses to questions where the client organization is to be compared against similar organizations. If, in a personal interview, the interviewer is asked the source before these questions arise, the respondent can be asked to wait until later in the interview or until the end of the interview for that to be revealed. An explanation of why the respondent is being asked to wait until then should also be given. If the respondent refuses to continue unless he or she is told, then they must be told and the interview terminated. Instructions to interviewers to this effect may appear on the questionnaire, or may be included in their training or in separate instructions.

Web-based surveys can carry a similar promise to reveal the name of the client at the end of the interview if it is thought that not to do so might reduce response rates. For postal surveys, this is not possible.

Cost to respondent

If taking part in the interview is going to cost the respondents anything other than their time, this must be pointed out. In practice it is usually only internet or web-based interviews that are likely to incur cost for the respondent (Nancarrow *et al*, 2001) and then only if they are paying for their internet connection on a per-minute basis. Occasionally, though, respondents will be asked to incur travel costs to reach a central interviewing venue such as a new product clinic. These costs, though, would normally be reimbursed.

Calling respondents on a mobile phone could also incur a cost for them. If they happen to be abroad at the time that cost could be significant. The questionnaire introduction should always establish not only whether it is safe for respondents to talk on their mobile phones, but also whether doing so is likely to incur any costs for them.

During the interview

Right not to answer

Researchers must always remember that respondents have agreed to take part in the study voluntarily. Should they wish not to answer any of the questions put to them, or to withdraw completely from the interview, they cannot be compelled to do otherwise. Part of the art of the interviewer is to minimize such occurrences by striking up a relationship so that respondents continue for the sake of the interviewer even when they would rather not. However, if a respondent refuses to answer or continue, this must be respected.

In Chapter 5 we examined the pros and cons of including 'Not answered/ refused' codes at every question and concluded that they should not necessarily be included as a matter of course. However, it should be possible to identify the questions that are most likely to be refused and to include a code for refusals as appropriate. Such questions are likely to be the sensitive questions listed above, and personal questions about income and family relationships.

With paper questionnaires the interview can progress even if a question is not answered, unless an answer is required for routeing purposes. In Chapter 10 the issue of electronic self-completion questionnaires was discussed and whether or not the researcher should build in an ability to move on to the next question following a refusal to answer. The alternative to allowing this can be that the respondent terminates the interview rather than answer the question. Different research organizations take different views on whether to accept termination of the interview or to provide another mechanism that allows respondents not to answer.

Maintaining interest

It could be considered an ethical issue that respondents must not be put through a process that is boring and tedious. The ethics of, for example, a telephone survey questionnaire that consists almost entirely of 200 rating scales that would take most people nearly an hour to answer, and on a topic that is of marginal interest to most respondents, must be questioned. This may be an extreme (although true) example, but questionnaire writers must look out for any tendency towards this.

Creating a boring interview is not just bad questionnaire design, which leads to unreliable data, it is also ethically questionable, fails to treat the respondents with respect, and damages the reputation of market research. Long and repetitive interviews should be avoided. This sometimes means that the questionnaire writer must find a creative way of asking what would otherwise be repetitive questions. Batteries of rating scales, in particular, can cause problems because of the desire to maintain a common format for analysis purposes.

Responsibilities to clients

Ethical behaviour does not just extend to the relationship between question-naire writer and respondent, however. The questionnaire writer also has a responsibility to behave ethically towards the client.

Much has been written in previous chapters about designing questions that are unbiased and strive to capture the best and most accurate data. This is not just a matter of good questionnaire design. There is also an ethical and moral duty to provide clients with data that is the best that can be obtained to meet their objectives and answer their questions.

The questionnaire writer has an ethical duty to ensure that the question-naire is fit for the purpose of the study. Deliberately introducing bias to support a particular point of view is unethical and is rarely of value to the client's organization.

The client should always be given the opportunity to comment on the questionnaire. Most quality control procedures require that the client signs off the questionnaire as having been agreed. It is the questionnaire writer's responsibility to ensure that the client has sufficient time to consider the questionnaire and any implications for the data to be collected before being asked to agree it.

By implication, questions to which the client has not agreed should not be included. It can be tempting to add questions on a different topic, possibly for a different client, where the sample definition for the two sub-ject areas is the same. It is unethical to do this without the agreement of both clients.

Also, where one client has paid for the development of a questionnaire, it is ethically unacceptable to use it for another client's survey. It is, of course, to be expected that the questionnaire writer will draw upon their experience when writing the second questionnaire, but usually the questionnaire is considered to be the property of the client who paid for its development unless specified otherwise in the contract. Questionnaires that the research company has developed itself, without being paid by a client to do so, are the property of the research company and can be used for multiple clients.

15

Social desirability bias

Response bias

No matter how carefully the questionnaire writer constructs the questions, the data collected is only as accurate as the responses elicited. Respondents give inaccurate answers for a number of different reasons. They do so consciously for reasons of their own, and also without any conscious awareness that the information they are giving is inaccurate. The researcher must be alert to these inaccuracies, try to minimize them and, where necessary, take into consideration the bias and inaccuracy in the data.

In previous chapters some of these biases were examined, including the problems of memory, inattention by the respondent and deliberate lying. This chapter examines a particular category of response bias known as 'social desirability bias'.

Social desirability bias

Social desirability bias (SDB) arises because respondents like to appear to be other than they are. This can occur consciously, because respondents want to manage the impression they are giving of themselves in terms of social responsibility, or subconsciously, because they believe themselves to be other than they are, possibly a form of denial. Thus SDB can manifest itself both in stated behaviour with, say, an overclaiming of environmentally friendly behaviour, or in the attitudes that someone expresses.

Sudman and Bradburn (1982: 32–3) identified the following topics as being desirable and therefore areas in which behaviour is likely to be over-reported:

- Being a good citizen:
    - registering to vote and voting;
    - interacting with government officials;
    - taking a role in community activities;
    - knowing the issues.

- Being a well-informed and cultured person:
  - reading newspapers, magazines and books, and using libraries;
  - going to cultural events such as concerts, plays and exhibitions;
  - participating in educational activities.
- Fulfilling moral and social responsibilities:
  - giving to charity and helping friends in need;
  - actively participating in family affairs and child rearing;
  - being employed.

They also quote examples of conditions or behaviour that may be under-reported in an interview:

- Illness and disabilities:
  - cancer;
  - venereal diseases;
  - mental illness.
- Illegal or contra normative behaviour:
  - committing a crime, including traffic violations;
  - tax evasion;
  - drug use;
  - consumption of alcoholic products;
  - sexual practices.
- Financial status:
  - income;
  - savings and other assets.

Until relatively recently, SDB was seen as an issue mainly affecting social research, as the above list suggests. Thus, it has been a problem in health care, where people might claim to lead a healthier lifestyle than is the case. It has been an issue for social researchers in a range of issues such as immigration, attitudes to minority groups, housing, public transport and the environment. If it has affected market researchers, it has been an issue mainly for a small number of specific categories in which there is a perceived element of social responsibility, or perceived social irresponsibility. In certain markets, such as tobacco, alcohol and gambling, both attitudes and behaviour are likely to be misrepresented. Many respondents will deliberately under-report their consumption in these markets so as to appear socially responsible, while others may over-report their consumption, particularly in the alcohol market, to appear more 'macho' to the interviewer. Researchers working in these fields have learnt that they cannot ignore SDB as an influence on the data they collect.

More recently, though, the rise in the association between many types of businesses and the impact they have on both the physical and social environments has meant that this has become an issue for researchers working in many more fields:

- For consumer goods companies and retailers it can arise with consumer concerns about the impact on the environment of excessive or inappropriate packaging.
- The social responsibility of food and confectionery manufacturers to their customers and suppliers has become a global issue.
- For manufacturers of consumer durables the impact of the disposal of their products can be a social concern.
- Cause-related marketing has been adopted by many organizations in recent years, in which the brand is linked to a good cause, such as supporting schools.
- Issues such as 'fair trade' products arise in individual markets.

It can no longer be assumed that SDB is an issue only for social researchers. Researchers in commercial markets now have to be equally aware of it. In many areas of commercial market research, if the questionnaire writer and researcher fail to recognize that SDB may be influencing responses, they may come to false conclusions from the research data.

Types of SDB

Impression management

Possibly the most common form of SDB is the need for approval, known as 'impression management'. This is partly a function of the individual and partly a function of the question, and its occurrence varies depending on a combination of the two. Some people will answer certain questions honestly but will not do so other questions where they feel the need for approval. The questions or topics on which people feel the need for approval may vary between respondents. However, within any one study it is most likely that if impression management occurs, it will do so on a small and consistent set of questions.

Ego defence and self-deception

Maintaining one's own esteem is a further cause of bias. Here respondents' intentions are not to manage the impression that they give to someone else, such as the interviewer or the researcher, but to convince themselves that they think and behave in socially responsible ways. This is less likely to be a conscious activity than is the need for approval, but can result in the same exaggeration of claimed socially responsible behaviour and attitudes. This type of behaviour may particularly affect future projections of likely behaviour, where the respondents convince themselves that they will behave in a responsible fashion in the future even if they do not do so currently. When this is carried out consciously it is known as 'ego defence'; when it is carried out subconsciously it is known as 'self-deception'.

Instrumentation

A further type of bias, and one that is totally conscious, is instrumentation (Nancarrow *et al*, 2000). This means that respondents give answers designed, in their view, to bring about a socially desirable outcome. Respondents may say that they will participate in a scheme or purchase a product, for example, although they know that it is unlikely they will. They do so because they believe the introduction of that scheme or product is desirable. A survey of attitudes to how lottery money should be divided between good causes and lottery administrators may suffer from this effect, for example. Respondents may deliberately give low estimates of the proportion that should be allocated for administration because they believe that if it is seen that the public wants a higher proportion to go to charities this could have an impact on the decisions of the regulatory body. This may be in addition to or in place of impression management, in which the respondent wishes to be seen by the interviewer to be generous to charities. Many respondents are relatively sophisticated with regard to marketing and to market research, and know that they have an opportunity to influence decision making through their responses to the survey.

Dealing with SDB

When writing the questionnaire care must be taken to identify question areas that are possible sources of SDB. If the questions ask about attitudes or behaviour on any subject that has a social responsibility component, then consideration should be given to how best to minimize any possible bias. Simply asking respondents to be honest has very little effect (Brown *et al*, 1973; Phillips and Clancy, 1972).

Research carried out under the MRS ESOMAR or CASRO code of conduct (see Chapter 14) should anyway tell respondents that their responses will be treated confidentially. This could be reinforced with a restatement of confidentiality as part of the introduction to the sensitive questions. However, the effect of this appears to be slight (Dillman *et al*, 1996; Singer *et al*, 1995) or even to reduce the level of cooperation (Singer *et al*, 1992). This reduction in cooperation could be because the additional emphasis on confidentiality highlights to respondents that the questions are particularly sensitive, and so increases their nervousness about answering them. With postal self-completion surveys there is evidence (Yang and Yu, 2011) that omission of a respondent identifier on the questionnaire decreases SDB. This suggests that assurances of confidentiality that are seen to have substance should have some effect. However, for surveys other than postal, there is still the interviewer, who will be aware of the responses or, for online surveys, whoever is receiving the data. Appealing for honesty and assurances of confidentiality are insufficient. Measures that are more positive are therefore required.

Removing the interviewer

With impression management, respondents are trying to appear more socially responsible than they already are. They may be trying to create that impression for the interviewer or for the unseen researcher. Many respondents will not appreciate that their responses are likely to be seen at an identifiable level by only the interviewer and, if using a paper questionnaire, by the person entering or editing the data. That may not matter in the sense that they just want to be 'known' as responsible people. However, the most obvious person for whom they want to create a good impression is the interviewer. Using a self-completion questionnaire, by removing the interviewer from the interface, should therefore eliminate much, but probably not all, of this particular problem. However, it will not eliminate ego defence/self-deception or instrumentation. Earlier work published on this topic (Booth-Kewley *et al*, 1992; Lautenschlager and Flaherty, 1990) had been inconclusive on whether removing the interviewer reduces SDB. More recently Poynter and Comley (2003), Duffy *et al* (2005) and Bronner and Kuijlen (2007) have all demonstrated that the admission of socially undesirable behaviour is greater with online surveys than with interviewer-administered surveys, so demonstrating the greater honesty that is achieved with this medium. In addition, Kellner (2004) demonstrated that there was less pressure on respondents to appear knowledgeable.

Self-completion questionnaires are also good to use where the subject is potentially embarrassing for the respondent, and they eliminate much of the bias that would otherwise occur. Both mail surveys and internet-based surveys benefit in this respect, with internet-based surveys possibly being seen by respondents as the most anonymous form of interview.

Random response technique

The randomized response technique was first developed by Warner (1965). It provides a mechanism for respondents to be truthful about embarrassing or even illegal acts without anyone being able to identify that they have admitted to such an act. This is achieved because the respondent is presented with two alternative questions, one of which is sensitive and the other not. No one other than the respondent knows which question has been answered.

To achieve this, two questions with the same set of response codes are presented for self-completion. One of these is the sensitive or threatening question, and the other is the non-threatening and innocuous one. Respondents are allocated to answer one of these questions in a random way, the outcome of which is unknown to the interviewer. This can be by having balls of two different colours in a bag and asking the respondent to draw one out without showing it to the interviewer, or tossing a coin out of sight of the interviewer. However, this can be a cumbersome process in most interview situations.

An alternative method, which would also work in online self-completion interviews, is presented in Figure 15.1. We know from other sources that 17 per cent of the population have their birthday in November or December and, given a sufficiently large sample, we can reasonably apply this proportion. So, of a sample of 1,000, it can be assumed that 830 will have answered the threatening question and 170 the non-threatening question. Of the 170, half (85) will have answered 'Yes' to the question about their telephone number.

If X out of the total sample have answered 'Yes' at all, we can deduce that, of the people who answered the threatening question, X – 85 answered 'Yes' to the threatening question. We can therefore arrive at an estimate of the proportion of the population who have used marijuana in the last 12 months, which is $(X - 85)/830$.

FIGURE 15.1   Random response question example

Below, there are two questions with only one place to record the answers. Please answer question A if you were born in November or December, and question B if you were born in any other month of the year. Don't tell me which question you are answering. As I do not know, and will not ask you, which month you were born in, no one will know which question you have answered. Please be honest about which question you answer and how you answer it.

A. TO BE ANSWERED IF YOUR BIRTHDAY IS IN NOVEMBER OR DECEMBER
Does your home telephone number end with an odd-numbered digit, 1, 3, 5, 7, 9? Answer YES if it does, NO if it does not.

B. TO BE ANSWERED IF YOUR BIRTHDAY IS NOT IN NOVEMBER OR DECEMBER
Have you used marijuana at all in the last 12 months?

YES ☐
NO ☐

It has been shown (Sudman and Bradburn, 1982) that the technique works effectively for subjects that are relatively unthreatening, eg having been involved in a case in a bankruptcy court, but that with more threatening subjects, eg drunken driving, it still significantly underestimates levels of behaviour.

This approach is limited to providing an estimate of the proportions answering 'Yes' and 'No' to the threatening question among the total sample, or among sub-groups that are of sufficiently large sample size for the assumptions regarding the proportions answering the non-threatening question still to hold. As it is not possible to distinguish individual respondents who answered the threatening question, we cannot cross-analyse them against any other variables from the survey to establish, say, the profile of those who admit to the behaviour and that of those who do not.

What the technique achieves is providing an opportunity for the respondent to answer honestly. This means that, while it addresses impression management, it can do nothing about self-deception.

Face-saving questions

Face-saving questions give respondents an acceptable way of admitting to socially undesirable behaviour, by including in the question a reason why they might behave in that way. For example, if the questionnaire writer wishes to measure how many people have read the new edition of the *Highway Code*, instead of asking, 'Have you read the latest edition of the *Highway Code*?' the writer could ask, 'Have you had time yet to read the latest edition of the *Highway Code*?'

The first question can sound confrontational, with an implication that respondents ought to have read the latest edition and be aware of current driving rules. This can force respondents on to the defensive, or to feel guilty about not having read it, and hence to lie and say that they have read it. The second question carries an assumption that respondents know that they ought to read it and will when they have the time. This is less confrontational, eases any guilt about not having read it and makes it easier for respondents to admit they have not.

Work carried out in the United States (Holtgraves *et al*, 1997) has consistently demonstrated over a series of studies that questions of this type can significantly reduce overclaiming of socially desirable knowledge (eg global warming, health care legislation, trade agreements and current affairs) and reduce under-claiming of socially undesirable behaviour (eg cheating, shoplifting, vandalism, littering). However, the work is inconclusive regarding the impact of such questions when applied to socially desirable behaviour (eg recycling, studying, attending concerts). Questionnaire writers therefore can use this technique confident that it reduces SDB where knowledge is being asked about, or where the task is to get respondents to admit to undesirable behaviour. However, caution should be applied before using this technique to reduce overclaiming of desirable behaviour.

Another technique that has the effect of reducing threat in questions of knowledge is to use the phrase, 'Do you happen to know ...' at the beginning of the question. Rather than ask, 'How many kilometres are there in a mile?' or, 'Do you know how many kilometres there are in a mile?' the question should be, 'Do you happen to know how many kilometres there are in a mile?' This softens the question and makes it less confrontational and has been shown to lead to an increase in the level of 'Don't know' responses, suggesting that respondents find it easier to admit their ignorance rather than guess.

Indirect questioning

A technique sometimes used in qualitative research is not to ask respondents what they think about a subject, but to ask them what they believe other people think. This allows them to put forward views that they would not admit to holding themselves, which can then be discussed. It can sometimes be possible to use a similar technique in a quantitative research question-naire. However, in qualitative research the group moderator or interviewer can discuss these views and use his or her own judgement as to whether or not respondents hold these views themselves or simply believe that other people hold them.

In quantitative research both the structured nature of the interview and the separation of respondents and researcher make this far more difficult to achieve. The researcher is therefore left with uncertainty as to the propor-tion of respondents who projected their own feelings and the proportion who honestly reported their judgement of others.

Question enhancements

The questionnaire writer can take a number of other simple steps in order to help minimize SDB.

Reassure that behaviour is not unusual

Where there is a concern that people may misreport their behaviour, state-ments that certain types of behaviour are not unusual can be built into the question, to reassure respondents that whatever option they choose, their behaviour will be considered by the interviewer or by the researcher to be normal. For example, 'Some people read a newspaper every day of the week, others read a newspaper some days a week, while others never read a news-paper at all. To which of these categories do you belong?'

Extended responses on prompts

In a similar way, extended responses on prompt material can suggest that extreme behaviour is not unusual and encourage honest responses (Brace and Nancarrow, 2008). For example, when asking about the amount of alcohol that people drink, the researcher can use prompts with categories that go well beyond normal behaviour, so that categories of mildly heavy drinkers appear mid-way on the list. This helps heavier drinkers to feel that their consumption might be of a more normal level than it actually is, and they may be more likely to be honest and not under-report. Care needs to be taken not to make light drinkers feel inadequate and so feel forced to over-report their weight of drinking. Having relatively small gradations at the lighter end of the scale, thus helping the lighter drinkers to see that they have more options, can help this (see Figure 15.2).

FIGURE 15.2   Two approaches to categories

Using one of the phrases on this list, please tell me how many units of alcohol you drink in an average week.

Approach A	Approach B
None	None
1 to 2 units	1 to 14 units
3 to 5 units	15 to 39 units
6 to 8 units	40 units or more
9 to 12 units	
13 to 17 units	
18 to 24 units	
25 to 34 units	
35 to 54 units	
55 to 74 units	
75 to 94 units	
95 to 134 units	
135 to 184 units	
185 units or more	

An alternative approach is to have broad categories, probably no more than three in total, so that respondents do not have to identify the amount too narrowly. The second approach is likely to be preferred by respondents because they do not have to specify closely, which they may be reluctant to do either because they do not want to admit it or because they find it difficult to calculate. However, for most research purposes the broad categories supply insufficient data to the researcher for the required analyses. This approach can be used as a first part of a two-part question. The first question is used to identify which of the three broad categories the respondent falls into and a second question is used to identify the amount more precisely within the category.

Identifying responses by codes

So that respondents do not have to articulate the response to the interviewer, code letters can be used against each of the prompted response categories and the respondent asked to read out the appropriate code letter. Respondents therefore do not have to read aloud the answer, which helps them to feel that a degree of confidentiality is being maintained. The interviewer of course knows to which response category each code applies, but respondent and interviewer do not have to share the information overtly (see Figure 15.3).

FIGURE 15.3   Use of code letters

ASK ALL IN PAID EMPLOYMENT.

SHOW CARD.

What is your personal annual income before tax or other deductions? Please read out the letter on this card next to the band in which your income falls.

J   UP TO £8,000

N   £8,001 TO £12,000

D   £12,001 TO £16,000

P   £16,001 TO £20,000

W   £20,001 TO £24,000

K   £24,001 TO £35,000

G   £35,001 OR ABOVE

Bogus pipeline

One other approach should be mentioned, though it has little application in normal market research surveys: the bogus pipeline. Respondents are physically connected to an apparatus that they are told can detect their true feelings and emotions. There is therefore no point in them not giving wholly truthful responses to the questions asked. This is, of course, not true, and the apparatus is bogus.

This approach has been shown to reduce social desirability bias. There is concern though that, although the technique does affect responses, it may be because respondents answer more carefully and with more thought rather than because they are trying to be truthful. However, because of the ethical issues it poses of deceiving members of the public about the capabilities of the apparatus and because of both the difficulty and cost of applying it, this is generally not an appropriate technique to use in market research surveys.

Determining whether SDB exists

It can be difficult to determine whether or not the responses to a question have been influenced by SDB.

Matched cells

One approach to determining whether or not there is a problem is to use one of the techniques described above and to have part of the sample as a control cell that is asked the same question but in a direct form.

The control cell must be matched on all relevant criteria to the rest of the sample and must be sufficiently large to enable reasonably sized differences to be statistically significant. If the responses from the control cell differ significantly from the rest of the sample, then this may confirm that SDB exists and that the questionnaire writer was correct to take the appropriate precautions.

This approach is likely to mean sacrificing a significant part of the sample on the appropriate questions, and the uncertainty resulting if no difference in responses is found. It is unlikely in most commercial studies that this technique can be justified. It is a better use of resources to assume that SDB does exist and to use an appropriate question technique that will minimize it.

Matching known facts

Where it is possible to cross-check responses against known data from other sources, this can highlight differences that may be due to SDB. The cross-checkable facts will tend to be factual or behavioural data, such as volume of product sold. Attitudinal questions cannot be checked in this way. Even with factual data it is frequently difficult to match external data sources with survey data because of differences in definitions, time periods and so on. Survey data can sometimes provide its own internal cross-checking. Pantry checks, to see what is actually in a respondent's store cupboard, can be used as a check against what the respondent has previously claimed to be there.

It has been suggested that, to check the level of SDB in attitudinal data, friends of the respondents might be interviewed and asked to evaluate their perceptions of the respondents' attitudes. This seems fraught with difficulties regarding both the accuracy of the friends' evaluations and their motivations. The scale and complexity of such a study is, anyway, likely to make it impracticable for commercial market research projects (Sudman and Bradburn, 1982).

Checking against measures with known SDB

For attitudinal questions it is possible to design a battery of scales that measure a sample's tendency to SDB. Such a battery would include behaviours that are common (majority of the population) and socially undesirable; and behaviours that are not common (minority of the population) but are socially desirable.

Consistently low scores on the first group (indicating low levels of undesirable behaviour) and a high score on the second (indicating high levels of desirable behaviour) would suggest that the respondent either falls into a small and angelic minority of the population or that SDB exists in the responses. Individual respondents with these response patterns can be identified, and if on another topic the sample has a higher than expected level of claimed desirable behaviour or a lower level of claimed undesirable behaviour, the researcher knows that there is an SDB problem with the sample as a whole.

There are several published batteries of scales to help the questionnaire writer, including Edwards (1957), Crowne and Marlowe (1960) and Paulhus (Paulhus and Reid, 1991). In addition, shortened versions of the Crowne-Marlowe scale have been tested by Strahan and Gerbasi (1972) and by Greenwald and Satow (1970) that may be more suited to market research interviews.

Rating the question for social desirability

Questions can be included that directly ask the respondents to assess the attitude or behaviour for social desirability (Phillips and Clancy, 1972). This can indicate the relative problem between different scales or questions. However, there must be doubt about whether such questions do not suffer from SDB themselves.

Noting physiological manifestations of unease

It is likely that there will be physiological signs that a respondent is trying to mislead an interviewer, such as facial muscle movement, galvanic skin response and pupil dilation. However, interpreting these even in laboratory conditions is problematic and outside laboratory conditions is likely to be impossible and beyond the skill set of most market research interviewers.

It will be seen that there are few ways of eliminating SDB with certainty. However, if researchers recognize the possibility or even probability of its existence, this may help them to design questionnaires that minimize its occurrence and to avoid misinterpretation of the data.

16

International surveys

Introduction

This chapter looks at the issues relating to international surveys. The term 'international' is used to mean a study that is being carried out in one or more countries different to that of the originator. This can include multi-national studies that cover many countries, or it could be a study in one country only.

There are many issues regarding coordination of fieldwork and analysis that will not be gone into in depth here, except in so far as they impinge upon the writing of the questionnaire. Similarly, reporting issues will not be discussed in detail here.

International surveys encounter all of the issues discussed in previous chapters, together with a number of unique problems. In the home country, the questionnaire writer should understand the conventions, nuances and subtleties of the language used in that country. He or she might not understand these issues in another country, even where it uses the same language.

Where an international study has been conducted for a number of years, the questionnaire is likely to be already written, tried and trusted in all the appropriate languages. Similarly with proprietary techniques administered by research companies, the wording of questions will be largely predetermined and is likely to have been tested in most major languages. However, the survey coordinator should still be aware of the issues relating to questionnaires in multiple languages, as there are invariably some variations between every study. If these variations are mishandled or mistranslated, they could jeopardize the remainder of the study.

Client presence

If you are conducting a multinational study, then it is possible that the commissioning organization, or client, has a presence in most if not all of the countries that are to be covered. However, the extent and expertise of that presence may differ between countries, depending on the size and the nature of their operation there. If the research is to assist in determining whether or not the client should enter the country, there may be no presence. This is significant because the extent of the client's knowledge of each country and its market will affect the information that the questionnaire writer has about each country, and how it is similar to or different from the same market in other countries.

With a strong presence in each country it is likely that much is already known about the market, and certain assumptions can be made when writing the questionnaire. If little is known, the questionnaire may need to be more open in the way it addresses topics, because of the danger of making wrong assumptions. The amount that is known about each market will have an impact on the way in which the same approach can be adopted across countries.

Common or tailored approaches

When faced with the prospect of conducting a study across a number of countries the first issue is whether to write a separate questionnaire for each country or a single questionnaire that varies only on items such as brand lists. This can only be answered by examining the objectives of the study and the known or likely differences between the markets. Downham (Worcester and Downham, 1978) lists the following differences that can have an effect upon the questionnaire:

- *Language.* There may be different languages not only between countries but also within countries. Is it necessary to include all minority languages in all countries? Apparently common languages may have different usages, eg English in the UK and the United States.

- *Ethnic differences.* Different ethnic groups may speak different languages. Where they don't, they may have different consumer habits and attitudes.

- *Religion.* This may be associated with ethnic differences, but may have implications for attitudes, lifestyle and consumption of products such as alcohol and meat, for which different questions will be required both to make sense and not to offend.

- *Culture and tradition.* It would be wrong to ignore cultural differences, and questions must allow for the machismo culture in some Latin countries, the issue of 'face' in the Far East, and the different levels of importance given to gifting in different cultures. Behling and Law (2000) draw particular attention to the difficulties that different cultures bring to the willingness to share personal information; what behaviours, attitudes and aspirations are thought acceptable to discuss with a stranger; expressing abstract ideas and concepts in universally understood ways; and finding the correct terms in which to express intentions and aspirations.

- *Literacy.* Literacy levels vary between countries, and even official statistics can overstate it. Low literacy levels among the sample mean that aids such as verbal prompt material cannot be used, let alone self-completion questionnaires.

- *Geography and climate.* Differences in climate can mean that product usage patterns are different, particularly with regard to food products that are suited to either a warmer or cooler climate, such as butter and olive oil. Issues such as water hardness can also create different usage patterns for the same product.

- *Institutional factors.* Different market backgrounds often require different questions to be asked. Baths are more common than showers in some countries but rarely taken in others; approaches to clothes washing, savings and credit cards all vary between countries for reasons of history and market development.

- *Distribution.* Supermarkets, hypermarkets and shopping malls dominate distribution of many goods in some countries but are unknown in others, where different questions may be needed.

- *Media and advertising.* The media that carry advertising vary between countries and, even more so, the access to the media may vary.

- *Infrastructure.* Different infrastructures may have an impact on usage and attitudes. The greater use of communal heating systems in some countries than others, different transport systems, different stages of development in telecommunications, and different approaches to healthcare may all affect the way in which the questionnaire is written for different countries.

It may be relatively easy to have a common format for a brand awareness and image study in the pasta sauce market across a number of European countries, for example. The same spontaneous and prompted brand awareness questions can be used, and the same format used to determine brand images. The brand list will almost certainly vary between countries in most markets and the image dimensions measured may need sensitive adaptation, but the structure of the questionnaire can remain the same. There are a number of reasons, though, why the questionnaire approach may need to be different.

Different usage of product

In some product fields and markets a study may require completely different approaches for different countries. Some products are used in completely different ways in different parts of the world. For example, milk-based products that are used as night-time drinks in Europe are frequently used as aphrodisiacs or body-building products in parts of Africa and the West Indies, and razor blades are used to shear sheep in some parts of the world. It is unlikely that a single questionnaire could be used that would adequately describe the usage patterns of these products in all regions.

Different market segments

Market segments that exist in one country may not exist in another. Low and mid-priced Scotch whisky segments, which can account for the majority of the market in Western countries, may not exist in some Asian countries where only luxury brands are available. The usage questions and image dimensions that are appropriate for a market segment with a strong mid-priced segment of many brands may not be of any use in countries where the competitive set is not just Scotch but other high-priced luxury drinks.

Brands in different segments

Brands may be in different segments in different countries. This can happen in any market and is quite likely to happen in countries where distributors are independent of the manufacturer and who have historically been given the authority to position the brand as they wish. Brands that in one country would be considered mid-priced may elsewhere be luxury brands. Good market data and local knowledge should identify this type of difference.

For most clients and researchers, the more the same questions can be asked in all countries under study, the easier it is to manage, analyse and report the study and the more likely it is that the client can adopt a common marketing approach. There can therefore sometimes be considerable pressure on the survey designer and questionnaire writer to adopt a common approach and set of questions. The client may want to adopt a common marketing strategy, but the researcher would not be doing his or her job if the client was led to believe that the markets possessed only a number of common characteristics and was left unaware of the differences because they were not asked about. The biggest danger is the assumption that because a questionnaire has been used successfully in one country it can be used in any country.

Comparability

Where a common research approach is adopted across countries, there are many reasons to try to make the questionnaires, and hence the data output, as comparable as possible. Downham (Worcester and Downham, 1978) suggests that:

- Time and money are saved by using a standardized approach.
- Life is simplified for the researcher.
- End-users often have greater confidence in a standardized approach, rather than one that has many variations.
- Absolute uniformity is essential in some cases, particularly in the data required for the technical development of products.

Having a common questionnaire is also likely to lead to fewer errors in survey administration than if there are a number of different ones. Given these reasons, most organizations would agree that a standardized questionnaire is always preferable and should be used unless there are good reasons why it would not be suitable for a particular country or group of countries.

One approach to writing questionnaires for a multi-country study is to start by writing the questionnaire with one country in mind. Once that has been refined, it should be tested for its appropriateness in every country in which it is to be used, even those sharing a common language. Amendments should then be made to accommodate differences between markets. This may require changes only in the brand lists, but it may also require changes in image dimensions, advertising media and prompts used, methods of distribution in the market, absolute prices, relative prices, the competitive product set, frequency of use bands, or completely different behavioural questions. The researcher can reach a point where the changes are so significant that it becomes a different questionnaire.

Coordinating common elements

Even if it is possible to conduct a study using a standard questionnaire across a number of different countries, there will nearly always be minor variations to be accommodated.

Brand lists

Almost invariably the brand list will change in most consumer markets. There may be local brands that are available only in that country or region, and the multinational companies may sell different brands in different countries. Some brands of Scotch whisky, for example, are sold only in the Asia Pacific region. Others only have a significant level of distribution in a small number of European countries. The brand list in many product sectors is unlikely to be the same in any two countries.

The questionnaire writer needs to be aware of these differences, which will affect the brand lists used both as pre-codes and as prompts for questions such as brand awareness, purchase and usage.

Brand image

Brand image questions are frequently asked of a small number of brands deemed to be important either in the market or in the direct competitive set to the client's brand. Even if the long list of brands available is similar in two countries, the short list of brands that are the most relevant to be asked about in image and brand-positioning questions may vary between countries.

Frequently the client will be able to advise on the appropriate brands for each country both for the long and the short lists. This may come from the company's marketing plans for each country and from the company's office, representatives or distributors. It is always worthwhile to check the list with local representatives, who may be aware of new local brands that have not yet made it into the company's global marketing strategy. It is also worthwhile for the research agency to ask its own representatives in each country for their views on the brand lists, for the same reason.

Image dimensions

Frequently the objective is to produce a single, global, brand image map on which variations between countries can be plotted. If insufficient care is taken in choosing the image dimensions relevant to each country, this can result in a misleading picture being produced for some countries.

To achieve the ideal set of image dimensions the researcher should determine all the relevant image dimensions for each country, bearing in mind that the positioning and the competitors could be different. A preliminary stage of qualitative research to explore the way in which consumers in each country perceive the market and the brands in it can be used to give the most appropriate image dimensions for each country. For studies across many countries, however, this is frequently too costly and time-consuming to carry out. Findings from qualitative research that has already been conducted in a country for other purposes can often be used to provide a consumer-led picture of the market structure and brand perceptions. If that does not exist, reliance will sometimes be placed on qualitative research carried out in a few countries that are thought to be representative of a group of countries. Where this occurs, it is particularly important to pilot the questionnaire in the countries in which no qualitative research was carried out.

However it is arrived at, a distillation of all relevant image attributes across the countries in the study can be compiled to form a 'master set' of image dimensions. If the intention is to use a technique such as correspondence analysis to produce a global map, all image dimensions may have to be used in all countries regardless of their relevance. There is a danger that the list, in trying to accommodate the key points for each country without becoming overlong, will contain too many compromises. While it will provide a global overview, it will not be sufficiently detailed to provide an accurate positioning in any one country. Supplementary questions specific to each country may be required for that to be achieved.

Attitudinal questions

Attitudinal questions can sometimes be difficult in maintaining comparability between countries. Not only may consumers have different attitudes to a market or product area in different countries, but what is important to them in arriving at those attitudes may also be completely different.

Frequently the attitude dimensions to be measured should be the same in each country, although with the expectation that response patterns will be very different between countries. If a battery of attitudinal rating scales is to be used, the wording of each dimension must be appropriate for each country, and care must be taken to avoid offence in relation to both cultural and religious attitudes.

Translating the questionnaire

Accurate translations are, of course, essential. But an accurate translation is not simply one that is literally accurate. Translations must be carried out sensitively so that meanings, shades of meaning and nuances are accurately retained.

Forsyth *et al* (2007) advocate a five-step process which they used when translating questionnaires from English into a range of Asian languages:

1 translation – using professional translators;

2 review;

3 initial adjudication to propose revision using bi-lingual adjudicators;

4 cognitive interview pre-test;

5 final review and adjudication.

Such a translate-test-review process represents the ideal for all multi-lingual projects, to tease out the nuances and shades of meaning that can ruin comparability between languages.

Possibly the most difficult to translate, with the greatest nuances and shades of meaning, are brand image and positioning statements, and attitude dimensions. There may be fine but clear distinctions in one language that cannot be translated into another. In English there is a clear difference of understanding between 'old-fashioned' and 'traditional'. In some languages this distinction cannot be made. Other words for which there may be no direct equivalent in certain languages include 'arrogant', 'rigid', 'proud' and 'ordinary'. The word 'warm' is frequently used as a brand image descriptor in English, to describe the warmth and affection of the relationship between brand and consumer. However, it is not infrequently translated into other languages as something equivalent to 'mildly hot'.

Even interviewer instructions can be ruined by a translator who is too literal and inexperienced in the language of market research. The instruction to 'Skip to Q5' has been seen translated as 'Run to Q5', and 'Probe fully' turned into an instruction to poke the respondent with a stick.

For all of these reasons initial translations should be carried out by people who understand the research process and the importance of capturing the sentiment rather than a literal translation. Oppenheim (1992) quotes the case where a question asking whether a house had 'running water', translated literally into other languages, was taken in some countries to mean having a stream or river running through the house. Wright and Crimp (2000) quote how 'out of sight, out of mind' became 'invisible, insane' in Mandarin Chinese.

Using native speakers

There are a number of different routes to achieving a good translation. Probably the most important step is for the first translation to be carried out by a native speaker of the language.

Native speakers are the most likely to understand the nuances of the language as they are understood by other native speakers. Many multinational research companies employ multilingual research executives or other members of staff who are from other countries. Forsyth et al (2007) advocate the use of professional translators, but they should also have some knowledge of the survey process if they are to avoid mistranslation of research terms.

However, native speakers living abroad may, depending on how long they have lived there, be out of touch with changes in the language as it is spoken locally. Subtle changes of meaning can occur with fashion or with a new usage. It is therefore important to have the translation checked by someone living in the country. The most likely candidate for this is someone in the agency that is going to be responsible for the fieldwork, provided that the person also has a good knowledge of the language in which the questionnaire was originally written.

A study is at a disadvantage if there is no fieldwork to be carried out locally (because it is being carried out online or by telephone from another country), as there is a lack of opportunity for local input. For such studies, it is worth finding someone resident in the country who will check the translation for usage of current language. This is becoming an increasingly common issue, with the growing use of multi-country and multi-language web-based internet studies. The multinational research companies, with offices around the world on which they can call for this, have an advantage in this respect.

Seen in print

This was seen in the English language version of a customer satisfaction questionnaire in a German hotel.

Please rate the following aspects of the restaurant from 1 to 5, where 1 is not at all satisfactory and 5 is very satisfactory.

	1	2	3	4	5
The quality of the food	–	–	–	–	–
The speed of the service	–	–	–	–	–
The table	–	–	–	–	–

Did they really mean the table itself, the workmanship that went into it, or the position of the table in the restaurant, or did they mean the food upon it? A native speaker might have queried what this question really meant.

Using the client's representative

If possible, the local representative of the client in each country should also check the translation. Local representatives may have had direct or indirect input to the questionnaire writer's understanding of the structure of the market in the country. They should be aware of any variations in technical terminology in the local market that the research-led translator may not know about. It may also be important to get local representatives' 'buy-in' to the questionnaire, if they are going to be responsible for implementing action that arises as a result of the research project. If they are not happy with the questionnaire, they may be less willing to implement the study's findings.

Back-translation

Finally, the questionnaire should be back-translated into the original language. This can show up changes in meaning, although it has to be determined whether they arise from the original translation or from the back-translation.

The process described here is what should ideally happen. However, it is quite possible for some of these steps to be omitted, depending on the ability of the translators and whether the questionnaire has been used before. It must not be overlooked that in some countries translation into a number of different languages and dialects will be necessary. Advice should be taken from the local client and research organizations as to how many and which languages are required. In a country such as India, for example, this can be a complex issue.

Demographic data

One area that often causes difficulty is the classification of demographic data. Many countries subscribe to a social-grade classification system that uses a grouping system described as A, B, etc. There the similarity often ends, with the number of groups and their definitions differing widely. The UK has a six-grade system (A, B, C1, C2, D, E), Ireland a seven-grade system (A, B, C1, C2, D, E, F) and India an eight-grade system (A1, A2, B1, B2, C, D, E1, E2). Many developing countries have no commonly acknowledged system of social-grade classification, and local researchers may all have their own approach. Level of education may be used as a surrogate for social grading or to complement it, but education systems similarly vary between countries. Terminal education age is something that can be measured in a consistent way between countries, but its implications are likely to be very different.

Alternatively, a measurement of living standards can be obtained by asking about ownership of durables. That too must be tailored to the local situation. Ownership of a moped, fridge or TV may indicate a very different level of social grade in, say, Vietnam and Germany.

Cultural response differences

In some cultures, people are more prepared to criticize than in others. In India, for example, it is considered rude to be critical of someone else's work. Responses to rating scales therefore tend to be more positive than in many other countries. Within Europe, as a rule people in Latin countries will tend to give higher ratings than in Nordic countries. Puleston and Eggers (2012) demonstrated high levels of acquiescence bias in India, but relatively low levels in Japan/Korea, North America and Northern Europe, with Southern and Eastern Europe in between. Similarly they found a much stronger propensity to 'like' something in India and South America than in Japan and Northern Europe.

Some researchers address the issue in the questionnaire, particularly where there are strong differences because the study includes both Western and Asiatic countries. One way is to use scales that have positive responses only. Thus a scale might run from 'very good' to 'fair', or a set of smiley faces might have five positive smiles of different sizes and no frowns or negative smiles. Alternatively, scales can be extended to 10 or 11 points with five positive responses to increase the discrimination, or extended numeric scales can be used to try to minimize the sense of criticizing by avoiding negative words.

Roster *et al* (2006) showed that the use of extreme points on scales can also vary between countries. This means that although the same question may be asked in several countries, the resulting data may not be directly comparable. Puleston and Eggers (2012) demonstrated that in their online surveys, respondents in India, China and South America were about twice as likely to agree to Likert scale questions as were respondents in Northern Europe and Japan.

The extent of the bias will vary depending on the types of questions being asked and the researcher must be careful not to rule out real differences between markets as being caused by cultural response differences. It may be possible to calculate compensation factors within a survey by asking questions with known responses, such as whether respondents were born in a particular month, and estimating the amount of overclaim from that. Such questions will need careful consideration at the time of questionnaire writing.

Another approach, cited by Wable and Pall (1998), is to use a 'warm-up' statement that distances the researcher from the product or advertisement being researched, so allowing the respondent to feel more able to criticize. This is a technique commonly used in qualitative research that they have transferred to quantitative questionnaires. They quote a typical warm-up as: 'I would like your frank opinion about this ad. You don't have to necessarily say nice things about it. Please feel free to give us any positive or negative opinion. We have not made this ad, so we will not feel bad if you don't have nice things to say about it.' They have shown that in India this has a measurable effect in reducing the level of positive comment, although it is not known whether it is sufficient to make the results directly comparable with all other countries.

Laying out the questionnaire

Where paper questionnaires are to be used the issue arises of how differences between the layouts can be minimized. This is generally desirable if the questionnaire is broadly common to all countries.

Layout conventions

However, it is also important that local agencies use their own layout conventions where these differ. Mistakes are more likely to be made by interviewers if they are presented with an unfamiliar layout. Where a co-ordinating agency e-mails a laid-out questionnaire to the local agency, it may be necessary to instruct the local agency staff to lay it out in their own format. Because it is easy to use the coordinating agency's file and simply type over the text in the local language, the interviewers may be presented with a completely unfamiliar style of layout. A further disadvantage of this is that the local agency executives do not become as familiar with the questionnaire as they would have done if they had had to lay it out for themselves. They are then less likely to spot unsuitable wording or be able to answer questions that may arise in the field.

Question numbering

A common question numbering scheme helps comparisons to be made easily for the same questions across countries. When the same question is being referred to there is a potential source of error if that question has a different number in each country. Checking of routeing instructions is also more straightforward if the same question numbers are used. However, a common question numbering scheme can mean that some question numbers are not used in some versions of the questionnaire. For example, where an additional question needs to be asked in one country only, that question number will not appear on questionnaires for all the other countries in the study. This must be clearly marked on the questionnaires or it can cause confusion amongst interviewers. If there are so many missing question numbers that it creates difficulties for the interviewers to follow instructions, then consideration must be given to abandoning common question numbering for the sake of minimizing interviewer error.

Similar issues arise where manual data entry utilizes a column-based format. To minimize data-processing errors, a common column-number and response code format is desirable. That decision, though, needs to be balanced against the likelihood of it leading to data entry errors.

APPENDIX 1
Example questionnaire

Introduction

The following, fictitious, case study is designed to demonstrate some of the techniques used in questionnaire design. The questionnaire has been written for this purpose rather than to meet precisely the objectives of the study, and deliberately includes examples of poor practice. It therefore should not be taken as a template for this particular type of project.

The output includes a flow diagram to show how the questionnaire is constructed, a discussion of each question, and the questionnaire itself.

Setting the scene

Crianlarich Scotch whisky is positioned as a brand for the off-trade, ie to be sold through off-licences and supermarkets and drunk principally at home. It has recently launched a marketing initiative to break into the on-trade business. The company is planning a press advertising campaign in England and Wales that will run for six months, appearing in a variety of newspapers and magazines. The aim of the campaign is to back a marketing initiative where pubs and bars are being encouraged to sell Crianlarich.

It is sold as a cheaper brand on the proposition that it is the brand drunk by the Scots, which is believed to be a key motivator of brand choice in this market, although this has not previously been researched.

The main competition is thought to be Grand Prix (another fictitious brand), which is expected to be advertising at the same time as Crianlarich.

The company wishes to conduct a study that will measure the position of the brand in the market and provide feedback on the success of the advertising campaign.

A pre-post advertising study has been designed. The research sample definition is all adults who have drunk whisky in the past month and who drink it at least once every three months. The objectives of the research are defined by the Marketing Director of Crianlarich as:

- to determine awareness of Crianlarich;
- to determine whether awareness of the brand changes over the course of the advertising campaign;

- to determine the perceptions of the brand on key product and image dimensions, and any change in those perceptions over the course of the advertising campaign;
- to determine the importance of the brand's key advertising proposition, that it is a brand drunk by Scots;
- to measure all of the above among both light and heavy off-trade Scotch whisky drinkers.

The same questionnaire will be used at both pre- and post-advertising stages of research. The pre-advertising stage will provide an initial measure of the brand's position prior to the campaign and the post-advertising stage a measure of how that has changed over the period of the advertising.

Questionnaire planning

To meet the objectives, the key measures that we need to establish are:

- *Spontaneous brand awareness of Crianlarich and key competitors.* This tells us how 'front of mind' the brand is compared to other brands. As one of the objectives of the campaign is to improve awareness, this will be an important measure to compare before and after the campaign.
- *Prompted brand awareness for Crianlarich and key competitors.* This measure relates to how well known the brand is, and tells us how many people in the market have still not heard of it. This is an important measure for new brands in a market, as they establish recognition. For established brands prompted brand awareness is already likely to be high and so unlikely to change greatly over the course of a single campaign.
- *Brand image perceptions.* These need to be related to the objectives of the campaign, so that we can measure any change in image perceptions over the campaign period. They need to be measured for Crianlarich and five other brands, including several brands that are more expensive. The purpose of measuring so many other brands is so that we can map the market and determine whether or not consumers perceive Crianlarich and Grand Prix, the brand we believe to be its closest competitor, as a sector distinct from the leading brands. The approaches to be considered are:
  - monadic rating of brands either on semantic differential or Likert (agree-disagree) scales;
  - brand image association.

  The brand image association technique is adopted because it is less time-consuming with this number of brands. A rating scale approach would have allowed only three brands to be rated by each respondent – Crianlarich and two competitors. Thus the competitor brands would have to have been rotated between respondents and measured on a reduced sample size, which we want to avoid.

- *Image importance.* We could derive the importance of the image dimensions to brand choice by correlation analysis. However, we want to be able to cross-analyse respondents to whom price is an important factor in their choice so as to determine their attitudes to and level of use of Crianlarich. A direct approach is therefore to be used. A constant sum allocation of 11 points between two dimensions has been chosen.

- *Behavioural information* on weight of drinking both on- and off-licence, and whether the respondent is influential in brand choice, is required for analysis purposes. Which brand or brands are bought is also required, for measurement, to see if it changes over the course of the campaign, and for analysis purposes.

- *Awareness of Crianlarich advertising* needs to be measured at a number of different levels, to determine whether or not respondents have seen or have remembered the advertising. How well the advertisement is branded will be measured by showing an unbranded ad for Crianlarich and for a competitor as a benchmark.

The question areas appear in the following order:

- screening questions;
- spontaneous brand awareness;
- spontaneous brands recall seeing advertised;
- prompted brand awareness;
- advertising awareness prompted by brand name;
- advertising source and content recall;
- behavioural information – where drunk, brands bought or specified, amount drunk;
- importance of image factors in brand choice;
- brand image associations;
- recognition of unbranded ads, with branding question;
- classification data.

Spontaneous awareness questions are asked first, before there has been any prompting of brand names. Behavioural questions come before brand image questions to avoid any tendency to distort behaviour in line with image perceptions. Showing advertising material comes last, to avoid influencing responses to the brand image questions.

Example questionnaire

Following is a description of each question, and why and how it is used. The wording of questions sometimes varies between the face-to-face and online questionnaires. The question numbers refer to the face-to-face paper questionnaire and the online questionnaires that follow.

The paper questionnaire is set out in columns for data entry into an analysis program that uses a column-based format. While common in market research, this type of analysis format is not universal. This is not required for the online questionnaire where data entry is built into the script.

Screening questionnaire

QA.

Face-to-face

SHOW CARD A.

Do you or anybody in your household work in any of the industries or professions on this card?

Online

Do you or anybody in your household work in any of these industries?

Following the introduction, QA is the security question designed to screen out anyone who works, or whose household members work, in key industries, as their responses could distort responses from those of the research universe as a whole or because knowledge of the content of the survey could provide a competitive advantage.

Although we are only interested in screening out people in the three sensitive industries (alcoholic drinks, advertising and marketing), a range of other industries is also offered. This disguises our interest somewhat, although as we have already said that the survey is about alcoholic drinks this is less than perfect. Just as important, it provides something to respond to for people who do not work in the three sensitive industries. Some people, trying to be helpful, may bend the truth somewhat and claim to have connections with one of whatever options are offered, no matter how distant or tenuous the link. Without the alternatives, they are more likely to be screened out unnecessarily, and an interview lost.

QB.

Face-to-face

SHOW CARD B.

Which of the products on this card have you drunk in the last three months either in licensed premises such as a restaurant, pub or bar, or at home or anywhere else?

Online

Which of these have you drunk in the last three months?
That could have been in licensed premises such a bar, pub or restaurant, at home or anywhere else.

QB is the first of the screening questions proper. Again our specific interest is disguised by offering a range of drinks that might have been consumed. If we asked 'Do you drink Scotch whisky?', this would allow potential respondents to second-guess our purpose and answer on the basis that they believed they were screening themselves in or out of eligibility rather than on actual behaviour.

The list offered is not extensive or exhaustive. This is because Scotch whisky may be an irregular or occasional drink for some of our research universe. If given too many options, these people may think of their more frequently consumed drinks first and fail to mention Scotch whisky. This would result in under-representation of light Scotch whisky drinkers in the sample.

Irish whiskey is included in the list shown. This is to ensure that drinkers of only Irish whiskey do not think that the term 'Scotch whisky' is meant to cover all types of whisky and so claim to drink it when they do not.

QC.

Face-to-face

SHOW CARD C.

Which of the phrases on this card best describes how often you drink Scotch whisky?

Online

How often do you drink Scotch whisky?

QC is an example of a scale question. Our interest is in determining whether the respondent drinks Scotch whisky more or less often than once every three months. The question could ask that directly. We don't use a direct question, partly again to disguise the precise point of our interest to stop people trying to opt in or out of the survey. Here, though, the subject matter could lead to some social desirability bias. Later in the interview we will ask in more detail about how much respondents drink, and the tendency may be for heavier drinkers deliberately to understate their consumption. The categories shown in this question already begin to suggest that drinking Scotch whisky several times a week is acceptable, hopefully encouraging heavier drinkers to be honest later on.

Main questionnaire

Q1.

Face-to-face

What brands of whisky can you think of? Please name as many as you can think of.

Online

What brands of whisky can you think of? Please type in as many as you can think of.

Q1 is a spontaneous question with no prompting. The interviewer is reminded not to prompt.

We are not interested in the precise wording used by respondents to describe the brands. If someone says 'Grand Prix', then that is all we need to know about what they have said. Therefore, the question does not have to be open-ended with verbatim recording of answers, and a pre-coded list can be supplied. This makes recording easier for the interviewer and for later processing of the data. The pre-coded list contains all of the brands that we believe are the most likely to be given. However, many more brands exist than we are able to put on the list, so space is provided for the interviewer to write in any others mentioned.

The brand Johnnie Walker has two main sub-brands – Red Label and Black Label. Respondents may specify the sub-brands or they may say just 'Johnnie Walker'. There is no prompting at this question so if someone says just 'Johnnie Walker' without specifying the sub-brand, we must accept that. A code is provided for that eventuality.

The first brand that is mentioned is recorded separately from the remaining brands. The respondent is not told this. By recording in this way we can provide a 'top-of-mind' measure as well as a measure of total spontaneous awareness.

A code is provided for 'None' but not for 'Don't know', as a 'Don't know' answer would mean 'None' in the context of this question.

Note the inclusion of Jack Daniel's, which is not a Scotch whisky. We know from experience that a significant number of respondents will say this, even though it is incorrect. It is therefore included partly to monitor the level of misattribution, and partly to reduce the amount of coding that would be incurred if it were to be written in under 'Other answers'.

Online, we require respondents to enter verbatim the brands that they can think of, as to present a list of brands would be to prompt. This can be an open text box, or a series of boxes to record the brands in order.

Q2.

Face-to-face

Which brands of whisky have you seen or heard advertised anywhere recently?

Online

Which brands of whisky have you seen or heard advertised anywhere recently?
Please type in as many as you can think of.

Q2 is another spontaneous question and uses the same list of pre-codes as Q1 for the face-to-face questionnaire. Online responses are again typed in verbatim.

There are three key phrases in this question. The phrase 'seen or heard' is used and not just 'seen'. Including the word 'heard' allows respondents to include radio advertising, which might otherwise be excluded from their consideration. Advertising recall tends to be dominated by TV. Including the word 'anywhere' indicates to the respondent that the advertising could have been in any media. We might have considered including the phrase 'on TV or anywhere else' in place of 'anywhere', specifically to encourage respondents to think of other media. However, there is a limited amount of Scotch whisky advertising on TV and this might have had the opposite effect of drawing attention to the few brands that do use that medium. The word 'recently' leaves it to respondents to define the time period to which the question refers. This can be dangerous, as some respondents may take it to mean the last six months and others the last week. However, most respondents will try to think of all the advertising for Scotch whisky that is stored in their mind, which usually (but not always) excludes anything that is very old.

Q3.

Face-to-face

SHOW CARD D.

Which of the brands of whisky on this card have you heard of?
Please include any that you have already mentioned.

Online

Which of these have you heard of? Please include any that you have already given.

In Q3 we are seeking prompted brand awareness. The list is shortened for the face-to-face questionnaire, consisting mainly of the brands in which we are principally interested as competitors to Crianlarich. Note that Jack Daniel's is not included, although is in the list of pre-codes for the spontaneous question. The prompt list includes the most salient brands in the market, whether or not they are seen as direct competitors. If these were omitted, respondents might overclaim awareness of smaller brands in order to appear knowledgeable.

The brand list on the show card will be rotated between respondents or, more likely, between interviewers in face-to-face interviewing. It should be rotated four ways, so that the brands in the middle of the list are also presented at the beginning and end in some versions, to equalize the primacy and recency effects. On the web-based questionnaire the order will be presented in a random order for each respondent.

Note that respondents are asked to include any brands they have already mentioned; without this reminder many will omit some of the previously mentioned brands. This is not necessarily a problem, as responses can be edited or recoded from the spontaneous question at the analysis stage. However, in this case, we need to take into account those who answered

'Johnnie Walker' at Q1 without specifying a sub-brand. Having given 'Johnnie Walker' once they may not say it again, but we want to encourage them to specify the sub-brands if they are aware of them.

In the online questionnaire brands will be presented in a random order for each respondent, except that the two Johnnie Walker brands will always appear adjacent to each other. If they are separated in the list there is a danger of satisficing, that is a respondent accepting the first Johnnie Walker variant he or she sees whether or not it is the one he or she was thinking of.

One possibility here would have been to show pack shots for each of the brands. This would give greater certainty that the brands nominated really were the brands thought of. However, for reasons given at Q24 we have chosen not to do this. In some markets, where there may be greater confusion between brands, sub-brands and variants than here, showing pack shots may have been of greater benefit for this question.

The set of brands that the respondent is aware of here becomes the set shown to them in later questions where brand lists are used in the online questionnaire.

Q4.

Face-to-face

SHOW CARD D.

Which of the brands of whisky on this card have you seen or heard advertised anywhere recently? Again please include any that you have already mentioned.

Online

Which of these have you seen or heard advertised anywhere recently? Please include any that you have already given.

Q4 is similar to Q3, this time asking for awareness of advertising. This question acts as a filter to route respondents to the following questions.

Q5.

IF CRIANLARICH MENTIONED AT Q4.

Face-to-face

Where did you see or hear advertising for Crianlarich?

Online.

Where did you see or hear advertising for Crianlarich?

This question is asked only of respondents who claim to have seen or heard advertising for Crianlarich at Q4. With the paper questionnaire the interviewer must follow this instruction. With the electronic questionnaires the routeing will be specified to occur automatically.

The question is not prompted in the face-to-face interview, although a list of pre-codes is supplied, but is prompted in the web interview. This is to avoid using too many open-ended questions in the web interview, unless they are clearly necessary (eg brand and advertising awareness). The fact that the question is not spontaneous for the web interview may encourage respondents to code more answers, as the pre-code list jogs their memory and suggests where they may have seen or heard advertising.

In all cases there is a potential ambiguity in the response list, which must be avoided. Many newspapers include a magazine supplement once a week. If the response list included only 'magazines' and 'newspapers' it would be unclear as to where newspaper magazines should be coded. By including 'newspaper (including magazine supplement)' we hope to avoid that ambiguity.

Q6.

IF CRIANLARICH MENTIONED AT Q4.

Face-to-face

Please describe to me everything that you can remember about the advertising for Crianlarich. PROBE: What was it about? What did it say or show? PROBE: What else?

Online

What can you remember about the advertising for Crianlarich?
Please type in as much detail as possible.

Q6 seeks both to confirm that what the respondent remembers really was advertising for Crianlarich and not for another brand, and to determine what the salient points are that have consciously remained with the respondent, in terms of either content or message. We should also consider whether we want to include a specific question to ask what was the main point or message the advertising was trying to convey, in case this is not elicited under probing here.

This is an open question with the answers recorded verbatim. Face-to-face, the interviewers will record these; on the web, the respondents must type in the response for themselves.

Q7.

IF GRAND PRIX MENTIONED AT Q4.

Face-to-face

Where did you see or hear advertising for Grand Prix?

Online.

Where did you see or hear advertising for Grand Prix?

Q8.

IF GRAND PRIX MENTIONED AT Q4.

Face-to-face

Please describe to me everything that you can remember about the advertising for Grand Prix. PROBE: What was it about? What did it say or show?

Online

What can you remember about the advertising for Grand Prix?
Please type in as much detail as possible.

Q7 and Q8 repeat Q5 and Q6 for Grand Prix. This provides a benchmark for levels of advertising recall that Crianlarich should expect from a brand believed to have a similar-sized advertising budget, and also to determine the success of Crianlarich's main competitor in its advertising.

Q9.

ASK ALL.

Face-to-face

Do you drink whisky only on licensed premises such as a restaurant, pub or bar, or only at home or someone else's home, or do you drink it both on licensed premises and at home?

Online.

Where do you drink whisky?

Q9 is a routeing question designed to identify respondents as in-home and/or out-of-home drinkers for subsequent questions. This question is also the start of a funnelling process that will end in determining the brands bought for consumption.

Note that the question does not ask about 'on-licence' and 'off-licence' consumption, as these terms may not be understood by all respondents, but asks about drinking 'at home'.

The question as worded presents a dilemma for the layout of the paper questionnaire. Listing the pre-codes in the same order as they appear in the question helps the interviewer to find the correct response code more easily. However, the routeing from this question is easier for the interviewer to follow if the two 'off-licence' codes and the two 'on-licence' codes are adjacent. That could have been achieved by having 'both' as the middle one of the pre-codes.

Note that the online question is shorter and uses the response codes to define the question.

Q10.

IF DRINKS AT ALL ON LICENSED PREMISES.

Face-to-face

How many glasses of Scotch whisky would you say you drank in the last seven days before today in pubs, bars or restaurants? By glasses I mean single pub measures.

Online

How many glasses of Scotch whisky did you drink in the last seven days before today in pubs, bars or restaurants?
A glass is a single pub measure.

Q10 is a numeric question. Note that the question specifies 'the last seven days before today', rather than 'in the last week', which might have raised ambiguities as to exactly what was meant, eg this could have been interpreted as meaning since seven days ago, or since the beginning of this week, or during the whole of the last complete week.

As the sample consists of people who have drunk Scotch whisky in the last month we must expect that a significant proportion will not have drunk any Scotch whisky in the last seven days. However, we can only ask what the respondents are competent to answer, and to provide details of weight of consumption over the last month would be beyond the capacity of most people's memory for this product field (particularly if they drink a lot!)

There is a risk here of social desirability bias, with some respondents deliberately under-reporting their consumption. Rather than ask for precise numbers of glasses we could have prompted the respondent with a list of ranges, say '0; 1 to 3; 4 to 8; 9 to 15; ...'. This would have required less of a feat of memory from respondents and, if the ranges went sufficiently high, say to 50-plus glasses, could have encouraged heavier drinkers to be more truthful.

Precise numbers as requested are not necessary for the researcher's purposes here. Responses separated into ranges would have given sufficient information to categorize the sample into heavy and light drinkers.

In the online questionnaire the definition of a glass is moved to below the question so as not to present a single large block of text.

Q11.

IF DRINKS OFF-LICENCE AT Q9.

Face-to-face

How many glasses of whisky would you say you drank at home, either in your own home or in anyone else's, in the last seven days? By glasses I mean the equivalent of a single measure in a pub.

Online.

How many glasses of Scotch whisky did you drink in the last seven days before today at home? That could be at your own home or someone else's.

Q11 repeats Q10 for off-licence drinking. With a respondent who drinks Scotch whisky on-licence, and has therefore answered Q10, interviewers using a paper questionnaire must check back to Q9 to determine whether they should ask Q11 or skip to Q23. An interviewer error here could mean the loss of a significant amount of data.

Q12.

IF DRINKS OFF-LICENCE.

Face-to-face

Do you drink Scotch whisky in your own home, in someone else's home or both?

Online

Whose home do you drink Scotch whisky in?

Q12 is a further funnelling question designed to identify people who drink Scotch whisky in their own home, to lead on to the brand or brands bought. Again, the online question uses fewer words and uses the response codes to define the parameters of the question.

Q13.

IF DRINKS AT HOME.

Face-to-face

Do you yourself usually buy the Scotch to drink at home or does someone else usually buy it for you?

Online

Who usually buys the Scotch that you drink at home?

Q13 is another funnelling question to determine whether the respondent is the actual purchaser.

Although not included in the question, 'given as a gift' is included in the list of pre-codes in anticipation that this will be the most common 'other answer', and we wish to minimize the number of unspecified 'other answers'.

Q14.

IF SOMEONE ELSE BUYS.

Face-to-face

Do you have a say in which brand of Scotch whisky they buy or do they decide, or do they always buy the same brand?

Online

Who decides which brand is bought?

Q14 is one more funnelling question to determine whether respondents exercise any brand choice if they are not the purchaser.

There is ambiguity in the routeing here from Q13. The purpose is to identify respondents with no brand choice, so we only need to ask this where someone else usually buys the Scotch. However, 'someone else' appears in two of the responses listed at Q13. To ensure that interviewers do not make a routeing error, an additional instruction to indicate the precise code is included in the paper questionnaire.

We anticipate that there will be households where the same brand is always bought and the respondent will see this as no brand choice being exercised. Without this as an option, the list of answers would be incomplete and cause these respondents difficulty in answering within the frame of the question.

Online, we seek to reduce the number of words in the question and the response options are consequently altered to provide more information.

Q15.

IF ALWAYS BUYS THE SAME BRAND.

Face-to-face

Which brand do they buy?

Online

Which brand do they buy?

Q15 is a spontaneous question in the face-to-face interview, so we use the longer list of brands as used at Q1, to minimize the number of written-in 'other answers'.

Online we use the set of brands that the respondent is aware of. This therefore may prompt slightly different responses. However, the danger would be greater if this was a multiple response question, when the list might remind the respondent of more brands than would be remembered without it. As this is a single response question that is not a danger.

Note that Jack Daniel's appears in the paper and CAPI versions where the respondent receives no prompting but it might be given, and not in the web version where the brands are prompted, as we do not want to suggest it is a Scotch whisky.

Q16.

IF KNOWS WHICH BRAND IS BOUGHT.

Face-to-face

Did you decide to always buy that brand, or was that someone else's decision, or a decision made by both of you?

Online

Who decided to always buy [INSERT BRAND FROM Q15]?

At Q16, having established which brand is bought, we try again to determine who the original decision maker was.

The 'Don't know' code is combined with 'Can't remember'. From this question, respondents who always buy the same brand skip to Q23. Online, we are able to reduce the number of words and insert the brand that was given at Q15.

Q17.

IF HAVE NO SAY AT Q14.

Face-to-face

Which brands do they buy? Which others?

Online

Which brands do they buy? Please tick all that apply.

Q17 is asked of those who have no influence on brand choice at Q14. More than one response is allowed here, as we want to establish the repertoire of brands bought. This is not prompted in the face-to-face interview but is in the online questionnaire. We may find, therefore, that a larger repertoire of brands is reported online than face-to-face.

Q18.

IF MORE THAN ONE BRAND BOUGHT.

Face-to-face

Which brand, if any, do they buy most often?

Online

Which of these brands, if any, do they buy most often?

If there is more than one brand in the repertoire, we now try to isolate the brand bought most often for drinking at home at Q18. One response only is allowed here. Online, only the brands given at Q17 are shown.

Note we must not assume that there will be one brand that is bought more often than any other, which is conveyed in the question by the phrase 'if any'. Without that phrase, respondents may feel that they have to nominate a brand even if there is no 'most often' brand. The list of pre-codes includes a category for 'No most often brand'.

Q19.

IF BUY IT MYSELF AT Q13 OR HAVE A SAY AT Q14.

Face-to-face

Is there one brand that you buy/ask for (AS APPROPRIATE) more often than any other?

Online

Is there one brand that you [buy – IF BUY MYSELF AT Q13, ask for – IF HAVE A SAY AT Q14] more often than any other?

For efficiency Q19 appears on the paper questionnaire as it is here, and the interviewer is expected to use the words 'buy' and 'ask for' as appropriate for purchasers and specifiers respectively. With electronic CAPI and online versions of the questionnaire, purchasers and specifiers can be routed to a version of the question that is worded appropriately.

Questions 19 to 22 are designed to establish the brand repertoire and 'most often' brand where the respondent is the usual purchaser or is the brand specifier. However, the question sequence is different to that asked in questions 17 and 18. In the previous section the interview established the repertoire first and then the 'most often' brand. Here it establishes the 'most often' brand first and then asks for other brands bought to establish the brand repertoire. Inconsistent sequencing of questions like this is to be avoided.

The different sequences are likely to result in different responses and make it difficult to combine data from the two sets of questions to provide an overall brand repertoire. Even where it is felt that the two sets of data are sufficiently comparable to be combined, the differences in the questions increase the likelihood of data-processing errors occurring. The second sequence requires four questions compared to two in the first sequence, so is less efficient. There is also more filtering of respondents through different question routes, so increasing the possibility of interviewer error on paper questionnaires or of a questionnaire programming error with electronic questionnaires.

Q20.

IF YES AT Q19.

Face-to-face

Which brand is that?

Online

Which brand is that?

Q20 establishes which brand is bought most often. As it is a spontaneous question in the face-to-face interview the code list is again the longer list of brands to minimize the number of 'other answers' written in. Online the reduced set of 'brands aware of' is shown.

Q21.

IF YES AT Q19.

Face-to-face

Which other brands, if any, do you buy at all?

Online

Which other brands, if any, do you buy at all?

Q21 is, again, a spontaneous response question in the face-to-face interview, so the longer brand list is used on the questionnaire. Online the set of 'brands aware of' is shown minus the brand given at Q20.

Q22.

IF NO AT Q19.

Face-to-face

Which brands have you bought in the last six months?

Online

Which brands have you bought in the last six months?

One of the inefficiencies of the approach adopted for questions 19 to 22 is that a separate question is needed for people with no 'most often' brand, as the question wording has to be different from Q21. Compare this with questions 17 and 18, where the same questions suffice for people with a 'most often' brand and those without.

Up to now, as all of the questions about buying have been asked in the present tense the time period has implicitly been 'these days' or 'nowadays'.

There is a danger that respondents will assume different time periods. Lighter purchasers are likely to assume a longer time period than heavier purchasers, as otherwise they may have no purchases to report. To avoid this, the questionnaire writer could have changed the questions to ask for brands bought or drunk over the last six months or some other specified period, as has now been used at Q22. For some respondents, particularly heavy drinkers with no fixed pattern of brand purchase, this might be difficult to answer accurately, while for light drinkers it might be difficult to answer accurately because of the low importance of the purchase to them.

Whichever approach is chosen it is important to be consistent and not to mix time periods or whether they are specified, as this would make it impossible to cumulate a full brand repertoire analysis.

Q23.

ASK ALL.

Face-to-face

I am now going to show you a number of pairs of words or phrases that describe some of the things that you might take into account when choosing a brand of Scotch whisky. For each pair I would like you to tell me which of the two is the more important to you when deciding which brand to buy by allocating 11 points between them. SHOW EXAMPLE ON SELF-COMPLETION PAGE. For example, the two phrases might be 'the depth of the colour' and 'the smoothness of the taste'. If one is much more important in your choice of whisky than the other, you might give 11 points to the more important and none to the other. But if you think that they are about equally important you would give 5 points to one of them and 6 to the other. You can give any combination of points provided that they add to 11. Do you follow me? IF ANY DOUBT REPEAT EXPLANATION.

Online

For each of these pairs of words, please allocate 11 points according to how important each is to you when deciding which brand of whisky to buy. If one is much more important than the other, you might give it all 11 points and none to the other. If they about equal, you might give 5 points to one and 6 to the other.

Q23 is a fixed-points allocation question to determine the relative importance of the key brand-positioning dimension against other factors believed to be key drivers of brand choice.

Note that respondents are asked to compare dimensions rather than attributes. We are not interested in whether they would be more likely to buy a brand drunk by Scots than a brand with a rich colour (although we will be able to deduce that) but in how important the dimension of Scottishness is compared to the dimension of colour richness. There are many ways in which this question could be asked, some of which would involve attributes rather than dimensions. Care must be taken with this type of question to distinguish between the two and use them appropriately.

The question as written above is for face-to-face interviews. It is long and not particularly easy for the respondents to follow. The length is alleviated by showing the example halfway through the question script. This is to try to involve the respondents and maintain their interest rather than present them with a lengthy speech from the interviewer. Avoid being condescending. The check question, 'Do you follow me?' or, 'Have I explained that properly?' is preferable to, 'Do you understand?' It is important to show an example for most self-completion scalar questions, particularly when the task is as complex as this is.

With seven dimensions, there are 21 possible pairs. To ask respondents to answer for all pairs is too great a task, which would lead to boredom and fatigue. We have chosen to ask each respondent to complete seven. There will be three alternative versions for the self-completion section on paper, which between them include all of the possible pairs. Each version will be asked of exactly one-third of the sample at random. A simple summation of the scores across all respondents will provide a ranking and a rating score for each dimension. Care must be taken with analysis of sub-groups to ensure that each sub-group contains an equal number of respondents with the three versions of the question. Data may have to be weighted to achieve this.

With the online questionnaire, the question is kept much shorter and the pairs of attributes will be shown at random, so that each pair is shown the same number of times across the total sample.

Q24.

ASK ALL.

Face-to-face

I am now going to read out a number of words and phrases that have been used to describe brands of Scotch whisky. For each one I would like you to tell me which of the brands on this card it applies to. SHOW CARD E. There is no right or wrong answer. Each phrase can apply to all of the brands, some of them or none of them.

Online

You will now see some phrases that have been used to describe brands of whisky. For each phrase, click on the brands to which you think it applies.

Q24 is a brand-attribute association question designed to determine the perceived brand images of Crianlarich and the five brands that are thought to be the main competitors. The question emphasizes that each phrase can apply to all, some or none of the brands.

This question is asked after Q23 – if it were asked before Q23, brand perceptions elicited at this question could force respondents into saying that something was important so as to appear consistent rather than because they think it really is. For example, if a respondent has said earlier that Crianlarich is their most frequently bought brand, and here they say that Crianlarich is a traditional brand, then they may feel compelled to say that tradition is an important dimension in their brand choice. They are less likely to say that Crianlarich is a traditional brand as a result of having said that tradition is important to them, because they are likely to have a more clearly defined brand image of Crianlarich than they do of what is important.

The attributes are chosen because they are believed to be the key image dimensions on which these brands are positioned. They would probably be a different set, though, if the client was a brand other than Crianlarich because the competitive set of brands would be different. Some attributes may be associated with most or all of the brands. While it may be important to know this, such a finding decreases the discrimination between the brands and makes it difficult to see if any brand 'owns' the particular attribute. Discrimination between brands can be increased by changing the question, for example to: 'Which one brand would you choose if you were looking for one with this attribute?'

The layout of the question on the paper questionnaire is in columns by brand rather than by attribute. This layout facilitates analysis of brand image profiles for the total sample and sub-analysis by those aware of a brand, brand users, etc.

A dynamic grid is used in the online questionnaire, with attributes appearing in a random sequence. This technique reduces flat-lining. The brands are presented in random order between respondents, but in the same order for individual respondents.

With the online questionnaire an option would have been to show pack shots for each brand. This has not been done because we want to assess the innate image of each brand held by respondents. In many markets, and in this one in particular, great effort is made to ensure that the packs communicate the desired brand positionings. Showing packs would prompt respondents and therefore mean that we would be measuring the effectiveness of the pack design rather than how the respondents view the brands in abstract.

Q25.

ASK ALL.

Face-to-face

SHOW AD N7.

Here is an advertisement for a Scotch whisky. Have you seen it before?

Online

Have you seen this advertisement for a Scotch whisky before?

The final section of the main questionnaire is advertising recognition. This is kept until after any brand image questions to avoid prompting and influencing brand image with the advertisements shown. Here we are showing a de-branded press advertisement for Crianlarich, to measure recognition.

Although not strictly necessary here, it is good practice not to label face-to-face prompt material in alphabetical order, as in some circumstances this may suggest a hierarchy and influence the findings.

Q26.

IF YES.

Face-to-face

Which brand is it for?

Online

Which brand is it for?

Responses to this question are spontaneous, so again the longer brand list is used in the face-to-face questionnaire. For the online version we might consider showing the full list including those previously not claimed to be aware of in case the ad jogs the memory.

Q27. ASK ALL.

Face-to-face

SHOW AD K3. Here is another advertisement for a Scotch whisky. Have you seen it before?

Online

Here is another advertisement for a Scotch whisky. Have you seen it before?

Q28. IF YES

Face-to-face

Which brand is it for?

Online

Which brand is it for?

Questions 27 and 28 repeat questions 25 and 26 for a competitor advertisement to provide a benchmark against which to assess results for the Crianlarich ad.

Classification data

Classification questions are usually asked at the end of the interview unless they are criteria for quota controls, when they must be asked as part of the screening process at the beginning of the interview. They may be seen as intrusive, and a greater rapport may have been built up with the interviewer by this time, which reduces the apparent intrusiveness. Any refusals at this stage will not endanger the rest of the interview, while age and social class can be estimated by the interviewer (and recorded as estimates) if refused.

Note that the minimum age of respondent is 18 years. For most surveys of adults this would be 16 years but is higher here because of the subject matter of this interview. Age is collected in six bands, although it would be unlikely that the sample size of this study would allow us to analyse by each band. However, having the six bands allows us to select age groups for analysis, which we would not be able to do if only three age bands were used. It costs no more to collect the more detailed information and not having it may limit the analysis possibilities. The minimum age requirement means that the online version asks age at the beginning of the interview to screen out anyone too young.

Social group is recorded in four categories, and not individually for each of the six groups. This reflects analysis needs and the information required to determine whether quota controls have been kept.

If the online survey is carried out using an access panel, then the classification data is likely to already be known and will not need to be asked again. If respondents are recruited to the survey through other methods such as pop-ups or other types of invitation, this will not be known and must be asked. As social grade cannot be asked in a self-completion questionnaire, the nearest approximation is job type.

Questionnaire flow diagrams

A flow diagram helps us to ensure that all respondents are asked the questions that they should be, and is an important aid in checking electronic questionnaires, where routeing instructions are not obvious.

The overview flow diagram (Figure A1.1) is relatively straightforward for this questionnaire. However, there is a complex sub-routine within the behavioural data section, for which a separate flow diagram has been prepared (Figure A1.2), as this is the area in which the final questionnaire (Figure A1.3) is most likely to contain routeing errors.

FIGURE A1.1   Overview flow diagram

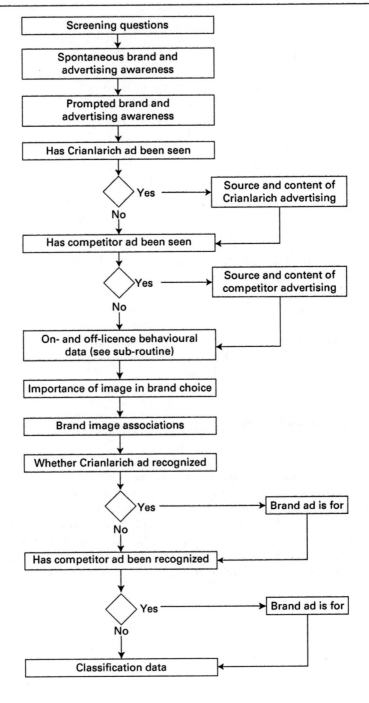

FIGURE A1.2 Behavioural section sub-routine

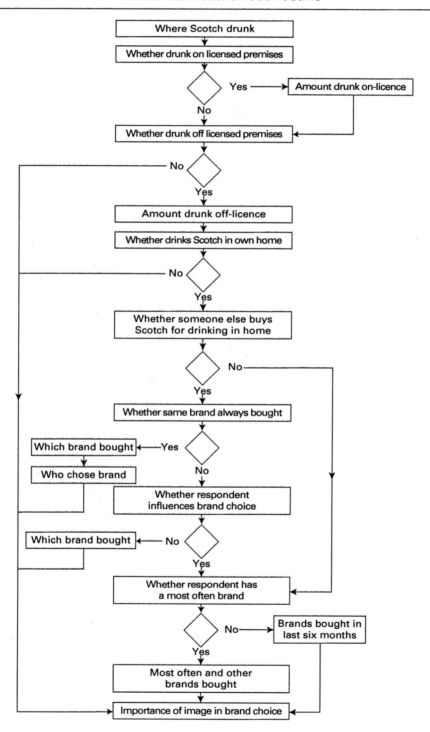

FIGURE A1.3   Example questionnaire

SCREENING QUESTIONNAIRE

Good morning/afternoon/evening. I am (interviewer name) from Acme Surveys, a market research company. I am carrying out a survey about alcoholic drinks. The interview will take about 15 minutes to complete, and is carried out in accordance with the Code of Conduct of the Market Research Society.

QA SHOW CARD A.

Do you or anybody in your household work in any of the industries or professions on this card?

		(120)
ACCOUNTANCY		1
ADVERTISING*		2
COMPUTERS OR INFORMATION TECHNOLOGY		3
MARKETING/MARKET RESEARCH*		4
ALCOHOLIC DRINK PRODUCTION OR RETAILING*		5
BANKING OR INSURANCE		6
GROCERY RETAILING		7
NONE OF THESE		0

IF ANY CODED*, THANK AND CLOSE.

QB SHOW CARD B.

Which of the products on this card have you drunk in the last month either in licensed premises such as a restaurant, pub or bar, or at home or anywhere else?

	(121)
ALE	1
LAGER	2
STOUT	3
WINE	4
GIN	5
SCOTCH WHISKY	6
IRISH WHISKEY	7
NONE OF THESE	0

IF SCOTCH WHISKY (CODE 6) DRUNK, CONTINUE.

IF SCOTCH WHISKY NOT DRUNK, THANK AND CLOSE

QC SHOW CARD C.

Which of the phrases on this card best describes how often you drink Scotch whisky?

	(122)	
MOST DAYS	1	
AT LEAST ONCE A WEEK	2	
AT LEAST ONCE A MONTH	3	
AT LEAST ONCE EVERY THREE MONTHS	4	CONT
AT LEAST ONCE EVERY SIX MONTHS	5	CLOSE

FIGURE A1.3   *continued*

MAIN QUESTIONNAIRE

Q1 What brands of whisky can you think of? Please name as many as you can think of. DO NOT PROMPT.

RECORD BRAND FIRST MENTIONED SEPARATELY ON LEFT BELOW.

RECORD OTHER MENTIONS IN CENTRE BELOW.

Q2 Which brands of whisky have you seen or heard advertised anywhere recently?
DO NOT PROMPT.
RECORD ON RIGHT BELOW.

	Q1 FIRST MENTION	Q1 OTHERS	Q2 ADVER- TISED
	(123)	(125)	(127)
BELL'S	1	1	1
CHIVAS REGAL	2	2	2
CRIANLARICH	3	3	3
FAMOUS GROUSE	4	4	4
GLENFIDDICH	5	5	5
GLENMORANGIE	6	6	6
GRAND PRIX	7	7	7
J&B	8	8	8
JACK DANIEL'S	9	9	9
JOHNNIE WALKER RED LABEL	0	0	0
JOHNNIE WALKER BLACK LABEL	X	X	X
JOHNNIE WALKER UNSPECIFIED	V	V	V
	(124)	(127)	(128)
TEACHER'S	1	2	3
WHYTE & MACKAY	1	2	3
VAT 69	1	2	3

OTHERS (WRITE IN AND CODE)

Q1
FIRST   4
_____

Q1
OTHERS   4
_____

Q2
ADVERT_____ 4
_____

                          NONE   5   5   5   Q3

FIGURE A1.3 *continued*

Q3 **SHOW CARD D.**

Which of the brands of whisky on this card have you heard of? Please include any that you have already mentioned.

RECORD BELOW ON LEFT

Q4 **SHOW CARD D AGAIN.**

Which of the brands of whisky on this card have you seen or heard advertised anywhere recently? Again please include any that you have already mentioned.

	Q3 AWARE	Q4 ADVER- TISED	
	(129)	(130)	
BELL'S	1	1	
CHIVAS REGAL	2	2	
CRIANLARICH	3	3*	
FAMOUS GROUSE	4	4	
GLENFIDDICH	5	5	
GLENMORANGIE	6	6	
GRAND PRIX	7	7*	
JOHNNIE WALKER RED LABEL	8	8	
JOHNNIE WALKER BLACK LABEL	9	9	
TEACHER'S	0	0	
WHYTE & MACKAY	X	X	INSTRUC-
NONE OF THESE	V	V	TION

IF CRIANLARICH SEEN ADVERTISED AT Q4 GO TO Q5.

IF GRAND PRIX SEEN ADVERTISED AT Q4 AND NOT CRIANLARICH GO TO Q7.

ALL OTHERS GO TO Q9.

FIGURE A1.3   *continued*

IF CRIANLARICH MENTIONED AT Q2 OR Q4

Q5   Where did you see or hear advertising for Crianlarich?

	(131)	
CINEMA	1	
DIRECT MAIL SHOT	2	
INTERNET	3	
MAGAZINE	4	
NEWSPAPER (INCLUDING MAGAZINE SUPPLEMENT)	5	
RADIO	6	
TELEVISION	7	
OTHER	8	
DON'T KNOW	9	Q6

IF CRIANLARICH MENTIONED AT Q4

Q6   Please describe to me everything that you can
remember about the advertising for Crianlarich.
PROBE: What was it about? What did it say or
show? PROBE: What else?
WRITE IN VERBATIM BELOW.   (132)

_____ 123
_____ 456
_____ 789
_____ 0XV

_____ (133)   SEE
_____ 123   IN-
_____ 456   STRUC-
_____ 789   TION
0XV

**IF GRAND PRIX SEEN ADVERTISED AT
Q4 ASK Q7.
OTHERS GO TO Q9.**

IF GRAND PRIX MENTIONED AT Q4

Q7   Where did you see or hear advertising for Grand Prix?

	(134)	
CINEMA	1	
DIRECT MAIL SHOT	2	
INTERNET	3	
MAGAZINE	4	
NEWSPAPER (INCLUDING MAGAZINE SUPPLEMENT)	5	
RADIO	6	
TELEVISION	7	
OTHER	8	Q8
DON'T KNOW	9	

FIGURE A1.3   *continued*

IF GRAND PRIX MENTIONED AT Q4

Q8   Please describe to me everything that you can
remember about the advertising for Grand Prix.
PROBE: What was it about? What did it say or show?
WRITE IN VERBATIM BELOW.   (135)
_____ 123
_____ 456
_____ 789
_____ 0XV

_____
_____ (136)
_____ 123
_____ 456
_____ 789
                                            0XV   Q9

ASK ALL.

Q9   Do you drink whisky only on licensed premises such as a restaurant,
pub or bar, or only at home or someone else's home, or do you drink
it both on licensed premises and at home.

                                                    (137)

ONLY ON LICENSED PREMISES	1	Q10
ONLY AT HOME/SOMEONE ELSE'S HOME	2	Q11
BOTH ON LICENSED PREMISES AND AT HOME	3	Q10

IF DRINKS AT ALL ON LICENSED PREMISES

Q10 How many glasses of Scotch whisky would you say you drank in the
last seven days before today in pubs, bars or restaurants? By glasses I
mean single pub measures.

WRITE IN BOX BELOW. USE LEADING ZERO IF UNDER 10.

(138)	(139)

eg 05

IF REFUSES WRITE IN 98.   SEE
IF DON'T KNOW WRITE IN 99.   INSTRUCTION

FIGURE A1.3 *continued*

IF ALSO DRINKS OFF-LICENCE AT Q9 ASK Q11.
OTHERS TO Q23.

IF DRINKS OFF LICENSED PREMISES

Q11 How many glasses of Scotch whisky would you say you drank at home, either in your own home or in anyone else's in the last seven days? By glasses I mean the equivalent of a single measure in a pub.

WRITE IN BOX BELOW. USE LEADING ZERO IF UNDER 10.

(140)	(141)

eg 05

IF REFUSES WRITE IN 98   Q12
IF DON'T KNOW WRITE IN 99

IF DRINKS OFF-LICENCE

Q12 Do you drink Scotch whisky in your own home, in someone else's home or both?

(142)

OWN HOME   1   Q13

SOMEONE ELSE'S HOME   2   Q23

BOTH OWN AND SOMEONE ELSE'S   3   Q13

FIGURE A1.3 *continued*

IF DRINKS AT HOME

Q13 Do you yourself usually buy the Scotch to drink at home or does someone else usually buy it for you?

(143)

BUY IT MYSELF	1	Q19
SOMEONE ELSE BUYS IT	2	Q14
SOMETIMES MYSELF, SOMETIMES SOMEONE ELSE	3	Q19
GIVEN AS GIFT	4	Q23
OTHER ANSWER	5	

IF SOMEONE ELSE USUALLY BUYS (Q13 CODE 2)

Q14 Do you have a say in which brand of Scotch whisky they buy or do they decide, or do they always buy the same brand?

(144)

HAVE A SAY	1	Q19
HAVE NO SAY	2	Q17
ALWAYS BUY SAME BRAND	3	Q15

FIGURE A1.3 *continued*

IF ALWAYS BUYS THE SAME BRAND

Q15 Which brand do they buy?

		(145)	
BELLS		1	
CHIVAS REGAL		2	
CRIANLARICH		3	
FAMOUS GROUSE		4	
GLENFIDDICH		5	
GLENMORANGIE		6	
GRAND PRIX		7	
J&B		8	
JACK DANIELS		9	
JOHNNIE WALKER RED LABEL		0	
JOHNNIE WALKER BLACK LABEL		X	
JOHNNIE WALKER UNSPECIFIED		V	
		(146)	
TEACHERS		1	
WHYTE & MACKAY		2	
VAT 69		3	
OTHER (WRITE IN AND CODE)			

                                    4   Q16

                            DON'T KNOW   5   Q23

IF SAYS 'JOHNNIE WALKER' PROBE
FOR RED OR BLACK LABEL BEFORE
ACCEPTING 'UNSPECIFIED'.

IF KNOWS WHICH BRAND IS BOUGHT

Q16 Did you decide to always buy that brand, or was
that someone else's decision, or a decision made
by both of you?

	(147)	
RESPONDENT'S CHOICE	1	
SOMEONE ELSE'S CHOICE	2	
CHOICE OF BOTH	3	
DON'T KNOW/CAN'T REMEMBER	4	Q23

FIGURE A1.3   *continued*

IF HAVE NO SAY AT Q14

Q17 Which brands do they buy? Which others? CODE ON LEFT BELOW.

IF MORE THAN ONE BRAND BOUGHT – OTHERS TO Q23

Q18 Which brand, if any, do they buy most often? SINGLE CODE ONLY.

	Q17 BOUGHT AT ALL	Q18 MOST OFTEN
	(148)	(150)
BELL'S	1	1
CHIVAS REGAL	2	2
CRIANLARICH	3	3
FAMOUS GROUSE	4	4
GLENFIDDICH	5	5
GLENMORANGIE	6	6
GRAND PRIX	7	7
J&B	8	8
JACK DANIEL'S	9	9
JOHNNIE WALKER RED LABEL	0	0
JOHNNIE WALKER BLACK LABEL	X	X
JOHNNIE WALKER UNSPECIFIED*	V	V
	(149)	(150)
TEACHER'S	1	1
WHYTE & MACKAY	2	2
VAT 69	3	3
OTHER (WRITE IN AND CODE)		
_____	4	4
NO MOST OFTEN BRAND	5	5
DON'T KNOW	6	6 Q23

*IF SAYS 'JOHNNIE WALKER' PROBE FOR RED OR BLACK LABEL BEFORE ACCEPTING 'UNSPECIFIED'.

FIGURE A1.3   *continued*

IF BUY IT MYSELF AT Q13 OR HAVE A SAY AT Q14

Q19   Is there one brand that you buy/ask for (AS APPROPRIATE) more
often than any other?

		(152)	
	YES	1	Q20
	NO	2	Q22

IF YES AT Q19

Q20   Which brand is that?
RECORD BELOW ON LEFT.

Q21   Which other brands, if any, do you buy at all?

	Q20 MOST OFTEN	Q21 OTHERS BOUGHT
	(153)	(154)
BELL'S	1	1
CHIVAS REGAL	2	2
CRIANLARICH	3	3
FAMOUS GROUSE	4	4
GLENFIDDICH	5	5
GLENMORANGIE	6	6
GRAND PRIX	7	7
J&B	8	8
JACK DANIEL'S	9	9
JOHNNIE WALKER RED LABEL	0	0
JOHNNIE WALKER BLACK LABEL	X	X
JOHNNIE WALKER UNSPECIFIED*	V	V
	(154)	(154)
TEACHER'S	1	1
WHYTE & MACKAY	2	2
VAT 69	3	3
OTHER (WRITE IN AND CODE)		
_____	4	4
DON'T KNOW	5	5
NO OTHER BRANDS BOUGHT	6	6 Q23

*IF SAYS 'JOHNNIE WALKER' PROBE FOR RED OR BLACK LABEL
BEFORE ACCEPTING 'UNSPECIFIED'

FIGURE A1.3 *continued*

IF NO AT Q19

Q22 Which brands have you bought in the last six months?

	(157)
BELL'S	1
CHIVAS REGAL	2
CRIANLARICH	3
FAMOUS GROUSE	4
GLENFIDDICH	5
GLENMORANGIE	6
GRAND PRIX	7
J&B	8
JACK DANIEL'S	9
JOHNNIE WALKER RED LABEL	0
JOHNNIE WALKER BLACK LABEL	X
JOHNNIE WALKER UNSPECIFIED*	V
	(158)
TEACHER'S	1
WHYTE & MACKAY	2
VAT 69	3
OTHER (WRITE IN AND CODE)	
_____	4
DON'T KNOW	5
NO PURCHASES MADE IN LAST SIX MONTHS	

IF SAYS 'JOHNNIE WALKER' PROBE
FOR RED OR BLACK LABEL BEFORE
ACCEPTING 'UNSPECIFIED'. Q23

FIGURE A1.3 *continued*

ASK ALL.

Q23 I am now going to show you a number of pairs of phrases that describe some of the things that you might take into account when choosing a brand of Scotch whisky. For each pair I would like you to tell me which of the two is the more important to you when deciding which brand to buy by allocating 11 points between them. **SHOW EXAMPLE ON SELF-COMPLETION PAGE.** For example, the two phrases might be 'the depth of the colour'and 'the smoothness of the taste'. If one is much more important in your choice of whisky than the other, then you might give 11 points to the more important and none to the other. But if you think that they are about equally important then you would give five points to one of them and six to the other. You can give any combination of points providing that they add to 11.

Do you follow me?

IF ANY DOUBT REPEAT EXPLANATION.

HAND SELF-COMPLETION PAGE AND PEN TO RESPONDENT.

WHEN COMPLETED TAKE PAGE BACK AND GO TO Q24.

FIGURE A1.3   *continued*

HOW IMPORTANT ARE THE FOLLOWING TO YOU IN DECIDING WHICH WHISKY TO BUY?

Please divide 11 points between each pair of statements depending on how important each one is to you in deciding which brand of whisky to buy.

EXAMPLE:

a) Whether or not it has a deep colour is much more important than how smooth the taste is.

THE DEPTH OF THE COLOUR	11	0	THE SMOOTHNESS OF THE TASTE

b) Whether or not it has a deep colour and whether or not it has a smooth taste are of about the same importance

THE DEPTH OF THE COLOUR	5	6	THE SMOOTHNESS OF THE TASTE

Please complete the rest of the page to show how important they are to you.

THE SMOOTH-NESS OF THE TASTE			HOW TRADITIONAL THE BRAND IS	(162 – 164)
HOW WELL YOU KNOW THE BRAND			THE RICHNESS OF THE COLOUR	(165 – 168)
HOW TRADI-TIONAL THE BRAND IS			THE RICHNESS OF THE COLOUR	(169 – 172)
WHETHER IT IS DRUNK IN SCOTLAND			THE SMOOTHNESS OF THE TASTE	(173 – 176)
THE PRICE OF THE BRAND			HOW DIFFERENT IT IS TO OTHERS	(177 – 180)
THE RICHNESS OF THE COLOUR			THE SMOOTHNESS OF THE TASTE	(181 – 184)
HOW TRADI-TIONAL THE BRAND IS			HOW WELL YOU KNOW THE BRAND	(185 – 188)

THANK YOU. PLEASE HAND PAGE BACK TO INTERVIEWER.

FIGURE A1.3 *continued*

ASK ALL.

Q24 I am now going to read out a number of words and phrases that have been used to describe brands of Scotch whisky. For each one I would like you to tell me which of the brands on this card it applies to. **SHOW CARD E.** There is no right or wrong answer. Each phrase can apply to all of the brands, some of them or none of them.

READ OUT:	BELL'S	CRIANLARICH	FAMOUS GROUSE	GRAND PRIX	TEACHER'S	WHYTE & MACKAY	NONE	DON'T KNOW
	(189)	(190)	(191)	(192)	(193)	(194)	(195)	(196)
Has a strong heritage	1	1	1	1	1	1	1	1
Is traditional	2	2	2	2	2	2	2	2
Is old-fashioned	3	3	3	3	3	3	3	3
Is different to the others	4	4	4	4	4	4	4	4
Is a cheaper brand	5	5	5	5	5	5	5	5
Is a more ex-pensive brand	6	6	6	6	6	6	6	6
A favourite of the Scots	7	7	7	7	7	7	7	7
A brand I like	8	8	8	8	8	8	8	8

Q25

ASK ALL.
SHOW DE-BRANDED AD N7.

Q25 Here is an advertisement for a Scotch whisky. Have you seen it before?

	(197)	
YES	1	Q26
NO	2	Q27
DON'T KNOW	3	

FIGURE A1.3 *continued*

IF YES

Q26 Which brand is it for?

	(198)	(200)
BELL'S	1	1
CHIVAS REGAL	2	2
CRIANLARICH	3	3
FAMOUS GROUSE	4	4
GLENFIDDICH	5	5
GLENMORANGIE	6	6
GRAND PRIX	7	7
J&B	8	8
JACK DANIEL'S	9	9
JOHNNIE WALKER RED LABEL	0	0
JOHNNIE WALKER BLACK LABEL	X	X
JOHNNIE WALKER UNSPECIFIED*	V	V
	(199)	(201)
TEACHER'S	1	1
WHYTE & MACKAY	2	2
VAT 69	3	3
OTHER (WRITE IN AND CODE)		
———————————————————	4	4
DON'T KNOW	5	5

*IF SAYS 'JOHNNIE WALKER' PROBE
FOR RED OR BLACK LABEL BEFORE
ACCEPTING 'UNSPECIFIED'.   Q27

ASK ALL.
SHOW AD K3.

Q27 Here is another advertisement for a Scotch
whisky. Have you seen it before?

	(202)	
YES	1	Q28
NO	2	CLASS
DON'T KNOW	3	AND
		CLOSE

FIGURE A1.3   *continued*

IF YES

Q28   Which brand is it for?

		(203)
	BELL'S	1
	CHIVAS REGAL	2
	CRIANLARICH	3
	FAMOUS GROUSE	4
	GLENFIDDICH	5
	GLENMORANGIE	6
	GRAND PRIX	7
	J&B	8
	JACK DANIEL'S	9
	JOHNNIE WALKER RED LABEL	0
	JOHNNIE WALKER BLACK LABEL	X
	JOHNNIE WALKER UNSPECIFIED*	V
		(204)
	TEACHER'S	1
	WHYTE & MACKAY	2
	VAT 69	3
	OTHER (WRITE IN)	4
	DON'T KNOW	5

*IF SAYS 'JOHNNIE WALKER' PROBE FOR RED OR BLACK LABEL BEFORE ACCEPTING 'UNSPECIFIED'.

COMPLETE CLASSIFICATION QUESTIONS, THANK RESPONDENT AND CLOSE INTERVIEW.

Online Questionnaire

The following illustrations show a selection of typical screens as they would appear in the online version of the questionnaire.

FIGURE A1.4   Q1 Spontaneous brand awareness

Please type in as many brands of whisky as you can think of.

This is Q1 in the face-to-face questionnaire.
Normally questionnaire numbers are not included in the online version because they mean nothing to the respondent and can confuse when there are skips or loops.

FIGURE A1.5   Q3 Prompted brand awareness

Which of these have you heard of?
Please include any that you have already given.

O Teacher's
O Johnnie Walker Black Label
O Johnnie Walker Red Label
O Bell's
O Grand Prix
O Glenmorangie
O Famous Grouse
O Crianlarich
O Whyte & Mackay
O Glenfiddich
O Chivas Regal

O None of these

This is Q3 in the face-to-face questionnaire.
The order of the brands is randomized between respondents, but
with the two Johnnie Walker brands always adjacent for clarity.
Brands not aware of at this question will not be included in brand
lists for future questions.

FIGURE A1.6   Q9 Where whisky drunk

Where do you drink whisky?

O On licensed premises (pubs, bars, restaurants etc.)

O At home/someone else's home

*This is Q9 in the face-to-face questionnaire. Online it is much
reduced because the answer codes define the response options
which have to be read out face to face.*

FIGURE A1.7   Q24 Dynamic grid

You will now see some phrases that have been used to describe
brands of whisky. For each phrase, click on the brands to which you
think it applies

O Teacher's
O Bell's
O Crianlarich
O Grand Prix
O Whyte & Mackay
O Famous Grouse
O None of these

O Don't know

*This is Q24 in the face-to-face questionnaire.
The list of brands will be constant for each respondent but randomized
between respondents.*

APPENDIX 2
Market research associations and codes of conduct

Market Research Society (**www.mrs.org.uk**)
   Code of Conduct: **http://www.mrs.org.uk/standards/code_of_conduct/**

ICC (**www.iccwbo.org**) and ESOMARICC/ESOMAR (**www.esomar.org**)
   International Code on Market and Social Research:
   http://www.esomar.org/publications-store/codes-guidelines.php

Australia AMSRS **www.mrsa.com.au**
   Code of Professional Behaviour: **http://www.amsrs.com.au/**
   professional-standards/amsrs-code-of-professional-behaviour

MRIA (Canada) **www.mria-arim.ca**
   Code of Conduct and Good Practice: **http://www.mria-arim.ca/**
   STANDARDS/CODE2007.asp

Declaration for the Territory of the Federal Republic of Germany
   concerning the ICC/ESOMAR International Code on Market and Social
   Research **www.adm-ev.de**

ASSIRM (Italy) Code of Professional Ethics **www.assirm.it**

JMRA (Japan) Code of Marketing Research **www.jmra-net.or.jp**

CASRO (United States) **www.casro.org**

Code of Standards: **http://www.casro.org/codeofstandards.cfm**

REFERENCES

Albaum, G (1997) The Likert scale revisited, *Journal of the Market Research Society*, **39** (2), pp 331–48

Albaum, G, Roster, C, Yu, J H and Rogers, R D (2007) Simple rating scale formats: exploring extreme responses, *International Journal of Market Research*, **49** (5), pp 633–50

Albaum, G, Wiley, J, Roster, C, and Smith, S M (2011) Visiting item non-responses in internet survey data collection, *International Journal of Market Research*, **53** (5)

Alwin, D F and Krosnick, J (1985) The measurement of values in surveys: a comparison of ratings and rankings, *Public Opinion Quarterly*, **49** (4), pp 535–52

Anderson, K, Wright, M and Wheeler, M (2011) Snap judgement polling: street interviews enabled by new technology, *International Journal of Market Research*, **53** (4)

Artingstall, R (1978) Some random thoughts on non-sampling error, *European Research*, **6** (6)

Baker, R and Downes-Le-Guin, T (2011) All fun and games? Myths and realities of respondent engagement in online surveys, ESOMAR Congress, Amsterdam

Basi, R K (1999) WWW response rates to socio-demographic items, *Journal of the Market Research Society*, **41** (4), pp 397–401

Bearden, W O and Netermeyer, R G (1999) *Handbook of Marketing Scales*, Sage, Thousand Oaks, CA

Behling, O and Law, K S (2000) *Translating Questionnaires and Other Research Instruments: Problems and solutions*, Sage, Thousand Oaks, CA

Booth-Kewley, S, Edwards, J E and Rosenfeld, P (1992) Impression management, social desirability and computer administration of attitude questionnaires: does the computer make a difference? *Journal of Applied Psychology*, **77** (4), pp 562–66

Brace, I and Nancarrow, C (2008) Let's get ethical: dealing with socially desirable responding online, Market Research Society Annual Conference

Brace, I, Nancarrow, C and McCloskey, J (1999) MR confidential: a help or a hindrance in the new marketing era? *The Journal of Database Marketing*, **7** (2), pp 173–85

Bradley, N (1999) Sampling for internet surveys: an examination of respondent selection for internet research, *Journal of the Market Research Society*, **41** (4), pp 387–95

Bronner, F and Kuijlen, T (2007) The live or digital interviewer: a comparison between CASI, CAPI and CATI with respect to differences in response behaviour, *International Journal of Market Research*, **49** (2), pp 167–90

Brown, G, Copeland, T and Millward, M (1973) Monadic testing of new products: an old problem and some partial solutions, *Journal of the Market Research Society*, **15** (2), pp 112–31

Cape, P, Lorch, J and Piekarski, L (2007) A tale of two questionnaires, *Proceedings of the ESOMAR Panel Research Conference*, Orlando, pp 136–49

Chang, L C and Krosnick, J A (2003) Measuring the frequency of regular behaviors: comparing the 'typical week' to the 'past week', *Sociological Methodology*, 33, pp 55–80

Christian, L M and Dillman, D A (2004) The influence of graphical and symbolic language manipulations on responses to self-administered questions, *Public Opinion Quarterly*, 68 (1) pp 57–80

Christian, L M, Dillman, D A and Smyth, J D (2007) Helping respondents get it right the first time: the influence of words, symbols, and graphics in web surveys, *Public Opinion Quarterly*, 71 (1), pp 113–25

Chrzan, K and Golovashkina, N (2006) An empirical test of stated importance measures, *International Journal of Market Research*, 48 (6), pp 717–40

Cobanoglu, C, Warde, B, and Moreo, P J (2001) A comparison of mail, fax and web-based survey methods, *International Journal of Market Research*, 43 (4), pp 441–52

Coelho, P and Esteves, S (2007) The choice between a five-point and a ten-point scale in the framework of customer satisfaction measurement, *International Journal of Market Research*, 49 (3), pp 313–39

Conrad, F, Couper, M, Tourangeau, R and Peytchev, A (2005) Impact of progress feedback on task completion: first impressions matter, Association for Computing Machinery, Conference on Human Factors in Computing Systems

Converse, J M and Presser, S (1986) *Handcrafting the Standardized Questionnaire*, Sage, Thousand Oaks, CA

Cooke, M (2010) The Engagement Agenda, Association of Survey Computing Conference, Bristol

Couper, M (2000) Web surveys: a review of issues and approaches, *Public Opinion Quarterly*, 64, pp 464–94

Couper, M, Traugott, M and Lamias, M (2001) Web survey design and administration, *Public Opinion Quarterly*, 65, pp 230–53

Cox, E (1980) The optimal number of response alternatives for a scale: a review, *Journal of Marketing Research*, 17, pp 407–22

Crowne, D P and Marlowe, D (1960) A new scale of social desirability independent of psychopathology, *Journal of Consulting Psychology*, 24, pp 349–54

Diamantopolous, A, Schlegelmilch, B and Reynolds, N (1994) Pre-testing in questionnaire design: the impact of respondent characteristics on error detection, *Journal of the Market Research Society*, 36 (4), pp 295–311

Dillman, D (2000) *Mail and Internet Surveys, 2nd edn, The Tailored Design Method*, John Wiley, New York

Dillman, D A, Singer, E, Clark, J R and Treat, J B (1996) Effects of benefits appeals and variations in statements of confidentiality on completion rate for census questionnaires, *Public Opinion Quarterly*, 60 (3)

Dolnicar, S, Grun, B and Leisch, F (2011) Quick, simple and reliable: forced binary survey questions, *International Journal of Market Research*, 53 (2)

Dolnicar, S, Rossiter, J and Grun, B (2012) 'Pick any' measures contaminate brand image studies, *International Journal of Market Research*, 56 (6)

Duffy, B (2003) Response order effects: how do people read? *International Journal of Market Research*, 45 (4), pp 457–66

Duffy, B, Smith, K, Terhanian, G and Bremer, J (2005) Comparing data from online and face-to-face surveys, *International Journal of Market Research*, 47 (6), pp 615–40

Edwards, A L (1957) *The Social Desirability Variable in Personality Assessment*, Dryden, New York

Eisenhower, D, Mathiowetz, N A and Morganstein, D (1991) Recall error: sources and bias reduction techniques, in (eds) P Biemer, S Sudman, and R M Groves, *Measurement Error in Surveys*, Wiley, New York

Esuli, A and Sebastiani, F (2010) Machines that learn how to code open-ended questions, *International Journal of Market Research*, 52 (6)

Findlay, K and Alberts, K (2011) Gamification – the reality of what it is ... and what it isn't, ESOMAR Congress, Amsterdam

Forsyth, B H, Kudela, M S, Levin, K, Lawrence, D and Willis, G B (2007) Methods for translating an English-language questionnaire on tobacco use into Mandarin, Cantonese, Korean and Vietnamese, *Field Methods*, 19 (3), pp 264–83

Greenleaf, E A (1992) Measuring extreme response style, *The Public Opinion Quarterly*, 56 (3), pp 328–51

Greenwald, H J and Satow, Y (1970) A short social desirability scale, *Psychology Rep*, 27, pp 131–5

Hogg, A and Masztal, J J (2001) A practical learning about online research, *Advertising Research Foundation Workshop*, October

Holbrook, A L and Krosnick, J A (2000) Violating conversational conventions disrupts cognitive processing of attitude questions, *Journal of Experimental Social Psychology*, 36, pp 465–94

Holbrook, A L, Green, M C and Krosnick, J A (2003) Telephone versus face-to-face interviewing of national probability samples with long questionnaires, *Public Opinion Quarterly*, 67, pp 79–125

Holtgraves, T, Eck, J and Lasky, B (1997) Face management, question wording and social desirability, *Journal of Applied Psychology*, 27, pp 1650–71

Ilieva, J, Baron, S and Healey, N M (2002) Online surveys in marketing research: pros and cons, *International Journal of Market Research*, 44 (3), pp 361–76

Johnson, A and Rolfe, G (2011) Engagement, consistency, reach – why the technology landscape precludes all three, Association of Survey Computing Conference, Bristol

Johnson, A J and Swinton, R (2011) Developing second generation mobile research techniques – How mobile research can enhance the enjoyment of media consumption, ESOMAR Congress, Amsterdam

Kalton, G and Schuman, H (1982) The effect of the question on survey responses: a review, *Journal of the Royal Statistical Society, Series A*, 145 (1), pp 42–73

Kalton, G, Roberts, J and Holt, D (1980) The effects of offering a middle response option with opinion questions, *Statistician*, 29, pp 65–78

Kellner, P (2004) Can online polls produce accurate findings? *International Journal of Marketing Research*, 46 (1), pp 3–21

Krosnick, J A and Alwin, D F (1987) An evaluation of a cognitive theory of response order effects in survey measurement, *Public Opinion Quarterly*, 51 (2), pp 201–19

Krosnick, J and Fabrigar, L (1997) Designing rating scales for effective measurement in surveys, in (eds) L Lyberg, P Biemer, M Collins, E De Leeuw, C Dippo, N Schwarz and D Trewin, *Survey Measurement and Process Quality*, John Wiley, New York

Lautenschlager, G J and Flaherty, V L (1990) Computer administration of questions: more desirable or more socially desirable, *Journal of Applied Psychology*, 75, 310–14

Likert, R (1932) A technique for the measurement of attitudes, *Archives of Psychology*, 140, pp 5–55

McDaniel, C Jr and Gates, R (1993) *Contemporary Marketing Research*, West Publishing Company, St Paul, MN, Chs 11/12

McFarland, S G (1981) Effects of question order on survey responses, *Public Opinion Quarterly*, 45, pp 208–15

McKay, R and de la Puente, M (1996) Cognitive testing of racial and ethnic questions for the CPS supplement, *Monthly Labor Review*, September, pp 8–12

Malinoff, B and Puleston, J (2011) How far is too far: traditional, flash and gamification interfaces for the future of market research online survey design, ESOMAR 3D Digital Dimensions Conference, Miami

Nancarrow, C, Brace, I and Wright, L T (2000) Tell me lies, tell me sweet little lies: dealing with socially desirable responses in market research, *The Marketing Review*, 2 (1), pp 55–69

Nancarrow, C, Pallister, J and Brace, I (2001) A new research medium, new research populations and seven deadly sins for internet researchers, *Qualitative Market Research*, 4 (3), pp 136–49

Nunan, D and Knox, S (2011) Can search engine advertising help access rare samples? *International Journal of Market Research*, 53 (4)

Oppenheim, A N (1992) *Questionnaire Design, Interviewing and Attitude Measurement*, 2nd edn, Continuum, London

Osgood, C E, Suci, G J and Tannenbaum, P (1957) *The Measurement of Meaning*, University of Illinois Press, Urbana, IL

Paulhus, D L and Reid, D B (1991) Enhancement and denial in socially desirable responding, *Journal of Personality and Social Psychology*, 60 (2), pp 307–17

Peterson, R A (2000) *Constructing Effective Questionnaires*, Sage, Thousand Oaks, CA

Phillips, D L and Clancy, K J (1972) Some effects of 'social desirability' in survey studies, *American Journal of Sociology*, 77 (5), pp 921–38

Poynter, R and Comley, P (2003) Beyond online panels, *Proceedings of ESOMAR Technovate Conference*, Cannes

Presser, S and Schuman, H (1980) The measurement of a middle position in attitude studies, *Public Opinion Quarterly*, 44, pp 70–85

Puleston, J and Eggers, M (2012) Dimensions of online survey data quality: What really matters? *Proceedings of the ESOMAR Congress*, Atlanta

Puleston, J and Sleep, D (2008) Measuring the value of respondent engagement – innovative techniques to improve panel quality, ESOMAR Panel Research, Dublin, October

Puleston, J and Sleep, D (2011) The game experiments – researching how gaming techniques can be used to improve the quality of feedback from online research, ESOMAR Congress, Amsterdam

Reid, J, Morden, M and Reid, A (2007) Maximizing respondent engagement: the use of rich media, *Proceedings of the ESOMAR Congress*, Berlin

Ring, E (1975) Asymmetrical rotation, *European Research*, 3 (3), pp 111–19

Roster, C, Albaum, G and Rogers, R (2006) Can cross-national/cultural studies presume etic equivalence in respondents' use of extreme categories of Likert rating scales? *International Journal of Market Research*, 48 (6), pp 741–59

Rungie, C, Laurent, G, Dall'Olmo Riley, F, Morrison, D G and Roy, T (2005) Measuring and modeling the (limited) reliability of free choice attitude questions, *International Journal of Research in Marketing*, **22** (3), pp 309–18

Saris, W E and Gallhofer, I N (2007) *Design, Evaluation, and Analysis of Questionnaires for Survey Research*, John Wiley, Hoboken

Saris, W E, Krosnick, J A and Schaeffer, E M (2005) Comparing questions with agree/disagree options to questions with construct-specific response options, http://comm.stanford.edu/faculty/krosnick, accessed October 2012

Schaeffer, E M, Krosnick, J A, Langer, G E and Merkle, D M (2005)Comparing the quality of data obtained by minimally balanced and fully balanced attitude questions, *Public Opinion Quarterly*, **69** (3), pp 417–28

Schober, M F (1999) Making sense of questions: an interactional approach, in (eds) M G Sirken, D J Herrman, S Schechter, N Schwarz, J M Tanur and R Tourangeau, *Cognition and Survey Research*, John Wiley, New York

Schuman, H and Presser, S (1981) *Questions and Answers in Attitude Surveys*, Sage, Thousand Oaks, CA

Schwarz, N, Hippler, H and Noelle-Neumann, E (1991) A cognitive model of response-order effects in survey measurement, in (eds) N Schwarz and S Sudman, *Context Effects in Social and Psychological Research*, pp 187–201, Springer Verlag, New York

Singer, E, Hippler, H-J and Schwarz, N (1992) Confidentiality assurances in surveys: reassurance or threat, *International Journal of Public Opinion Research*, **4** (34), pp 256–68

Singer, E, Von Thurn, D R and Miller, E R (1995) Confidentiality assurances and response: a quantitative review of the experimental literature, *Public Opinion Quarterly*, **59** (1), pp 67–77

Smyth, J D, Dillman, D A, Christian, L M and Stern, M J (2006) Comparing check-all and forced-choice question formats in web surveys, *Public Opinion Quarterly*, **70** (1), pp 66–77

Stern, M J, Smyth, J D and Mendez, J (2012) The effects of item saliency and question design on measurement error in a self-administered survey, *Field Methods*, **24** (1), pp 3–27

Strahan, R and Gerbasi, K C (1972) Short homogeneous versions of the Marlowe-Crowne social desirability scale, *Journal of Clinical Psychology*, **28**, pp 191–3

Suchman, L and Jordan, B (1990) Interactional troubles in face-to-face survey interviews, *Journal of the American Statistical Association*, **85** (409), pp 232–41

Sudman, S and Bradburn, N (1973) Effects of time and memory factors on response in surveys, *Journal of the American Statistical Association*, **68**, pp 805–15

Sudman, S and Bradburn, N (1982) *Asking Questions: A practical guide to questionnaire design*, Jossey-Bass, San Francisco, CA

Taylor, H (2000) Does internet research work? *International Journal of Market Research*, **42** (1), pp 51–63

Thomas, R, Couper, M P, Bremer, J and Terhanian, G (2007) Truth in measurement: comparing web-based interviewing techniques, *Proceedings of the ESOMAR Congress*, Berlin, pp 195–206

Toepoel, V and Dillman, D A (2010) Words, numbers and visual heuristics in web surveys: is there a hierarchy of importance? *Social Science Computer Review*, **29**, pp 193–207

Toepoel, V, Das, M and Van Soest, A (2008) Effects of design in web surveys – comparing trained and fresh respondents, *Public Opinion Quarterly*, 72 (5), pp 985–1007

Toepoel, V, Das, M and Van Soest, A (2009) Design of web questionnaires – the effects of the number of items per screen, *Field Methods*, 21, pp 200–213

Tourangeau, R (1984) Cognitive science and survey methods, in (eds) T Jabine, M Straf, J Tanur and R Tourangeau, *Cognitive Aspects of Survey Methodology: Building a bridge between disciplines*, National Academy Press, Washington, DC

Tourangeau, R, Couper, M and Conrad, F (2004) Spacing, position, and order: interpretive heuristics for visual features of survey questions, *Public Opinion Quarterly*, 68 (3), pp 368–93

Tourangeau, R, Couper, M and Conrad, F (2007) Color, labels and interpretative heuristics for response scales, *Public Opinion Quarterly*, 71 (1), pp 91–112

Tourangeau, R, Rips, L J and Rasinski, K (2000) *The Psychology of Survey Response*, Cambridge University Press, Cambridge

Van Schaik, P and Ling, J (2007) Design parameters of rating scales for web sites, *ACM Transactions on Computer–Human Interaction*, 14

Wable, N and Pall, S (1998) You just do not understand! More and more respondents are saying this to market researchers today, ESOMAR Congress

Warner, S L (1965) Randomized response: a survey technique for eliminating evasive answer bias, *Journal of the American Statistical Association*, 60, pp 63–9

Weijters, B, Geuens, M and Schillewaert, N (2010) The individual consistency of acquiescence and exteme response style in self-report questionnaires, *Applied Psychological Measurement*, 34 (2), pp 105–21

Wood, O (2007) Using faces: measuring emotional engagement for early stage creative, *Proceedings of the ESOMAR Congress*, Berlin, pp 412–37

Worcester, R and Downham, J (1978) *Consumer Market Research Handbook*, 2nd edn, Van Nostrand Reinhold, Wokingham

Wright, L T and Crimp, M (2000) *The Marketing Research Process*, 5th edn, Pearson Education, Harlow

Yang, M-L and Yu, R-R (2011) Effects of identifiers in mail surveys, *Field Methods*, 23 (3), pp 243–65

Zaichkowsky, J L (1999) Personal involvement inventory for advertising, in (eds) W O Bearden and R G Netemeyer, *Handbook of Marketing Scales*, Sage Publications, Thousand Oaks, CA

INDEX

NB: page numbers in *italic* indicate figures or tables

CPSIA information can be obtained at www.ICGtesting.com
Printed in the USA
LVOW10s2245160414

382063LV00002B/21/P